D1737278

A WALKING FIRE

SUNY Series,
The Margins of Literature

Mihai I. Spariosu, Editor

A Walking Fire

A Novel By

Valerie Miner

STATE UNIVERSITY OF NEW YORK PRESS

Production by Ruth Fisher
Marketing by Nancy Farrell

Published by
State University of New York Press, Albany

For information, address the State University of New York Press,
State University Plaza, Albany, NY 12246

Library of Congress Cataloging-in-Publication Data
Miner, Valerie.
  A walking fire / Valerie Miner.
    p.   cm. — (SUNY series, the margins of literature)
  A retelling of the King Lear story.
    ISBN 0-7914-2007-8 (acid-free).—ISBN 0-7914-2008-6 (pbk.: acid
-free)
    1. Vietnamese Conflict, 1961–1975—Protest movements—Fiction.
    2. Women political activists—United States—Fiction.   3. Fathers
and daughters—Oregon—Fiction.   I. Title. II. Series.
PS3563.I4647W35   1994
813'.54—dc20   93-35569
                                                                    CIP

10 9 8 7 6 5 4 3 2 1

"Look, here comes a walking fire." Fool, Act III

The Tragedy of King Lear by William Shakespeare

OTHER BOOKS BY VALERIE MINER

FICTION
Trespassing and Other Stories
All Good Women
Winter's Edge
Murder in the English Department
Movement
Blood Sisters

NON-FICTION
Rumors from the Cauldron: Selected
Essays, Reviews and Reportage

CO-AUTHORED
Her Own Woman
Tales I tell My Mother
More Tales

CO-EDITED
Competition: A Feminist Taboo?

For
Deborah Johnson, Eve Pell, Douglas Foster, Raul Ramirez
and David Weir.

ONE

Fall, 1988
Washington, D.C.

The sky was bleak. Silent, shivering, the two walked toward the Vietnam Memorial. Cora reflected that she was a forty-year-old woman with a grown child. The war was over. Fran dragged one step behind, her attention darting from the booth soliciting support for MIAs to the knots of families carrying thermoses and flowers. She paused to listen to a middle-aged man in a wheelchair singing "Greensleeves" under a tree. Cora refrained from hugging her daughter, who was wisely absorbing the present rather than racing through history.

She studied Fran, taken aback once again by the mix of familiar and unfamiliar: the tall, thin frame was classic Casey as was the strong jaw, fair skin and brown eyes—genuine Irish, Pop would have a chance to say any day now. In many ways Fran was the spit of herself, although Cora's hair was black, not red, and lately she had found secret stores of cellulite and new wrinkles. Then there was the difference in style. Chic, cool Fran, her hair sculpted into spikes at the front and drawn into a ponytail at the back. Did she envy or admire her daughter's ease? Her daughter—who, on alternate days, could pass for twelve or twenty-one—this young woman. Had they really come here, back home, below the border, together?

White stars, red stripes, American flags everywhere—on t-shirts and purses and tiny plastic sticks. Cora steeled herself to be angry, to respond, if necessary, to nitwits speaking slogans, calling the vets heroes. *Every* war had its heroes. Once you had honored the heroes then you got on with . . . with the next war perhaps. As they walked across the grass from the parking lot, Cora was filled with palpable fury—at the arrogance, the stupidity, the waste. Innumerable people, still the count continued, slaughtered. Miles of land completely destroyed. And now the fires continued elsewhere. She thought

3

of the petitions and articles and marches which had brought her to the point of ignition. Recalling how her family cut her off, Cora felt that cold, hard place inside herself that she feared and cherished. If Ron or George or Pop had died in the war, they would have deserved it. They knew what was going on. They refused to talk, to listen. She would have grieved heavily if they had died—more than she grieved now—but they would have been responsible. What a terrible thing to believe.

Fran paused again and Cora was forced to look at a bronze statue of three soldiers, clearly weighed down by exhuastion and what was it? Despair?

"Beautiful," a short man behind her was saying as he focused his zoom lens on the statues' faces.

"Beautiful?" she responded, in spite of herself. Fran reached for her elbow.

The man had not heard her. Cora knew it was pointless to argue that the statue romanticized the agony of three handsome individuals; to ask, What about those who had half their faces blown off? This statue was saying: All war is the same. Young men suffer. Suffering is virtue. Heroes earn honor. Heroes? Victims, maybe—or survivors. The best she could come up with was survivors.

Suddenly the hillside was sliced with dark marble. From this distance Cora could tell the lines across its face were names. Thousands of names.

She and Fran walked down a concrete ramp past people who were tracing the name of a friend or relative. They were not as she expected—neither the dead nor the living. No rhetoric here about freedom, courage, sacrifice, leadership—this was a family affair. Children skipped ahead of parents who sought brothers and friends. Old people supported one another as they lay down flowers. Poems to departed husbands were plastic-wrapped against the rain. In front of the blocks of endless names were teddy bears, flags, books, photographs.

The endlessness of those names was what finally broke Cora—each a person killed during her lifetime. She had seen war memorials before—to Canadians who fought in World War II, in World War I, in the War of 1812, in the struggle between Wolfe and Montcalm. But they had been bearable in their distance and magnitude. Usually they expressed an air of local commemoration: Peterborough honoring its war dead or Saint Mary's parish praying for immortal souls. Here, however, military anonymity was at its most brutal. The cold words honored no one, represented no place. Tears raced down her cheeks.

Nothing about that time was as simple as it seemed. That time, if only she *could* compartmentalize it. But now at the end of the monument, they were adding more people—women and men who had somehow been overlooked, lost among the lost.

She felt herself turning back, walking down to the center, promising to memorize at least one name on each panel. But she didn't make it past five men.

Daniel. Eugene. Juan. Frederick. James. She wiped her wet cheeks with the back of her shaking hand. What right did she have to weep in front of these mourning families? But the tears would not stop. She began, slowly, to realize that it was *for* these young men she had fought all that time. She allowed herself to think—as she hadn't in twenty-odd years—of the dozen boys from her high school class who had gone straight into the army. She remembered those scared kids who came through the draft counseling center in Oregon—and later the gawky deserters who had somehow made their way to Canada. Deep down, she knew it had been for *these guys* she had been fighting. And they had been too unlucky or too cocky or too misinformed to see she had been on their side. Somewhere along the line—after she had lived in Canada several years, she had come to see the U.S. soldier as the enemy. Of course some of them were, as they returned home and joined the protestor-smashing police. But others became active against the war. For a decade, she had nightmares about uniformed men: campus police wielding billy clubs; National Guardsmen posing with bayonets; Green Berets slitting the throats of little Vietnamese girls.

They became her enemy, those men in uniforms, when in fact she had just wanted them released from their own wrongheaded notions of duty and sacrifice. After everything was said, recollected and psychoanalyzed, she had loved her father and her brothers. She understood now, fully for the first time, how *she* had been one of the losers of that war. So what if she had been right about pulling out? So what if she were halfway innocent of the deaths? The rest of her family were allowed to live safely here below the border. At home.

"What about the people who were wounded or died protesting?" She asked her daughter. "All this belated welcome-home nonsense is not so much reconciliation as *reconstruction*. What about the COs, the people who went to prison, the ones who would never return from abroad?"

She did not ask who would welcome her home.

Fran shook her head sadly.

Cora had been aware of Fran's concern. The girl had quietly clasped her elbow as they walked the length of the memorial. Still she wasn't ready to return to being a mother yet. She looked over Fran's head at the family groups leaving the parking lot, at the single men and women who had come here to commemorate a soldier's birthday or wedding. Cora had a ridiculous impulse to turn to Fran and ask permission to stay. But she could not bear the seriousness she would find in the eyes of her daughter who had grown up in the threatening shadow of a mad grandmother. Cora pulled herself together.

Jacques told her she was too controlled, but he didn't understand maternal responsibilities. Calmly, Cora nodded toward the Potomac.

Resting against a railing, she stared at the grey river and felt sadness trickle from her. She was conscious of a light arm around her shoulder and of a shaking. This was unreal, as Fran liked to say. Cora had never permitted herself to lean on her daughter; she was too busy protecting her and apologizing to her. Now she was filled with an entirely new poignancy. Fran's arms were sure. She could smell the coffee on her daughter's breath.

TWO

Summer, 1988
Toronto

Cora arrived early, a motherly gesture, perhaps, but she wanted to secure a quiet table at the back. She and Fran had agreed to meet as adults on neutral territory, and Dimitri's Taverna was an old favorite of her daughter's.

Normally she would wait to drink until Fran arrived, but it had been a tough day. Her eyes filled as she thought about her Aunt Min's letter. *Still* she had finished the article. Yes, this was a celebratory meal. Bravo to her article and Fran's acceptance to dance school. Cora breathed in the aromas of garlic and roasting meat. The sunlit liquid brought to mind white Cretan houses, cobbled streets, southern skies.

Cora shifted from imagination to memory, preferring, as always, the later. Now she recalled the cheap California burgundy she drank at college. While most political people smoked dope, she never trusted grass which was so much less predictable than booze. Cora didn't want to trail her mother into oblivion. Now she felt her shoulders loosen; the resin scent put her at ease.

Enter the daughter in glittering pink top, navel exposed, purple tights and leg warmers. Cora's breath caught at Fran's disappointment in failing to spot her mother.

"Over here, sweetheart!" Sweetheart, her nineteen-year-old hated being treated as a child. Still, Fran grinned broadly and floated forward, kissing Cora's cheek and finding her seat in one fluid movement.

"Howrya doing, Mom?" She leaned forward on her elbows. "Say, terrific dress. Wild red lace!"

Dimitri served the taramosalata and hummus.

"Fabulous, Dimitri, how did you know I was *starving*?"

Cora exchanged a smile with the bald waiter, briefly feeling more kinship with him than with her effervescent daughter.

7

"So, you finished the latest muckraking masterpiece?" Fran poured herself a half-glass of retsina (she always drank abstemiously to maintain her dancer's body) and raised a toast.

"At noon today," Cora reached for her earlier euphoria. "Should come out next month. I'm sure they'll put it on the cover."

"Outstanding!"

"Another toast to you—when does the course begin?"

Fran grinned and tugged on the third feather hanging from her left ear. "Middle of the month. Oh, I still can't believe it, Mom, I still can't believe it."

Neither could Cora. After a childhood as the daughter of a single mother, after years in progressive schools and weekends at antiwar marches, teach-ins and feminist rallies, her daughter had decided to become a dancer. A hoofer. Not your radical Isadora Duncan political art, not even your classical ballet, but show dancing. Ed Sullivan kind of dancing to popular music in lavish variety shows. The only "political" thing about Fran was her lesbianism. Cora knew her response was unsound, but she hoped Fran would outgrow that. What could she do about any of Fran's choices, Fran's life?

"Come in, Mom." Fran leaned back, one leg wrapped under the other, yawning widely, earrings jingling. "Earth to Mom. Hello there, Mom."

Cora blinked. "I was just appreciating my stunning dining companion." She bit her tongue to stem a critique of Fran's make-up.

"I'll be going south of the border." Fran raised a speculative eyebrow.

Cora gulped retsina. "When?" Her voice was cool.

"Next weekend. School recommends that we catch as many New York shows as we can. So me and Nancy are going on one of those all-in-one culture and hotel deals." She noticed her mother's open mouth. "OK, Nancy and *I*."

"It's not . . . that." Cora shook her head vaguely. Did she resemble Mom in this vagueness? Her mother had died when Cora was eight, but had disappeared long before that. "I, I don't know. I was going to wait until after dinner until I told you, but, well, Grandpa is sick."

"Who?"

Cora didn't check her annoyance. "My father. Your grandfather. He's . . . dying."

Fran waited cautiously.

"And I've decided to go back."

"To the States?" She blinked.

"Well, to Oregon. To Grandview." She spoke defensively, as if visiting her family were not the same as returning to the whole country.

"Is it safe, Mom? I mean, are you sure?"

Cora shrugged. She waved to Dimitri, who picked up his pad and approached.

"I'd like the lamb kebabs, please."

"Greek salad, please," Fran said distractedly.

Cora drifted. During the first two years in Canada she couldn't sleep a full night for fear of the Royal Canadian Mounted Police barging into the flat and extraditing her to the States. Could they take her daughter, who had been born Canadian? Would they leave her behind? As years passed and the U.S. authorities seemed to forget antiwar protests, she wondered how much of the danger she had invented.

Fran was horrified. "You can't go to Oregon, Mom, be reasonable."

"Some things are beyond reason." She brushed crumbs off her blue napkin and folded it into smaller and smaller squares.

"Well, how about sense? You're always harping on me about common sense." She looked as if someone had knocked all the air out of her. "Why would you go back to see that old fart? What has he ever given you but grief? Why would you even want to say good-bye?"

"It's more than that," Cora protested, overcome by her irritation. "It's more than good-bye. There's everything left to say."

"What's that supposed to mean?" Fran persisted in the same annoying, protective tone.

"I don't know." Cora blurted, too loudly. Heads turned and she lowered her voice. "I don't even know if I'm *going* to Oregon . . ."

"Well," Fran interrupted, "if you go, I go."

"No, honey, you don't understand. He's sick. If I go, it could be months. You have your classes. Besides . . . "

"Besides, what?"

"Besides, it may not be safe."

"That's what I *said*."

"You really are infuriating."

"No, I just don't fit into your story the way you want." Her eyes grew more anxious. "You can't place my remarks in the appropriate paragraph. You can't edit life the way you edit your articles."

"I knew I never should have paid for that psychotherapist," Cora laughed.

"Anyhow, I'm coming." She ignored her mother's warning glance. "I might as well have a *look* at my grandfather."

"Enough." Cora raised her hands in an exasperated gesture one might inherit from a daughter. "There's plenty of time to talk about this. Let's get back to celebrating school acceptances and article conclusions so that we can," she nodded toward Dimitri as he neared the table, "digest the meal."

* * *

Eight hours earlier, Cora had assumed that the one remarkable thing about her day would be finishing the article. And by noon she *was* finished at last, after four months.

Cora leaned back in her chair looking past the clutter of books, tapes and paper to Mr. Caputo across the street. The old man raked his lawn. Scrape. Scrape. It was still summer. She had spent the entire summer writing about refugees from Guatamala and El Salvador. Wincing, she recalled how she had once dramatically regarded herself as a refugee, from "Amerika." She picked up a mug of cold coffee and sipped absently. Scrape. Scrape. There *had* been some painful parallels. Mr. Caputo raked slowly, methodically. If she didn't move, he would start on her yard. Ninety years old and every day out in the garden. Always ready with a friendly word and the persistent, "Take it easy!" Before she met Mr. C., she had believed that guardian angels had to be one's own sex.

The coffee tasted strangely sour. Ugh, yesterday's mug, with the milk going off. She smiled at the mess in her small study: files sandwiched between plastic bags and library books; used manila envelopes she had meant to refile once she had found a spare drawer; photos of the Dominion Day picnic stuck between old copies of *Saturday Night* and *This Magazine*. Finished, what a relief.

Downstairs, she found a copy of "Proud Mary" and put it on the stereo. The Minellis were away this week, so she could turn the music up full blast. "Rollin', rollin', rollin' down the river . . . " she sang as she gathered books, files and spare clothes. Cora shook her head at the selective vision she always developed in the last stages of a big project. "Proud Mary keep on burning . . . " She had never really understood this song, but she liked it for the same reasons she liked Helen Reddy's "Delta Dawn" and "Leave Me Alone." Outdated feminist instincts, Fran would say. She shrugged. Creedence Clearwater, lovely name.

The bathroom was beyond words. Throw away the magazines first. Yes. Cora sat on the toilet, urinating, leafing through a copy of *Maclean's*, reading a memoir about Jackie Gleason and crying, sobbing. Tough, fat, Irish, working-class wisecracker makes good; gets drunk; loses money; makes good. This was her father's story. Jackie Gleason dead? Reginald Van Gleason dead? The Pour Soul? Ralph Kramden? Not Ralph Kramden, the immortal bus driver.

Scrape. Scrape. She yanked up her pants and flushed the toilet. Scrape: the stereo needle weeping over the vacant plastic. She selected an album from Perth County Conspiracy, one of the first records she had bought in Canada. Outdated, too, *and* very scratched.

Cora stood at the living room window, hands on her modest hips, listening for the hits of grass and speed in the agitprop lyrics. She remembered one hot late night at a Toronto folk club, as people passed a joint from one stranger to another—wondering if she would some day learn the line between the possible and the impossible—wondering if she wanted to be restrained by borders of reality.

Mr. Caputo slowly lifted the pile of leaves into the garbage can. Straightening, he noticed Mrs. Bardotti opening his gate. Sturdy, dour Mrs. Bardotti was only eighty-eight but stiffer in the joints than Mr. Caputo. Soon she would unpack her picnic basket at the backyard table under the maple tree. Might as well enjoy the fine weather, Cora could hear Mr. Caputo say. After lunch they would both nap somewhere in his house. In the same bed? Cora hoped so. She would not have to guess what would happen at 6 o'clock. Mr. Caputo would walk around the corner to Mrs. Bardotti's house for supper and television.

The Perth County Conspiracy; Mrs. Bardotti; a half-empty bag of pumpkin seeds near the television; a completed article upstairs. Christ, there was no point in finishing an assignment if you didn't get it to the magazine. "Where's your keeper?" she could hear her brother George say. She checked her watch, 12:10. If she hurried, she could deliver it to the office while Arthur was still at lunch, avoid a confrontation about submitting a week late and be back here in time to finish a good portion of the cleaning. Jacques was due home on Tuesday. Surely she would have dug her way out of the mess by Tuesday.

Outside, two envelopes protruded from the mailbox: a boring brown one from the bank and a letter from Aunt Min. She would save the letter from Aunt Min as a treat on the way home from the office. She returned the bank statement to the mailbox, willing it to disappear.

Hurrying along Dahlia Street, Cora inhaled the almost autumnal air. She loved the melancholy of fall. In a few months, these lusty green trees would be bare. Not all of them. She preferred the dignified, nude trees to the ones with leaves straggling until March or the first buds in April.

On the subway home, Cora closed her eyes. Once Arthur read the article, he would forget the deadline. She didn't always feel so confident, but she knew this piece was good, as well as important. Not enough of her work had been important. OK, she usually wrote serious stories—with the occasional foray into comparative bagels or cheap holidays—but it had been ages since she had believed in an issue the way she believed in sanctuary for Central Americans. She sucked on her bottom teeth, fretting, still, that she had not been completely honest with them. Of course they hadn't asked if she were American; no one asked any more, for they were in a new stage of refugee history. Besides, by learning the Canadian way of saying, "been, about, again," she could pass. What did her birthplace matter now, almost two decades after finding her own sanctuary?

Cora glanced around the train. She liked to travel midday, when people were less guarded. Their bodies took up more room. Emotions crossed their faces. By contrast, the morning and evening commuters often seemed to be erasing their memory banks and replacing the content with news from

The Star or *The Globe and Mail.* This was a very Toronto crew—an old Portugese woman wearing black, sitting next to an even older Portugese woman,
whose dress had faded to a dark grey. Would they be buried in these clothes
they wore to mourn their husbands? Cora recalled her own contained presence when she had arrived in Toronto, so full of ideas and plans, so practiced
in assimilation and camouflage.

The letter. This mooning was getting precisely nowhere, that's what
her aunt would say. Next to God, perhaps even before God, Aunt Min believed in family. She was the only one with whom Cora kept in touch. In recent years Cora had begun to look forward to these letters as a strange
lifeline.

She fished the envelope from her shoulder bag, then glanced around to
watch three kids playing pitchpenny against the wall and the Portugese
women silently studying their laps. This intimate, impersonal company afforded a queer feeling of safety, and she hoped none of them would disembark until she had read the letter.

> *Dear Corey,*
>   *This is hard to write.*

She looked around possessively at the other passengers. Family, Gordon had
told her when she reached Vancouver, was simply a social construct.

> *Your father is very ill. The emphysema is worse and they've found can-
> cer in both lungs. The doctor thinks he has two, maybe three months. I
> know, Corey, that you've had a hard time with your Pop, but it's im-
> portant to say good-bye.*
>   *I hope you'll consider coming home. But he's still as explosive as ever.
> He's no pussy cat, making peace on his way out.*

His way out. His way out. His way out. She had waited years for this letter, had forecast her distant, angry victory as her brothers whimpered over
his grave. Now Aunt Min wanted her to come home. *Home?* She stared at the
Portugese women whose eyes were shut.

> *But I think he needs you now. He refuses to go into a hospital. Your
> brothers say this is crazy because the insurance would pay for it and
> they don't have the money to hire private nurses. And I can't do it my-
> self. I haven't wanted to burden you with this, dear, but because of some
> glaucoma, I'm not good for much any more. This is a lot to ask. I know
> how you've felt about your father. If this makes it easier, think about
> coming home for ME. It would be wonderful to actually SEE you while
> that's still possible. Think about it . . .*

Aunt Min, Cora shook her head sadly, she could not understand the woman's implacable loyalty to that boor. Pop never respected his younger sister, always treated her as a servant, even when she flew to his house after his wife left (was taken away?) and raised his children. Here she was, at sixty, still looking after the bastard and arranging for Cora to fill in. That's what women did all over the world, trained younger women to fill in. It made a mockery of the last two decades, of her rejection of what Pop stood for, of her new life in Canada, her independence, her sanity, her relationship with Jacques. Who knows what she would be risking if she went back? And for what?

o   o   o

That night she lay in bed thinking how quickly Fran had grown. Although—or because—she had consumed almost an entire bottle of retsina, Cora couldn't sleep. She yearned for Jacques. Jacques listened as no one else could. He would worry about her returning to the States. He wouldn't want her to go.

Cora switched on the light and peered across the room at a couple of small, framed photos. She was filled with pleasure as she observed the two scruffy people hunched under heavy packs, posed stiffly, waiting for the automatic shutter to click. Jacques had introduced her to backpacking, cross-country skiing and a new sense of herself as a physical person. The other photo had been taken by her old friend Oscar at a peace march. She and Jacques were bundled in quilted jackets, blowing on their fists for warmth. She felt at once frightened about being without Jacques and guilty at the prospect of leaving him. What melodrama! Oregon was only two thousand miles away, just across the continent. One state down from British Columbia.

No, she mustn't think about it. When her mind raced like this she couldn't make even a simple decision. She should be planning her next project, how she was going to bring more money into the house. No, she shouldn't be thinking at all; she should be sleeping. But yes, she would like to accept that invitation to Nicaragua. On the way south, she would write about Guatemalan and Salvadoran refugee camps in Mexico. Her Spanish was good now, and she had made lots of contacts through the last article.

What would Pop say if he opened the door to her? The dream, of course, was that he would beg her forgiveness. *Pop and her brothers*. No, it was too much to ask remorse from all of them. *He* was the one from whom she needed to hear . . . something. She had spent so many years feeling stunned and bitter that this man was actually her father. So many years wishing him dead. Why did she care now?

No, she rolled over, pulled the duvet above her shoulders and put the blue striped pillow over her head. She needed to sleep. She imagined November and counted snowflakes.

When she had left the States, she had felt as if she had worn away most of her skin in frustration and anger and failure. During the last twenty years she had embroidered a pattern over the dangerously thin places. Even as she did this, she knew X marked the spot. The sources of her success in Canada were patterned in her failures as an American.

Was the cancer painful? Did he have trouble breathing? She sat up and wondered what time it was in Oregon now. One A.M. here, so 10 P.M. there. He would be in bed because he always awoke at 5 A.M., dutiful sailor. No, she shivered, he would be in bed because he was always in bed these days. Dying men do not walk the dogs before dawn. Did he have bed sores? Was he eating properly? How much could he eat? He was always such a child—consuming quantities of the worst foods despite his already erratic heart. She used to imagine he would go quickly in a cardiac arrest. He must be furious at deteriorating like this. Of course he would not want to go to an instituion. How could George and Ron be so thick? So selfish?

A window slammed downstairs. Next door. The Minellis were home early from their holiday. For years Cora had had trouble adjusting to the intimacy of row houses. She felt intruded upon when people took showers. She dreaded the muffled conversations seeping through the bedroom walls. And the roaches. It did absolutely no good exterminating if your neighbors didn't do it with you. People often asked her what the biggest change had been for her living in Toronto. It had been the colors and the space. Because she didn't want people to identify her too precisely, she didn't mention the Pacific. She missed the ocean most.

Obviously he would want to die in that house. You couldn't see the water from the hospital. Why didn't those jerks understand that? They used to be so tight—George and Ron had been the sons he wanted, and he was the strong, blustering father they aspired to be in their own families. Why weren't they nursing him? And why did she care?

She thought she had recovered from that hateful man years and years ago. She had lived half her life in Canada. She must be at least half Canadian. Why did it matter where you came from if you knew where you were . . . and where you were going? She felt tears running inside her throat, sweet rather than salty. Either she was going home or she was going crazy. Was there a difference?

No, she couldn't possibly return to Oregon. She had responsibilities to Fran and Jacques. And friends here who needed her. She would not desert them out of filial sentiment. She would not be a fool.

The toilet flushed next door. Cora could hear the Minellis talking in bed. She slid back down under the duvet and felt her body surrender.

THREE

Fall, 1988
Toronto

Outside in the mild rain, Cora leaned against the porch railing and allowed water to run through her glistening black hair and down her flushed face. Jacques had opted for a more conventional shower, but Cora was drawn to the rain. She grew melancholy with the smell of lovemaking washing off her mouth and cheeks. Her hands felt young as she ran them through her hair.

Was Mr. Caputo speculating on her craziness from his darkened parlor now? She returned to her body, relaxed, satisfied, tired and again sad. Sad about the possibility of leaving Jacques for months. About the prospect of Pop's death. About returning to the U.S. More sad at the memory of leaving years before.

She heard a rap on the picture window and turned to see Jacques inside lifting a pot of tea. Yes, she nodded to the handsome curly head. Perfect. Yet she was reluctant to relinquish the rain. It poured in Oregon from October to May. Her wet hair dripped into the thin cotton of her T-shirt.

Inside, Jacques handed her a large white, fluffy towel they had nicked from a motel in Sudbury. His touch was electric. Immediately she wanted to return to bed. Still, she knew Jacques had work to do, that they both had decisions to make. She had always wanted more.

Cora draped the towel over her shoulders, unwilling to dry the rain from her hair just yet. Jacques watched disapprovingly. Cora picked up the chipped, brown tea pot, swished it around and filled Jacques's mug. As she poured her own, she studied the Darjeeling turning the milk a silky grey. "Great tea."

"My pleasure."

"Hmmm." Cora looked at this strong, slightly chunky man warming his hands on the cup. She admired the pink fingers that had given her such delight. Cora cherished his tenderness and hunger and corny humor. How could she think about leaving him?

"Now, don't worry about me," Jacques read her mind. "Of course I don't want you to go. But you must do what you want. Or *need*."

"That doesn't make it any easier." Cora frowned. She wished she could leave it to the opposing forces to determine the outcome. She was just the rope in the middle—let one of them pull harder for her. Of course life was never as simple as being chosen by people who wanted you.

After a long silence, Jacques reached over and touched her knee. "*Ça va?*"

Cora shrugged. "Sometimes I hate choice. The worst part of my journalist personality emerges—all the dogged, conflicting questions."

"Doggedness is one of your charms, that and a certain tendency to over-seriousness." Jacques winked.

"I just don't know how to make this decision, honey." Cora stared out the window at sun igniting yellow leaves. If she left now, she would miss the autumn, her favorite time in Toronto. Suddenly the glare caused her to bend her head. Fingering her hair, she could feel water weighing down the curls. Heavy. Momentary ripeness. Already some of the ends had dried. She shivered.

"Well, pneumonia could make the decision for you." Jacques observed softly.

"Sorry?"

"Come on," Jacques said.

Cora looked up expectantly.

"*Voici.*" He handed her another towel.

* * *

The rain had disappeared by the time Cora reached Queen's Park. She might have fantasized the shower if it were not for the puddles and the dampness of red and gold maple leaves. Often she walked here to think. There was something reassuringly limited about the tranquility of this small park surrounded by urban bustle. In the center, you could almost imagine the traffic vanishing, but not quite. Unlike outlying High Park or the ravines, where you could get lost, here in midcity there was always a comforting screech of truck gears or police sirens from the park boundaries.

She had fallen in love with the statue of Victoria in Queen's Park Crescent nineteen years ago. The empress was hardly an ideologically acceptable role model, but she felt for the fat, marble lady. They were both outsiders in this cold capital. Few of her Canadian friends were as fond of Queen's Park as she. "You want to picnic in the middle of the city?" Jacques would demand. For most Torontonians, it was a pleasant detour to and from work. Cora understood that her enjoyment of Queen's Park was one of the things that marked her as an outsider.

She glanced at the greyworsted workers scuttling down narrow paths to the subway and the parking lot. She considered her tennis shoes, old jeans, and the bulky sweater her friend Elana had knitted eight years before. From a distance she could pass—did pass—for a college student. But now, examining the lines creasing her fingers and the spots appearing on the backs of her hands, she wondered how much longer she would pretend that the girl inside would grow up and become someone else.

She walked east through the Annex, crunching leaves—squishing most of them—for wet was inhibiting her autumn pilgrimage. Tomorrow the leaves would be dry again, crackling in full fire. Autumn in Oregon was grey and brown. She was angry at Pop for taking her away just as she was about to celebrate her twentieth Canadian fall. Well, she didn't know if she were going, if she *could* go. Oscar would tell her.

◦ ◦ ◦

Oscar's comfortable waiting room exuded an aura of establishment and security without threatening clients with the notion that it would be redecorated next month on the strength of exorbitant fees. The young secretary was busy, so Cora sat on a mauve velvet couch, running her finger back and forth across the upholstered fur. They were meant to be friends from the start, nothing more, she told Oscar one night when he was treating her to dinner on a corporate account. She would never forget his soulful reproach: "Nothing *more*? What's *more* than friendship? You have some pretty antiquated notions for a feminist."

That was true.

"Mr. Green is on an international call." The new secretary's curiosity was masked by remote politeness. She sat up straight, smoothing her short burgundy skirt over bare thighs. "May I get you coffee or tea?"

"Oh, no thanks, I mean I'll get it. I've known this office for ages." She visited the ancient Mr. Coffee, poured herself a cup, then ducked into the minifridge below for milk. Oh, yes, she shut the door against the smell of memory; it still reeked of garlic. The night she met Oscar, they had wound up making love on the sofa in the small front office.

The secretary picked carefully at her mousse nest of blond hair and smiled thinly as Cora sat down. She wore that possessive look Oscar cultivated in his assistants. Really, it was too ridiculous, Cora would have to tell him, they were getting younger and younger while he . . . but the worst of it right now was that the woman felt vaguely threatened by her. Perhaps she should just speak broadly enough to be recognized as American. Perhaps the secretary would believe she was one of Oscar's cousins.

Their friendship had been sustained by the very Americanness they tried to shed. They still talked enthusiastically about the intelligent modesty of Canadians, the cosmopolitan quality of Toronto, the three-party system, bilingualism. Jacques had developed an understandable cynicism about these things.

"*But* it's so much better than the States," Cora and Oscar would chorus.

"Why must you always compare us with them?" Jacques would demand.

Us. Them. She was neither. She was evolving. The nature of evolving during one's own lifetime was that at any given moment one was always the end product.

"Cora."

Oscar was a little balder than last month and as gawkily eager as ever. Filled with affection, she stood on her toes, kissing his clean shaven face.

"Madeline," his voice was flustered. "Let me introduce you to my old friend Cora."

Had he emphasized the word *old*?

"Cora and I are like family."

"Cousins," Cora laughed.

She sank into the brown leather chair and surveyed the office furniture, covered in discreet beiges, browns and blues. Very comfortable, but she missed the small cubbyhole at the front of the building. She did not feel quite stylish enough for this office. She recalled the randomness of her own house—the odd tables and chairs needing new seats. She and Jacques did intend to frame the prints in the living room.

"I'm thinking about going home." It slipped out.

"You just got here." He cocked his head and settled behind the desk.

"No," she smiled at his concern and at her own distractedness, "back to the States."

"For a visit," she rattled on hopelessly. "A longish visit, maybe. My father's very sick. Dying."

He took her hand, "I'm sorry, Cora. How are you feeling?"

"Fine. I mean confused. Tired." She shrugged. "I guess I came to ask if you think it's safe."

He stared. "I doubt I know anything you don't know at this point. I've always told you it would be safer to take out Canadian citizenship."

This had been a sore point between them, for Oscar had become Canadian at the first opportunity while she had kept stalling.

"As we've discussed," his voice was slower, more lawyerly, "there's no statute of limitations on something like this. In theory, the FBI could keep the case open forever because of the death and possible conspiracy charges."

She listened intently to the familiar analysis. The blood vessels in her face throbbed.

"On the other hand, some of those antiwar cases were simply forgotten. If there's never been an arrest warrant, chances are all the secrets died with

Ralph. No one from the movement is going to start talking after all this time. It's a calculated risk . . ."

She imagined watching them from the doorway: the anxious, middle-aged client and the supportive, professional attorney. Two old comrades still calculating the odds after all these years.

" . . . but are you sure you *want* to go?"

"*Want* isn't the word. The man is dying." She sighed, then spoke too loudly, "My father is dying."

He shook his head. "You never really left."

The choices over Canadian identity divided many of her friends. People like Oscar changed citizenship as soon as they could, to demonstrate their loyalty to Canada, to settle their lives. Most people who had become Canadians were less angry at the U.S. Cora knew her own anger was a tie with home and that's what prevented her changing citizenship.

"You never settled here."

She forced steadiness into her voice. "That's not true. I have my writing. My family." What *did* she hope to accomplish by going back? Why did she feel responsible for Pop? What about her work—wasn't the Nicaragua story more important than her own individual family odyssey? Who *were* her family—Fran and Jacques or Pop and her brothers? It was crazy, simply crazy to return to all that.

"I knew you would go back."

She resisted the familiar guilt. "That's a little dramatic, as if I were using Toronto as a guerrilla base . . ."

"Maybe as therapy . . ."

"Enough," Cora shouted. "I'm just going to help him die. I'll be back." She broke down in sobs. "This is my home."

He leaned forward, his face worried, but his voice still hard, "So you had decided all along."

"I don't know! Christ, I come to a friend and I get criticism/self-criticism." She stood. "I just don't know."

"Wait," he softened. "Let's talk. If you decide to go, let me give you the name of a lawyer I know in Portland." His eyes were reassuring. "Not that I think there's anything to really worry about."

* * *

Cora knew it was a dream. She kept waking and falling back over the blurred lines. She was walking to the beach, as she had done a thousand times. As she had not done in twenty years.

Sharp rocks penetrated the thin soles of her veteran running shoes. The wind was high and cold and the sun low enough in the sky to strike her chest. A perfect/imperfect Oregon evening. While her Toronto friends lusted after luscious Caribbean beaches, Cora ached for the rugged Pacific coast. Her pleasure was fused with fear and she reached for a deeper sleep.

Cora timed her breaths to the rise and fall of the waves. In . . . out. In . . . out. The separation of ebb and flow was too long, the reflex for air too strong. She inhaled, gulping—a pathetic land animal devolved from her ancestral amphibian—still, she belonged to the water. The pungent brine was tinged with scents of Pacific fir and pine. How often she had walked alone here as a girl, away from the voices. How old was she now? Surely no longer a child. Cora shook her long dark hair, mostly dark save for what Jacques called the lunar streaks. She reminded herself she was a mother, a lover, a writer, a daughter returning of her own volition. She had a new country and after twenty years, three new layers of skin. She would not be imprisoned. She had created a new life for herself. And when she walked along the Oregon beach, she would be free.

Cora picked across the gravel and boulders, careful not to trip or twist an ankle. If anything, the beach was more rocky than during the misty gloom of her girlhood summer afternoons. She had always missed the sea, had never felt truly safe midcontinent. She yearned for these soft, moist movements and rich aromas, for the brisk climate and the enveloping waves. When she made love she returned to the Pacific rhythms.

Scanning the southwestern sky for predictions of sunset, Cora prayed the cumulus clouds would scatter long enough to streak sacramental blood across the sky. Sunset on the water: mirror image of the host ascending over red wine. Cora imagined herself in an organdy communion dress kneeling on a nurse log. The girl wondered if she were a witch. The woman wondered about the coast between originality and madness. Meanwhile, which way was hubris?

She continued toward the lighthouse, recalling childhood walks with Pop and later solitary teenage rambles in the same direction. At her feet was an "I Like Ike" button—a shiny new red, white and blue campaign badge with a round picture of the smiling, bald golfer. The beach had always been scarred by litter. "Safe sex" promised the giant-size condom box. So much garbage. A cracked orange hula hoop. Half a Sony Walkman. An old TV set with Arthur Godfrey singing "The Hawaiian Wedding Song" off key. Again, she reached for a deeper sleep, matching breaths with the tides. In . . . out. In . . . out. She would linger between land and sea.

Wet, cool, yes, this was the Pacific Ocean on her bare toes waking her— the opposite of lulling—waking her to the joyful mystery of a Western sunset. West coast. Last coast. Often during the past two decades she wondered whether her immigration had more to do with going to Canada or going inland. The coast was different from the rest of the continent. This was the edge. Oregon was more related to Baja and British Columbia than any Yankee place further east. Yet even as she stood inhaling the western spray, she was afraid. "*J'ai peur.*" The French implied fear was something you possessed rather than something that possessed you. Even as she merged with the salt air, she conjured prison as she hadn't in years. Who would capture her? How and why? No, this was ridiculous. She had been baptized in the daring of the west; her family was here; the lapping water reminded her she was safe.

Cora stood, barefoot at the west of the West. When you traveled on from here you moved east—to Japan, Vietnam, China—aross the international dateline. Oregon was way out, far out, far away. Oregon was the end.

FOUR

Fall, 1965
Oregon

The view from the kitchen was restful: dark clouds and grey ocean framed by giant pines. She could smell the lumber yards and the salt air, even through the closed window. Cora planned to make the best of her first weekend home from college. Pop, George and Ron were watching football on TV as she cooked. She had ordered at Franklin's Restaurant every Sunday since Aunt Min married John Earle. So it was expected that Cora would fix chicken when she came home. In her more petulant moments, she wondered if they were looking forward more to her return or to the chicken dinner.

As she basted turnips, pleased to see they were all evenly brown, she considered that the visit could have been worse. While it's true that no one had greeted her with confetti, that so far they had spent two boring evenings watching television, there hadn't been any major blowups. When it wasn't chicken, she was a happy cook—so there had been compliments all around yesterday. She didn't mind their going bowling this afternoon because that had given her time to study.

Cora felt grateful her big brother was home from the war and wished he wouldn't ship out again. It was someone else's turn to risk his life. She had read terrible things about what the Vietcong did to American soldiers. She did not want George coming back missing a leg or an arm. She did not want him returning in a body bag. She wanted him home, practicing his swing. He was still young enough to have a shot at the major leagues. And now Ron talked about enlisting when he graduated from high school. Wasn't there some law against both sons in one family fighting in the same war? She had hoped to have a moment with Ron this weekend, to invite him to campus. Perhaps if they got away from home for a few days, away from George and Pop, she could convince him to apply for college instead of the army.

Considering the clouds again, she realized she liked these melancholy days better than the bright blue ones. They felt safer. She recalled Sara's criticism last week—was she timid? Well, as Aunt Min would say, this wasn't the way potatoes got cooked. Cora reached into the sack and began to peel—three each for the boys and two for herself. She supposed they were big eaters. Whenever she visited Sara's family she was astonished by the small servings. After all, Dr. Riley was a rich surgeon. Then, again, he was a frail creature next to whom Pop looked like Godzilla. Pop wasn't fat—just large-boned and healthy. Smiling, she thought how nothing meant as much to Pop as family loyalty.

The TV volume increased with the Olympia beer commercial. "It's the water; it's the water . . . " a woman sang in a thin, clear and—Cora imagined—Artesian voice.

Pop appeared in the doorway. "Dinner on schedule?" He demanded, then winked.

"Yes sir," she saluted.

"Good, good," he barked. "Glad to see you haven't lost all your female instincts in those libraries." He pulled a Budweiser out of the refrigerator.

Cora shook her head. She knew he was damned if he was going to buy Olympia just because they sponsored the football games.

"Smells great." He snapped open the can, talking with a cigarette in his teeth, "If only the galley on the ship did this good. 'Course there's not much they can do for produce once we get to Saigon. Best stuff goes to the military. Bloody Pacific. Japs, Koreans, Gooks. Wish we could blast them out of the ocean, then fill it with concrete. That'd solve our parking problems." He was laughing as he returned to catch the last quarter. His limp was surprisingly mild for such a cold day.

Cora stared out the window again at the ocean, imagining she was running across the sand, swimming around knots of seaweed, deeper and deeper into the waves.

Would it be too much to ask that they avoid talking about the war tonight? Did she believe in praying? It probably *was* too much to ask George. And she admired her older brother's courage. Last night's dream surrounded her as if she were still sleeping. George crouched in high grass. Helmet on his sweat-slicked head, a clip of ammunition down his back, like rattles on a snake. One hand gripped a rifle. The other brushed grass out of his face. How were they going to get him? By air? From the front or the side? With a grenade? Bullets? A land mine? What could she do to save him . . . Now Cora blinked and steeled herself to keep silent at dinner.

"If you're not part of the solution, you're part of the problem," according to Sara's bumper sticker.

The chicken, what was that smell, Christ, burning already.

◦ ◦ ◦

"Not bad, Sis," Ron said.

George grinned. "I got nostalgic for charbroiled chicken in those swamps, I got to tell you."

Cora looked down at her plate. Ridiculous to take his teasing seriously. Suddenly she felt exhausted from a late night studying for midterms and the last two days cooking and cleaning. Cheer up, it's only a weekend. She was lucky Pop had allowed her to go to college. She was lucky to have a scholarship. Lucky, she should feel, not tired.

"If you're smart, George," Pop paused to swallow his potatoes, "you'd keep your eyes open for land over there. After the war, we'll be building charbroilers and soda shops and spaghetti houses. It'll be like the Philippines, only better—because we'll do it right this time."

"You think we have a chance of winning?" Ron looked down at his plate.

"Only if we get off our airy fairy asses and start bombing the hell out of the North," George said. "Ridiculous way to run a war. You'd think we had a bunch of faggots in the White House."

o o o

Cora thought back to that first night at the Pancake Palace with the girls from the dorm. She could hardly contain her anger with that smug pacifist sophomore Becky. Pop had warned her about these people who had no real contact with the war, who didn't even know why we were fighting. If you left the country to them, he said, we'd all be speaking Chinese.

"I think," she heard herself telling the girls, "we need a clearer, more aggressive policy. We could end the war, stop the suffering in a few months, if we simply engaged in a more concentrated bombing campaign." She noticed how articulate she sounded.

When she read about the war she thought about George and Pop over there in a world with mangrove swamps, rice paddies, lagoons, typhoons. It was a different planet with extra terrestrial names: Khe Sanh, Mekong, Bien Hoa, Nui Coto. What were they doing over there—Pop and George and the others? She knew this question was disloyal—just the kind of doubting the girls wanted to hear. Cora stared at her pancakes and listened to them argue.

o o o

"Otherwise that war could go on forever," George persisted. "The Viet Cong know the swamps blindfolded. If Johnson doesn't get off his ass, we're going to lose thousands more good American men."

"What if we pulled out?" Cora heard herself asking. (She tried not to think of those political cartoons urging L.B.J. to perform coitus interruptus, but she felt her face redden. Everything was coming at her at once these days—midterms, sex, politics.) "What if we just left it to the Vietnamese?"

"Where did you pick up that language, missy?"

She watched her father's jaw stiffen. "No place for treason at my table, understand? This is a patriotic home. I'm proud of my contribution transporting ammunition. Proud of George. I'll be proud of Ron when he's old enough to get involved too." He lit a cigarette and passed the pack to George.

Cora detected anxiety beneath her younger brother's compliant smile.

"It's these Commie professors." George helped himself to more potatoes. "I told you we shouldn't let her get mixed up in college. Next thing you know . . ."

The dog started to bark under the table. George reached down to calm her. Tenk had always been partial to George.

"No!" Pop declared. "You don't have to worry about Cora. She has a head on her shoulders. She's no traitor. Like Father Larsen said, she's a credit to the family."

Fall, 1966

Flourescent lights hummed in the empty editorial office. Almost empty. Cora looked up now and then at Lenny, the cute night editor, awaiting her copy on the anti-ROTC demonstration. He was eating M & Ms and listening to Mary Wells belt out "My Guy" on his transistor radio.

Cora found herself going home from college less often during her second year. The bus trip seemed to take forever. She had more friends on campus, particularly on the student newspaper, where she was spending too much time for the good of her studies.

Cora ran her finger through the sweat in her eyebrows. The campus police had been brutal. She had to describe that. The demonstrators had been rowdy at times, but the word *inspirational* was her main response. They had been willing to risk their grades, their enrollment, their lives to stop the war. "Stop the bombing. Stop the war. Stop the bombing. Stop the war." Northwest State University might be small, but the antiwar movement here was one of the best organized in the country.

"Yesterday's demonstration was . . . inspirational. . . ." No, of course she couldn't write that. She didn't even want to feel it. But she knew tonight, as she had suspected for months, that she had moved to the other side. The more she read and listened and argued, the more she realized the Americans shouldn't be running Vietnam. She had asked Pop about this several months ago, and he had practically laughed her off the phone. Didn't she know we were just supporting the Vietnamese people until they got back on their feet? Didn't she understand that Ho Chi Minh was backed by Peking? Didn't they teach her anything about the domino theory in college? What was she studying—underwater basketweaving?

Cora stared at the beige copy paper in her typewriter, thinking about U.S. military violence, peace, democracy, loyalty, the campus police, free speech. Sara and Becky teased her about bringing her "Catholic conscience" to college. What was wrong with morality, she asked. They tried to explain that politics and morality were two separate things.

For several weeks Cora had stayed away from Sara and her other friends. She refused to call home. She simply focused on her class assignments and her shift at the cafe and tried to sort out her opinions about the war. Increasingly it was hard to sleep and eat. She did become fixed on red-and-white striped mints, sucking them through her lectures and as she studied. The humming of flourescent lights and the ticking of clocks made her very nervous. She bought earplugs, but still the rhythmic sounds drove her crazy. Crazy? Like her mother? Now that she thought of it, Mom's trips to the hospital were always preceded by times of isolation. Cora was more afraid of craziness than anything. She would have to sort out her ideas about the war some other way.

So she forced herself to talk to people. To go to the movies with Sara. She wrote to George and Pop—hoping the letters would reach them wherever they were. Once a month she phoned Ron, who didn't seem to be doing much of anything since he graduated from high school except part-time yard work and sitting in the Grandview house, making up his mind about which branch of the service to enter. Assiduously, she stayed in touch with the family—telling them about her double major in English and sociology and her afternoon job at the cafe. She did skip over her love affairs. And she was wary about mentioning the school paper.

The page in her typewriter was still blank. Oh, why had she agreed to cover the demonstration? She wished the whole thing hadn't happened. Wished she hadn't listened to stories about soldiers destroying villages. Wished she hadn't heard those lectures about American international ambitions. Wished she could go back to the last year and take different classes and make different friends. She did not want to know what she knew. She was beginning to understand that the most real person in her life didn't know everything about the real world. It was up to her to save Pop's life.

"Cora," Lenny called from across the newsroom, "the printer charges doubletime after midnight."

Cora thought how this short dark guy with thick glasses had daunted her for the first two months. Now she was almost sure he had a crush on her.

"Ten more minutes," she pleaded. The humming from the flourescent lights was maddening.

He nodded back. Cora thought he was overdoing it with the eyeshade. He was just a junior, a year older than herself. She remembered the green visor that she and Ron used to wear when they played bus driver. Well, Lenny *was* right about the deadline. Objectivity, she told herself, don't editorialize in the *Blaze* news columns. Tomorrow she would ask to be switched to the cultural beat. She wondered if you could get cancer from flourescent lights. Other people heard them humming, didn't they?

Spring, 1967

Fog wisped along the beach. Kites sailed through the high, flawless blue as Cora and her father walked to town. He was talking about his parents' last days in Ireland and the dreadful ship they took to New York. A wonder he became a seaman after that, he always said. She had heard the story a dozen times, but he was never sentimental like this with her brothers.

Sandpipers skittered in front of them. She was glad she had skipped classes today to spend time with her father before he shipped out again. Although he would never admit it, he was lonely now that George was gone. When he had phoned her at school asking, "Can you keep an old man company this weekend?" she had dropped everything assuming an emergency. Emergency or no, she owed him this, for he had stuck with the family as Mom had not.

"So what are you going to do with a college degree?" He hadn't asked this question in six months.

"Teach, I think," she said for Aunt Min had always hoped she would become a high school teacher. "Or write, maybe." Why was she confessing this? "Become a journalist. Maybe."

He looked at her the way he sometimes looked at Mom during her bouts of craziness.

She marshaled her defenses.

He peered silently out to sea. Finally, "You can make a living at that? Doesn't sound very secure to me."

"Oh, Newspaper Guild wages are terrific," she began, then realized he was faintly intimidated by her exotic interests. Who knows if she could make it anyway? She didn't want to fail him—Roy Casey's pretentious daughter goes to college and flunks out of life. Now she found herself staring at the waves. Funny, she considered how she had inherited most of her ideals from Pop—a sense of possibility, a commitment to say what you believe, a dedication to larger goals.

She tried to think of something to change the topic, to keep their conversation away from the war. She didn't want to argue with him on this beautiful day. God knows when—if (no, she wouldn't think like that)—she would see him again.

"Australia in that direction," he nodded to the southwest. "Had a good time there during the war. Good time in Sydney, that is. Brisbane people were cold. Angry that American servicemen were stealing Aussie girls, but if you ask me, you could just as well accuse the Aussie girls of stealing the American men. I never did any of that." He turned more serious. "I was always faithful to your mother." His voice was hollow. Still he grieved terribly twelve years after her death.

Ahead of them the beach was pocked with shallow puddles of water, glimmering like sheets of glass. She slipped off her sandals, enjoying the warm sand squeezing between her toes as she padded toward town with her father.

Summer, 1967

Cora thought this was an ideal chance for Ron to visit campus. He had a lot of time on his hands, and Pop was gone for the summer. She knew her younger brother was smart. George was, too, but he wouldn't have the patience to sit in a classroom.

"The university has a great geology department," she tried one evening after dinner, avoiding his eyes. She looked into the quiet livingroom—at the ceramic Ho Tai standing on top of the silent TV and at the sunset pink drifting in through the picture window.

"I'm sure it does." He picked at the chocolate frosting of his favorite marble cake. "So why don't you take some classes."

"I was thinking of *you*." She kept her voice light. "You still have time to apply for spring semester."

"It would be a long commute from 'Nam."

"You don't *have* to enlist, you know. I'm sure you can get a student deferment." Calmly she told herself. Slowly. She noticed a line of doubt cross his eyes. Damn George: it was one thing for him to maneuvre an extra long stint in Vietnam for himself; it was quite another for him to lure Ron there. To keep herself from pressing him she went into the kitchen and returned with the coffee pot.

"Sure, I'm afraid of the war. God knows what I'll wind up doing. But it's more than that, I'd feel, I don't know, disloyal, if I didn't go."

Cora concentrated on the brown arc of the flowing coffee between pot and cup. In her most conversational tone she asked, "Do you think it's *our* war? Do you think we belong there?"

"Yes, I think that America stands for freedom. We are a strong, wealthy country, and we have a responsibility. Besides, we *are* there—like it or not— Pop and George are there. It's up to us to defend *them*."

Sipping her coffee, she studied his face. "I don't want to lose all of you."

"Oh, Cora, you're not going to lose us. Look, we'll have those VCs on their asses in no time. I may not even have a chance to fire a shot. You're not going to lose anyone, Cora."

She bit her lip and stared at the blank TV screen. She tried again, in her most gentle voice.

"Why don't we just drive out there this weekend and I can show you my old dorm. I have this cute friend, Becky, who is doing summer school."

"For Christsake, Cora," he slammed his fist on the table, reminding her of when he was ten and she realized he had grown physically stronger than she. "For Christsake."

Instinctively Cora backed down. "I didn't mean to upset you. I only meant . . . " No, she would not fade into the wallpaper like Mom. "I only meant to save your life."

She got up to clear the table.

Fall, 1967

The room was smokey: tobacco, pot, hash. Becky had brought a hookah and the guys near the door were giggling over their noisy bubbles. Cora leaned her head back and allowed a sigh to course through her body. Three years in college and she was still uncomfortable with this hippie paraphernalia. What did it have to do with politics, anyway? She worried about her Chaucer exam tomorrow. Lenny walked in with that new girl, Barbara MacGregor, hand in hand. She looked away and pretended not to notice.

"All right, you guys, let's get organized." Henry Rhinehart, a tall, blond senior spoke from behind the desk. "We've got to get the media campaign straightened out, or we're going to wind up with the same kind of noncoverage after each demonstration."

We need a revised image," explained Lenny. He paused, blew on his new rimless glasses and wiped them with the sleeve of his workshirt. "Someone who can charm the pants off them."

Cora saw Barbara smile knowingly. Did she hate herself or Barbara more? Of course it was possible to hate Lenny.

"OK," Henry persisted. "So we need someone articulate and straight, who won't immediately offend."

"How about Julie Andrews over there?" Lenny smiled mischievously.

Why had she told him her high school nickname? Why had she believed that things said (and done) in bed were confidential?

"Cora?" Henry frowned. "You think we should have a *girl* as a press spokesman?"

"Why not?" Barbara asked. "We *are* part of the organization. Besides, it might be a novelty. Might distract them."

Ralph Blake, the new graduate student, sat forward. "We want to persuade them, not distract them. They're already distracted enough."

Ralph was right about that, Cora thought, although she was disappointed that he didn't support her. Everyone said Ralph was a brilliant engineer, but a little wacko. Cora wondered if people were just frightened by his intensity. He seemed perfectly sane to her; if anything, he was more focused than the others.

"We could certainly use a softer touch," said James. Cora hoped people didn't think James was defending her because they were sleeping together.

"Softer touch!" balked Ralph. "We're not exactly selling toilet tissue."

"Even if we *are* trying to wipe out our shitty foreign policy," Henry laughed, alone. "But seriously . . . Cora, how about it?"

"Well, on the *Blaze* I've met a lot of reporters from around the state. I get along with them OK. At least I know where they're coming from, who's the most sympathetic and so forth. Yeah, sure, I'll give it a shot." Although she was nervous, she didn't believe anyone else could do a better job. She would not think about what Pop might say if he read anything about her in the Sunday *Herald*. "Sure," her voice was louder now and—she hoped— more confident. "Sure, I can handle that."

She sat back, concentrating on the meeting, ignoring the pride creeping into her line of vision. Yes, she could be of use. She focused on the report being given about the Chicago group. What had Barbara thought when Lenny nominated her? She had supported the idea. Barbara wasn't so bad. Actually, Cora admitted to herself, she and Lenny never would have lasted. She could get used to seeing him with Barbara. She grew more alert as James described the antimilitary campaign in the high schools.

"It's going OK. Better now at Henley Collegiate than with the rednecks at Wiley. Hopeless consciousness there. Hopeless."

Cora shifted uncomfortably on the floor.

"Pathetic," Henry shook his head. "Naive bastards. Like lambs to the slaughter."

Cora felt that old fury with her brother. "College pap," Ron had dismissed her arguments about the war. She believed she had failed completely, for what use were marches and articles and impassioned letters to the editor if you couldn't convince *your own brother*, if you couldn't save your own family. Lenny had told her to relax, that they were all brothers and sisters in the movement, that they were breaking down the nuclear family. Just because Ron was too thick to listen to her didn't mean she couldn't save her other brothers. She tried hard to think of these guys as her brothers.

Henry was warming up. "You know what one asshole did? Ran his motorcycle right through the rally we were holding outside Western High screaming, 'Kill the Commie bastards.'"

Cora closed her eyes and saw George in jungle fatigues, trying to sleep despite the noise of crickets, machine-gun fire and helicopters. She thought of the last time she heard from him—a short "Hi, Sis" on the back of that postcard which showed a soldier talking to his guardian angel, "When I die I'll go straight to heaven because I've served my time in hell."

Henry was still speaking, "And the kid on the motorcycle wasn't talking about the Viet Cong."

Admiring, anxious laughter rippled through the room. Henry regularly put his body on the line. He worked the longest hours of anyone in the group.

"After all the information they have, those guys who go deserve what they get," whispered Sara.

Cora didn't notice herself standing. She didn't know she was going to speak. "That's stupid, *dangerous* rhetoric." Her voice gained strength. One day this anger could get her in a lot of trouble. "Protest is one thing for you guys. For most of you, it meant getting a college deferment. And if you're clever with your middle-class education, you'll escape Vietnam after gradua-tion. But for kids at Western High or Wiley, there's no choice. For a lot, the military is the way out of unemployment or dead-end jobs."

"What is this?" Henry flushed. "Neo-Marxist shit?"

"They'll wind up dead in one sense or another," Sara said.

"They don't have the same choices as you or the kids graduating from Henley Collegiate. How many of them have families who can pay for lawyers? How many of them know they have options about the draft?"

"Them?" inquired Lenny.

Ralph leaned forward, watching her closely.

"Them?" Lenny asked again.

She hated the intimacy in his voice.

"Aren't you one of *them*? You came from that world and here *you* are. Isn't it patronizing to say that they don't have the same choices?"

"I was lucky," she steadied her voice for she was betraying the family by acknowledging her difference from them. "Besides, they don't draft girls." Did she belong here? Had she deserted Pop, George and Ron by protesting the war? By going to college? Was she playing an elaborate charade? What was the line between treason and lunacy?

"Three folks from Ann Arbor are coming next week," Lenny interjected in a conciliatory voice. "They'll need housing. They'll be doing an educational before the meeting . . ."

Cora reread the agenda. She would end up like Mom if she persisted in this fuzzy thinking. Next time she planned to take minutes; that would help her concentrate.

FIVE

Spring, 1968
Oregon

The enormous living room was filled with the noise of roaring rapids. Inside the beveled glass French doors, twenty tired people sprawled on chairs, couches and the deep pile green rug.

"OK. What's on the agenda?" Henry stood by the bookcase."Cora, why don't you write down the list. Then we'll prioritize."

She pulled out a green binder and uncapped her pen. The air smelled of cigarette smoke, sweat and burgundy.

Lenny leaned forward, "I think we need to talk about McCarthy and Kennedy. About what kind of time we're giving to the primary campaigns."

"You're full of it, Keller." Becky shouted, "We agreed no electoral politics. If you want to waste your *own* time with this fantasy about the Democratic party, be my guest."

Cora lit a cigarette. They always took a while to get focused, she thought, stretching her neck from side to side. Even though she was exhausted, she had to admit this Friday night session was a good idea. At least they wouldn't waste so much time tomorrow.

When Henry Rhinehart initially proposed the weekend retreat, Cora had been torn. Who had time to retreat for two whole days? The entire nation was exploding, and he wanted twenty activists to *cool out* in the country and talk? Still, they had been spinning their wheels these last two months, with members debating each other about vigilante tactics and the definition of the New Left.

Cora had almost stayed home. The movement work had put her so far behind she would have to attend summer school if she planned to graduate on time. Henry warned Cora not to be rigid about her studies. What use were Blake and Milton when the country was burning down? Henry

33

acted as if he had all the time in the world to get his degree. Cora feared that if she didn't finish school now she would run out of nerve as well as money. She simply couldn't overcome her "obsession with courses," so she hid her studying from the group. School was not a sound reason for veto-ing the retreat.

Henry's family place was outside Springfield, overlooking the McKen-zie rapids. The vast yard was scattered with fragrant, wet needles from the luxurious canopy of dark trees. The Rhinehart house had five bedrooms, a liv-ing room, a recreation room and a large verandah. There was no chance his family—who were in London for two weeks of theatre—would learn about the retreat. He thought it best no one know their whereabouts. Cora had grown used to secrecy during the last two years. They all knew someone who had been turned in by an agent. For a while, she had wondered about Henry's credentials, but she knew that paranoia was more of an epidemic than subversion.

"Yeah, Lenny," Henry was pacing in front of the huge slate fireplace. "If you want to be 'clean for Gene,' that's OK with me. Personally, I'm happy to keep my hands dirty with more important matters."

"Draft counseling." Barbara cut through the argument. "We have to talk about that tomorrow. And the Canadian immigration stuff. I have a re-port from Gordon Winters in B.C."

◊   ◊   ◊

Cora was very tired. Her mind wandered to that letter from George. As movement spokesman, she was visible enough at college, but that was a fair distance from Grandview, let alone from Vietnam. Her older brother's letter, as Sister Matthew would say, was "the soul of brevity."

> *Dear Cora,*
> *I hear you're making a ripe fool of yourself at that college. Burning flags and cheering Mao. Also hear you've become an advocate of free love. How do you think Mom would have felt? And Pop? Listen, I'll give you a chance. I won't tell him a thing if you write and promise me you're going to start behaving like a Catholic girl, an American, again.*

This had been the last letter between them. She steeled herself for her father's retribution and grew obsessed with the question of who had told George—someone from the ROTC unit on campus? The FBI?

Of course it had been impossible to respond to George. For him it was black and white. He was being loyal to his country, his family. And in dis-agreeing she was a traitor. Ron took the same view—as if he had been given a graft from George's cortex. She had lent Ron articles and books from the draft counseling center. She had argued with him. But he refused to think deeper than the platitudes. Refused to visit campus.

"You have to serve your country." He looked at her carefully to make sure she understood his words. She remembered Pop looking at Mom to see if she were still on track.

"But there are *other* ways to serve. You could work with old people or make parks or go to college and become a teacher."

"I want to support the President—as a good American should."

"Is that like being a good German?" She snapped.

"Are you calling me a Nazi?" He reddened.

"I'm saying if you join the service, you're responsible for what happens."

"Responsible. Yes, that's the word I'd used to describe standing along-side Pop and George. Loyal. Responsible."

She shook her head.

"What about you, Cora?"

                                    ✿   ✿   ✿

"Cora. Come in, Cora." Henry loomed over her. She blinked and looked at her sheet.

"Yes?" She stifled a yawn.

"I asked if you thought we had enough of an agenda for tomorrow morning," Henry laughed. "But I can answer that—looking at the ten-point-list on your page and the glaze in your otherwise lovely brown eyes." He turned to the group. "Anyone move we adjourn until tomorrow?"

Lenny nodded.

"Second," said Ralph.

Although Cora was exhausted from the three-hour drive here, she found the living room floor hard and couldn't sleep amidst Jenny's snoring and the rustling sleeping bags and Ralph's ridiculously loud ticking clock.

About 4 A.M. she found her way out to the verandah. Pulling her buttonless pea coat tightly around her, she watched a slivered moon shining in the rapids.

Pop had often talked about taking them on vacation down here. He had seen the McKenzie on his first trip to Oregon. The boys, he said, would love the water. But they never made it. She realized now that she had no idea if Pop were in Grandview or in the middle of the Pacific or just about to land in . . .

"Penny for your thoughts."

She gripped the handrail as blood drained from her face. Henry's voice, she recognized it almost immediately. No reason to be frightened.

"Oh, just thinking how peaceful it is here." She drew a long breath. "And enjoying the smells. I love the scents of late spring . . . "

A profound, inexplicable fear engulfed Cora. What was wrong with her? Henry was a bright, thoughtful, gentle man. She had known for weeks that he was interested in her. Her own response flickered on and off. Of course, even if she didn't want to live happily ever after with him, they might enjoy a night together. No reason to be a prude. He had terrific wavy yellow hair and sweet green eyes.

"Chilly out here," he said. "Can I warm you up?"

No, on second thought, she felt sure she would not enjoy that at all.

He didn't wait for an answer. Setting his hands on her shoulders, he nuzzled close. "I'm glad you were restless too."

"Chronic problem," she reached for a clincial tone. "I get insomnia when I'm doing too much."

He kissed her lips fully, longingly.

"No, really." She pulled away. "I'm behind on the press releases."

His right hand on her waist, he swiveled her toward him. She drew away, but it was futile: 180 pounds versus 120 pounds, confidence versus confused fear. OK, she would let him kiss her. Once. Maybe she could be coy: not-tonight-I-have-my-period sort of thing. And then never again, she warned herself, would she go out alone on a verandah after dark.

But he would have none of her protests. He touched his tongue to her ear, licking deep, deeper. He pulled the coat off her shoulders. Just as she was on the point of shouting—should she shout? Should she wake the others simply because she wasn't in the mood for sex?—Sara wandered out sleepily.

"Oh," she was startled. "Sorry, I didn't mean to intrude . . . "

"No." Cora took the opportunity to step back, shamefully tugging the peacoat back over her nightgown.

❄ ❄ ❄

The next day Cora avoided both Sara and Henry. This wasn't hard. She had got so little sleep that the best she could achieve was attention to the minutes and a comment or two in discussion. At 11:30 she and the other girls left to fix lunch.

Stainless steel double sink. Dishwasher. Refrigerator and freezer. Ice-blue appliances set against white tiles and varnished wood cabinets. The room was cool. The smell of fresh coffee revived her.

War news rattled on the radio. Battles. Bombings. Enemy casualties. Like the weather, it had become a routine part of her day. As she switched off the radio, she wondered where her father was now. She thought Aunt Min said he was on the way home.

"I don't care if you think feminism is a self-indulgent deviation." Sara argued as she sliced the tomatoes into perfect wheels. "I say you have to look at how this organization works to see the kind of society it will create."

Barbara shook her head. "Means and ends . . . an old counterrevolutionary argument if I ever heard one. Where would we be if Lenin had been constrained by rigid moralism."

"Try East Berlin," suggested Sara, brushing a strand of her chestnut hair out of her eyes. "The real question is, Where would we be if people had listened to Emma Goldman?"

"You're not going to bring up that ancient anarchist trip."

As the two argued, Cora appropriated the sandwich-making. She hated debates about women's liberation; they filled her with that old feeling of being crazy. Life was too urgent to investigate every tiny process. Barbara and Sara, on the other hand, *loved* these arguments.

What really wounded Cora was the letter from Ron, which came several months after George's note. Three weeks after Pop had returned a birthday present unopened. Ron's letter was long, briefly mentioning the heat of the Mekong and a woman he had met and describing the experience of watching friends get hands and legs blown off. He wrote detailed accounts about the deaths of his two best buddies. Ron concluded with something called "a plea."

> *When George told me what you were doing, I tried to pretend it didn't matter. Then it started to gnaw under my skin. One night I dreamt that my unit was crouching in an abandoned temple as you walked in carrying a grenade, looked all around until you spotted me and then lobbed it straight in my direction. Listen, Corey, I don't know what's going on with you. I don't know if it's some adolescent rebellion against Pop or what. But you have to WAKE UP. This is treacherous work and you're making it a hell of a lot tougher—maybe impossible—to believe I'll come back alive.*

As she heated chili for the group, Cora thought how she lived smack in the middle of her brothers. Although she was much closer in age to Ron, she looked more like George for they both shared their father's height and dark coloring. Perhaps Mom was too worn out to pass on much by the time fair, pale Ron was born. Cora's temperament was in the middle, too; she teetered between Ron's self-doubt and George's command of destiny. While young George never let on how he felt; Ron as a boy was always shouting and crying. When she thought about it, she was simmer on the scale of still to boil. For a time, she felt safe in the middle and got used to being a bridge between the two boys, between them and Pop. If she wasn't happy, at least she knew her place. It was confusing when the boys grew tall on either side, leaving her in the shadow, as they talked bowling and watched football games. For a long time, it seemed too dark to move.

The afternoon meeting was long and heated. Ralph waved his cigarette in the air, describing the vigilante tactics of groups in Columbus and Seattle. "Press releases, marches, slogans,—All we've done is fiddle with words. Where has it got us? Where did it get thousands of people killed last year in 'Nam? Where did it get King?" He was more jittery than usual, Cora noted. Ralph's anxiety always unsettled her. Probably those rumors of him slitting his wrists were untrue. Probably she just had a hard time with intense people because they reminded her of Mom. She focused on the discussion.

"What do you want us to do?" demanded Becky.

"Oh, it's his usual *Battle of Algiers* romantic crap about bombs and shots in the night." Henry leaned forward. "Just what the Establishment wants—an excuse to discredit serious political opponents, to say we were thugs all along."

Cora felt dizzy from arguments and smoke and lack of sleep. She poured herself a full mug of black coffee. Henry had a point. A band of inexperienced students could hardly smash the state. On the other hand, she was beginning to believe she had to *respond*. She thought of those people in Watts and Detroit responding. She thought of George's strange new vocabulary—rules of engagement, conventional operations, recon mission, point man. God, she hoped he was all right. Letting this war go on was *madness*. She understood Ralph's urgency while she feared it could lead to disaster. Her body temperature rose ten degrees.

The debate continued over dinner on the verandah this strangely warm evening. The men argued late into the night. Cora sat quietly and listened. There were many reasonable, conflicting points and lots of rhetoric. She had never learned to debate; she had never even learned to interrupt.

By Sunday morning, the majority had clearly dismissed violence as counterproductive. Ralph slumped silently in the rocking chair. Just before lunch, he rose to his feet. "I'm leaving now. I just believe in other strategies. It's a hard decision."

Cora looked around at the startled, angry, uncomprehending and relieved faces of friends and comrades—friends?—who had worked with Ralph for years.

"I know you'll understand why I can't say more."

Henry clinked his pencil against a coffee mug. "Nothing like a high drama exit, old Ralph. Look, it's almost noon, why don't we break for lunch and those of us who are interested in being serious political people rather than joining Curly, Moe and Larry can reconvene at one o'clock."

People poured into the kitchen. Cora could not believe that no one was saying good-bye to Ralph. She went forward to shake his hand and heard herself saying, in a voice that betrayed too much caffeine and too little sleep, "Can I call you when I get back to campus? I want to . . . help."

Ralph shrugged, "I guess so."

"I want to do something, too."

He nodded.

She watched him walk toward the door, balancing along a line of resignation and purposefulness. Heat licked against her temples. She had meant what she said.

Ralph waved.

Turning back toward the kitchen, Cora noticed Henry holding open the door, observing her.

* * *

Several weeks later Cora read Sara Pop's letter disowning her. They sat across from each other on the twin beds in their small apartment. Cora's voice remained even.

"He's bluffing." Sara sat forward. "You know your Pop, he's full of hot air. He'll calm down."

"No." Cora smiled ruefully. "This is one thing I know better than you. That's it. Finis. No more *mi casa es su casa.* No more $50 a month."

"Oh, he'll get over it." Sara lit a cigarette for both of them. My dad and I have fights all the time. He's a real MCP."

"No." Cora sucked on the Marlboro. "With Pop it's different. He sees this as a test or something. He actually thinks I don't love him enough because I oppose the war. I keep trying to explain that I hope we pull out because I want to save his goddamned neck. I keep telling him that my position is much more true to the principles he raised us with . . . "

"Oh, you and your dad do go on. Blowhards, both of you. He'll recover. Just wait."

Cora closed her eyes. With mixed feelings, she absorbed the news that she could expect no more support for school and that she was not welcome back in the Grandview house. She felt relieved to acknowledge she did not belong in that family. So it's settled, she told herself; I'm my own person now. I don't have to worry about them or feel guilty or even angry. They are not my family.

Now she had the absolute freedom to believe, to be, to do what she wanted. The graceful spring light was extending each night and her sense of hope with it. This anticipation, it had to be admitted, balanced on a fine line of terror.

"You know," she said to Sara, "my whole life I've felt alone. I knew something terrible was going to happen to Mom, but everyone said, no, no. I knew Pop drank too much, but Aunt Min said only once in a while." What Cora did not say to Sara was that she knew going to college had meant saving her life at some profound expense. Now she had learned the cost. She would be alone.

Sara came over and sat beside her on the bed. "You have Aunt Min."

Cora shrugged. "Aunt Min has tried with Pop. But she has her own life with John Earle and the twins."

"Well, you still have *family.* I mean you can spend Christmas and Thanksgiving with them. And you can always come to our house. My dad is crazy about you."

Cora held back the tears as she shrugged away her friend's comforting arm. "Well, the financial thing will probably be OK. I can add hours at the cafe. So I get a little less sleep."

Sara moved back to her own bed.

Cora continued. "But I know *we're* right. Someday Pop will see that I'm the one upholding family principles. Draft counseling, demonstrating, these are patriotic activities."

Sara stamped out her cigarette and pulled the covers over her head. "Why do you care about those jerks? You're nuts, Cora."

Summer, 1968

Cora and Ralph were sharing a pizza at the Heathcliff Bistro when they first started to talk about doing something. Ralph was chain-smoking fast and eating slow and talking about the French student movement and some of the other groups he admired in Europe—Bader Meinhoff and the Italian Red Brigade and the IRA. "Those people have a sense of history."

She listened, watching the smoke from his cigarette thicken the gray saloon air. The Heathcliff was eerily quiet in the summer. She looked over Ralph's shoulder, wondering what Henry and Barbara and Lenny were doing now.

Luckily, Sara and Becky also had to do summer school and would continue to share the rent. She was surprised and pleased when Ralph announced that he would be around too. While it was nice to have a breather from some of them, the summer desertion of her comrades made her even more frustrated and impotent about the war. As she watched the late night news with Sara and Becky, she felt more and more responsible for the body count. Still, when people came back together in the fall, she told herself bitterly, they would be as ineffectual as ever.

"How did you get so knowledgeable about these European groups, Ralph?"

He shrugged. "I did one of those junior years abroad in London. Took some politics. Read *Kapital*. Kept up with the press."

"It's unusual for an engineer to be so politically active."

"What is this—the third degree?" He lit another Camel.

She knew not to press him further although she was fascinated by his contradictions: rich kid who wore the same pair of ragged jeans all week; family involved in state government who sent him no money. Sara was suspicious of Ralph's background, but Cora told her no one had a choice about parents.

Ralph offered, "Europeans are more sophisticated about social change."

In the past, she had found him a little too ideological, detached from practical and personal questions as he spun ideas about the just world. But Cora came to see cerebral Ralph as the kindest of her comrades. He was a good listener as well as a good talker. And he had something to say.

Now Cora took a deep breath. In a low voice she said, "We talked about doing something, ourselves."

He looked at her blankly, almost blankly. There was a line of distrust in those sad, alert eyes.

"After the retreat at Henry's," she cajoled.

"We don't have a movement here," he sighed.

She stared at her beer. "You only need two people to make a movement."

He rolled his eyes.

"Hey Louie, Louie," from the juke box. She moved her upper body back and forth to the rhythm of the Kingsmen. Stupid song. They were all stupid, what great music.

"What's on your mind?" she asked as nonchalantly as possible.

"Well. . . . " He paused.

Cora felt her heart open. Yes, go ahead, she urged him silently.

"I've been thinking about the draft board."

She waited. Was he going to enlist and try to do something from the inside? She'd heard that lots of good work was being done at the bases. And that was more dangerous than trying to do something as a civilian. But Ralph wouldn't care about danger. How could she help him if he joined the service?

"Johnny B. Goode" now, Chuck Berry belting it out.

"Yes," she coaxed.

"Oh, nothing," he said warily. Then, looking around the bistro, "I was thinking of torching it."

Her eyes widened.

"I'm probably a fool to trust you."

"We're two of a kind, Ralph. We've talked about it often." Conscious of the impotency and despair that had plagued her for the last six months, she savored the exhilaration of her anger, her commitment.

Cora had nightmares for ages after she got Ron's letter. When she helped send medical supplies to the National Liberation Front, she worried that the NLF might blind or kill one of her brothers or even Pop if his ship slipped into vulnerable waters.

He was silent.

"We're in this together."

He shook his head.

She cut him another slice. "Come on," she spoke gently.

"They take vacations in the summer, too. Unfortunately, not all of them, but it isn't nearly so well manned."

She wanted to interrupt and ask how he knew these things, but she was afraid to raise his distrust again, so she waited.

"I think it would be easy enough, about an hour's work, some night."

"You couldn't do something like that alone," she said without conviction.

"Oh, I don't know." He lit another cigarette.

She lit one herself and coughed. "I want to help." Again she teetered on the edge of hope.

"You can't make a serious decision this quickly," he said.

"I know my mind," she answered firmly.

"Well, I don't know," he watched her. "I'm fond of you, Corey. I know you're sincere. But I want you to take some time to think about it. We both need time."

                                                           o o o

That night when Cora returned to the apartment, Sara was eating licorice and studying *The Fairie Queene* in the living room. The Kingston Trio were revolving on the hi-fi with "Hang Down Your Head, Tom Dooley." In her chartreuse baby doll pajamas and shiny long hair, her friend looked like a fairy. Cora herself was light, contented, almost free of the anxiety she had felt at the bistro.

"Where have you been?" Sara looked over her reading glasses and turned down the music.

"At the Heathcliff." She smiled.

"Doing?"

Suddenly Cora felt guarded, remembering how much Sara had mistrusted Ralph. God, why couldn't one person in her life get along with another?

"Eating pizza. Pepperoni."

"With . . . Oh, I know, with Robert, that cute cook at the cafe. Have you guys gone to bed together yet?"

"I wasn't with Robert."

"Who, then? Peter? Dave? I have trouble keeping track of your boyfriends."

"For godsakes, Sara, you sound like my Pop."

Sara dodged and continued, "With our more-radical-than-thou friend?" She raised her fist in a mock power-to-the-people salute.

"You've never understood Ralph."

"And I suppose you do."

"In a sense I think I do. I guess I feel as if we're both outsiders. Sort of soul mates."

Sara pursed her lips, holding back. "Be careful, Corey." She took off her glasses and studied her friend.

"What's that supposed to mean?"

"Look," she leaned forward, "Ralph is a decent guy. A committed political person. But the man lives in his head. He doesn't have, I don't know, certain kinds of practical instincts."

"Again, what's that supposed to mean?" Cora turned toward the bedroom.

"Why do I try with you? You won't listen. You know you're as stubborn as your father. So I'll just say two things: One, be careful around Ralph. Two, I love you and I don't want you in danger."

"Thanks for number two." Cora entered the bedroom and closed the door.

Exhausted, she dropped her clothes on the floor, then climbed into bed. The day passed by in review: 4:30 breakfast shift. 9 o'clock class. Mad dash back to the apartment to finish her paper for Professor Whitman. Delivery of paper just before office hours closed at 5 P.M. Dinner shift at cafe. Talk with Ralph for, what, three hours. She felt tired, very tired.

That night Cora descended to hell, looking for Persephone, Jesus, Mom, looking frantically. Cardinal Spellman appeared, a flak jacket over his ruby robes, holding an M16 assault rifle. "Ambush!" he shouted. George and Ron ducked. "Ambush!" It was hot, very hot, until she opened a door and walked into a wall of flame.

o o o

They met at Serimelli's coffee shop four days later—between her afternoon and evening shifts at the cafe.

Ralph was sipping his mocha as she sat down. He nodded.

"Twenty-eight days until the end of the month," she said.

"Yes," he nodded.

"I want to join you." She looked at him directly.

"You're sure?"

Why was everyone always asking her if she was sure, telling her to be careful?

"Yes," she said, "I'm sure. Absolutely sure." Enough of the wavering. She was proceeding now with deliberate fury. A walking fire.

SIX

Fall, 1988
Toronto and Washington, D.C.

Jake scratched at the back door.

"Just a second," Cora called to the dog as she poured boiling water into the pot. Six A.M. She would steep the tea until 6:05 before taking it up to Jacques. Terrible: waking a person to say good-bye.

As she held the door open for Jake, crisp autumn air stung her eyes. The dry leaves hinted of coming frost. Seasons changed so much faster here. Canadian Thanksgiving occurred six weeks before American Thanksgiving. She had promised herself that she would be in Toronto before American Thanksgiving, a holiday she always detested. Maybe she was part Indian. Maybe she just hated pumpkin pie. Jake started to bark. "Shhhh, you'll wake up Jacques." She remembered the tea.

Jacques lay with a pillow over his head to protect himself from alarms and dogs and deserting lovers.

"Tea's ready," Cora set the pot on their nightstand, then gently massaged Jacques's neck.

"*Bien.*" He emerged, squinting.

Cora loved Jacques best at this, his most vulnerable time of day.

"Yes, I know," he murmured with more determination, sitting up and bracing his arms around Cora. "You'll have to call me every morning from Oregon to wake me up." He managed a half smile.

"And wire tea!" Cora also tried to smile. She scraped her hand on the dark morning stubble of his chin.

They were both in tears.

"It can't last long." Cora pulled back. "Aunt Min thinks he only has a few months left. At most."

"Take as long as you need," Jacques spoke deliberately.

Cora lifted the cracked brown pot and poured them each a steaming mug. Too agitated to sit still, she walked over to the window. Leaves swirled around the car on the street below. Otherwise the world seemed still. "I do feel guilty about taking the stationwagon."

"Forget it. I'll carpool with Lawrence. And when that doesn't work, I'll take the subway; you do it all the time."

Cora frowned at Jacques's sudden alertness. His waking moments were so precious. Two sips of tea and Jacques was in high gear. Cora grew distracted again. "I wish it had gone better with Fran yesterday afternoon."

Jacques waited.

"I mean it was completely ridiculous for her to think I would give in at the last minute and take her. I can't afford to skip work and pay for the trip, myself, let alone feed another person along the way. Besides, she knows there is some kind of danger. But she's as stubborn as . . . "

"Her mother?" Jacques bestowed his miracle of a smile.

Cora nodded distractedly. Noticing the tightness in her chest, she understood she didn't want to breathe because she didn't want to know how scared she was—of crossing the border, of seeing her father and brothers.

Jacques was still smiling.

No, she would not allow herself to panic. She kissed Jacques's hand. "You have Aunt Min's number. I'll call back here as often as I can."

"It's all arranged, *chérie.*"

Cora searched Jacques's face for certainty and instead found sadness, a touch of fear, an edge of fatigue and the regular intensity. Jacques would be at the print shop in two hours. Stunning to think that life would proceed this normally. Please, god, it would.

"Well," she released a long sigh. "I guess I better be going."

"Let me help you with the gear."

"No, remember what you promised—that you'd stay right here, so I could remember you in our warm bed to which I *will* return. And you know, you sneak, that I packed the car last night."

Jacques nodded. Cora hugged him, inhaling the almondlike scent of their bed.

With a sharp snap, she shut the front door and refused to look back. The air was just as cold as when she had let Jake into the kitchen. Damn, she would miss the best part of autumn. Setting her purse and briefcase beside the car, she was startled by a figure sleeping in the back seat under a blanket. The feathery red hair gave Fran away. Christ almighty, this child was impossible. Cora burst out laughing. Fran slept on, oblivious. Cora heard a rap from the upstairs window.

She swiveled, waved to Jacques, then pointed to the car, shaking her head and mouthing "Fran!"

Jacques nodded, grinning widely.

Cora shook her head in exasperation. Angry about being disobeyed, she checked herself: she would not become like her father.

Fran was an adult now. She had as much right to come as Cora had to worry about her.

Cora weighed the arguments one more time. Yes, Fran was right, she would be perfectly safe; she had never trespassed against the U.S. government. With an unsettled conscience, Cora allowed herself to feel how much she might enjoy her daughter's company.

She returned Jacques's smile and threw up her hands.

"You on a trip?"

She turned to Mr. Caputo.

"Yes." She was dismayed she had forgotten to say good-bye to the old man. "To the States, to see my family."

He studied her. "You are a American?"

"Yes," she said, practicing the smile she had prepared for the border guard. "Born in Portland, Oregon."

"Ah, very nice to see the family," The old man smiled back. "Have a good trip. Take it easy."

She nodded, then turned to wave once more to Jacques.

The body in the back didn't stir as Cora opened the door. Did she imagine a momentary tightening of Fran's shoulder muscles? Cora slipped behind the wheel and inserted the cold key in the ignition. During the several minutes it took the engine to warm up and the windows to defrost, the stowaway remained still. Momentarily, Cora feared Fran might have frozen overnight, but through the rearview mirror she detected the reassuring breath shifting the blanket up and down.

∗ ∗ ∗

Somewhere outside Hamilton Fran emerged. Cora heard a rustle of covers, then a crackling of paper. Fran leaned into the front seat.

"Hi, Mom," her voice was heavy with sleep.

"You know," Cora found her way through a tangle of terror, anger and affection.

"Now Mom, don't get hyper."

Cora clenched her teeth. "I do not think this is wise." She paused, to make sure she was saying the right thing. "But you're an adult."

"Yes," Fran said, expectantly.

Cora didn't like feeling pushed. She was almost ready to stop the car. Grudgingly she continued, "You have a right to come, I suppose."

"That's the spirit," Fran kept her voice light.

"It's times like this," Cora shook her head in ironic surrender, "that I know they didn't switch babies on me at the hospital—that *you* must be my willful daughter."

Fran sighed, feigning relief. "And to prove it," she reached into a white paper bag, "a cherry danish."

"My fav," Cora said. "You *are* the perfect traveling companion."

"I was hoping you'd come to that conclusion." She kneaded her mother's neck.

Cora bit into the pastry, allowing the sugar to revive her. Touched by Fran's desire to meet her family, she reminded herself they were her family too.

"You think we'll have trouble at the border?" Fran asked.

"Oh, no," Cora said unconvincingly.

She had practiced the speech. "American citizen," she would say if asked. Then, if she had to show her driver's license, she would explain she was a Canadian Landed Immigrant returning to the States for a holiday. Telling the truth about Pop would take too long.

"Good, Mom, I'm sure you're right. Nothing to worry about."

"Nothing to worry about. Nothing to worry about." Cora said this mantra over and over during the next one hundred miles. Nothing to worry about.

As they pulled up to the U.S. border, a tall, young guard bent into the car and looked past Cora.

"Morning," he smiled broadly at the young woman. "Cold enough for you?"

"Yeah. Hey," Fran talked across her mother. "You got little heaters in those cubicles?"

Cora concentrated on the light in the guard's eyes.

"Little ones," he smiled. "Mother and daughter?" he asked, again addressing Fran.

"How d' ya guess?" she asked. "Our haircuts are completely different."

He laughed. "Nationality?"

"Americans," Fran grinned again, "coming back."

Cora couldn't look at her child who had always claimed vehemently to be 100 percent Canadian. She registered her own small pleasure in Fran's identification.

"Welcome home." He waved them through.

◦ ◦ ◦

Cora consented to a day in Washington. Jacques was probably right that she needed to acclimate to this country. Cora would have skipped Washington altogether if it hadn't been for Fran. Insisting that they enjoy the journey, Fran was making her feel like a cranky teenager.

"You don't want to do *anything*, Mom."

Cora was tired, irritable. "This trip isn't meant to be a vacation."

"Mom, how many times do you get to see the great capitalist capitol? The reflecting pond? The Lincoln Memorial. The Smithsonian, the cherry trees."

She struggled with her daughter's familiarity and enthusiasm, then answered petulantly, "It's September. We'll have to wait a long time if you want to see cherry blossoms."

Cora knew she could not go to Washington without visiting the Vietnam memorial. The pilgrimage lasted from morning until late afternoon . . .

As they walked from the commemorative tablets back to the car, she heard a voice.

"You OK, Mom?"

The voice was unbearably mature. No, Cora wanted to answer. I'm not OK. But her fragility seemed infinite, and she found herself nodding, "Sure, fine." She was glad to be able to ask, "But do you feel like driving back to the motel?"

"No problem."

Cora peered at the map, cursing herself for not getting a pair of cheap reading glasses as Jacques had urged her to do. What an indignity to hold the page a foot forward. She looked at Fran who seemed to be driving quite capably through the traffic.

"Whew, this is really something." Fran shook her head. "Look at these shanty houses. All the people living on the streets. The bottles and garbage on the sidewalks."

"Ummm," Cora nodded, ashamed of her self-absorption.

"Looks like South Africa," Fran said.

"Or Washington," Cora was exasperated.

"Like something on TV, anyway?" Fran concentrated on avoiding a motorcyclist.

Cora stared at her daughter, wondering at the difference between her Canadianness and her own Americanness. Surely Fran knew about American ghettoes. And it wasn't as if white Canadians welcomed black people into Rosedale or Don Mills. But it was true she had never seen anything like the crowding, the noise, the poverty of this street on the Capitol's fringes. Cora was grateful for the inocence and foreignness of Fran's observations, which provided a distance from her daughter that was comforting after their recent intimacy.

Thomas's Atlas Motel was located on the grim side of modest. Cora's heart sank as she opened the door, for she had half-hoped the room would transform itself while they were gone. However, this was the same tiny, sanitized cell with brick walls, turquoise bedspreads and plastic television stand which also served as bureau, desk and table. The broken bathroom fan whirred off-key. Cora was of two minds about that because it did help block noise from the other guests. The people on the left listened to MTV at full volume and the kids on the right ran up and down the corridor. Both families kept their doors wide open. When Cora asked the MTV people to lower their television, they looked at her as if she were crazy. Well, she shrugged to Fran, they would be leaving in the morning, and no one watched TV all night, right?

Fran cocked a doubtful eyebrow.

Cora picked up *The Lives and Times of the She Devil*, but after two pages, even Fay Weldon wasn't distraction enough.

"Ah, Mom, quit your pacing." Fran smiled. She lay on the bed, painting her nails. "If the noise bothers you so much, just turn on the TV. Fight fire with fire."

Cora winced and rotated the dial until she found a news program: American constantnews, on twenty-four hours a day. She reckoned there would have been a lot of changes since she left the country. Improvements? She would see. First, she *listened*, for the accents were so marked. Of course she heard American accents all the time in Canada—in films, on the radio, among friends like Oscar and Susie. Today, however, she had been saturated. Instead of concentrating on the reports about boring Bush and Dukakis and the budget bill in Congress (Congress, not Parliament, she reminded herself, alarmed by her twinge of nostalgia) she heard only the broad vowels; the lowered voices at the ends of sentences; the wide painful "ow" in *about*. This was a harder, sharper, coarser accent than the Canadian way of speaking, and she recalled how her Toronto friends used to tease her about pronunciation.

He appeared and broke through her reverie. She still had a hard time believing Ronald Reagan was President. She remembered when he was elected governor of California. As the news came over the wire on the campus paper, she was sure it had been some sort of teletype prank.

She stared at him, blocking the words momentarily, trying to calculate the appeal of this apple-cheeked, wide-eyed boy/man. Howdy Doody bore the same charming certainty; the same slick mop of virile brown hair; the same button nose. The liver spots would do for freckles. The same wooden noggin. Perhaps Bill Bennett was Buffalo Bob. Ed Meese was Clarabell. George Schultz was Mr. Bluster. Nancy was the ever-young Princess Summerfallwinterspring.

Fran looked horrified as she listened to the words.

" . . . continue to support the freedom fighters in Nicaragua . . . "

She shook her head. "It's all so much more real here, somehow. He's actually crazy. They're all crazy."

"They?" Cora kept her voice steady.

"They, the Americans." She was absorbed, again in the presidential homily.

Cora fought automatic defensiveness. Why did she care? *She* had dismissed Americans often enough. Yet she felt complicitous in a way her Canadian daughter never could. She was conscious of that slight resentment she felt toward Canadians' innocence, safety and sanity.

"Americans aren't *crazy*," Cora mused, "so much as afraid. The arrogance is part of that fear, I think."

Fran stared at the TV.

Cora continued. "You get used to driving eighty miles an hour through the world, and you don't notice warnings about budget deficit, nuclear buildups, environmental decay. You get used to seeing yourself as a leader, and you think you control the earth."

The thin, black anchorwoman was relating a story about a turtle race in Tallahassee. Fran's eyes were fixed on the screen; she waved her red fingernails in the air to dry.

"Of course, maybe you're right," Cora lowered her voice. "Maybe that's what craziness is—refusing to see the reality around you while the danger increases—the danger to yourself and others." She lay back on the bed and shut her eyes. Michael Jackson entered her brain via the TV in the next room. She lay there, listening to "Thriller" and the mellow tones of CNN feature reporting and the slight whistle in Fran's breath as she blew on her fingernails. Yes, maybe that's what she was, crazy for coming back here, for going on to Oregon.

Abruptly sitting up, she summoned her faith in action as an antidote to madness. Certain kinds of action. "Dinner? Got any ideas about dinner?"

Fran nodded at the TV, cheered the winning turtle, then turned to her mother. "Let's just go to the motel coffee shop. I'm too wiped out for much else."

Cora nodded. "It's been a long day for both of us."

They found a table by the window and studied the plastic menus. Hamburgers. Reuben sandwiches. Chops and mashed potatoes. Cora smelled grease mixed with ketchup and A.1. Sauce. This was so much not Fran's kind of place. She herself found a certain familiarity, which brought both discomfort and pleasure for this was just the sort of restaurant where Pop would take the family once every couple of months as a treat. She could see him now, grandly ordering roast beef for five and sending it back if it were not rare enough, steaming in deep purple juice. They would order milkshakes with dinner and then strawberry shortcake afterward, and if the service were good, Pop would leave a big tip. If it were not up to par, the rest of the family would skittle out the door while he left a big piece of his mind.

"Tuna salad," Fran looked at her mother quizzically. "Not much they can do to tuna salad."

Cora shrugged.

After the waitress took their orders, Fran pulled out a road map. "Let's look and see where we're going, shall we?"

The large, multicolored map crinkled open over the Arborite table. Cora moved the saltshaker and smiled at Fran.

SEVEN

Fall, 1988
American Highways

Cora leaned back against the headrest with heavy lids. She was being driven across country by her daughter. Turning, she opened one eye—no, she wasn't dreaming. Here was Fran—red spikes, makeup to beat the band, tattered purple sweatshirt over a blue turtleneck and enormous metal earrings, far more than she cared count. Her daughter. Driving out of Washington, through Virginia. Driving her home. How different from the trip they had made in the other direction—one of them invisible, the other scheming ways to make herself invisible.

Cora pretended to sleep again. How *crazy* to think this beautiful young woman was *her* daughter. *Crazy* to think that she herself could be forty. Aging was an antisocial process. Sometimes when she was with Fran and her friends, she couldn't tolerate the noise and constant movement. Conversely, they must find her unbearably stodgy. Hormones—no one had told her about hormones when they introduced the sixth and ninth commandments. Even in her CR groups they never talked about hormones except in the form of birth control pills.

OK, let's try again, she breathed in the fragrance of Indian summer. Let's consider the gains. She felt more realistic now—both more accepting of other people's foibles and more skeptical of their ideals. Humor came a little easier. She was less self-conscious, less afraid of drowning. Still, sometimes she got discouraged. Was life more complex than she had imagined or was she simply tired? Circumspection. Judgment. The examination of conscience had always caused more trouble than the sinning.

Outside Washington, the South was opened into storybook landscape. Cora gazed at rolling hills; trees with greeny blue leaves; ancient, white columned houses; lulling cattle and sheep. Actually, she knew more about

Canadian than American geography because she had traveled so much more north of the border: Fraser Canyon, Mount Revelstoke, Banff, Manitoba plains, Great Lakes, the Gaspé Penninsula, Montreal, Quebec City, the Bay of Fundy, Cape Breton Island. Her mind wandered to weekend trips with Jacques—Guelph, Kingston, Niagara-on-the-Lake—tantalizingly close to the American border. Now she was across that border—home?—and she was surprised by how much she knew about this American South. Washington, Jefferson, Lee, Carver, Sojourner Truth, Flannery O'Connor, Zora Neale Hurston. Driving through the South for the first time was, strangely, like coming home. With sweet familiarity, her body relaxed. Home. Would that she could feel this easy when they crossed the border to Oregon.

That was a long way off and their pilgrimage would take a circuitous route. Meanwhile, her attention was caught by sun lighting up the thick dust on her grey dashboard. For a year she had been intending to vacuum the car. Now she also noticed the coke cups and the gum wrappers stuck into the map rack. The maps, themselves, were ragged and torn, filed between parking stubs and gasoline receipts. She resolved to clean the mess when they reached tonight's motel.

They drove along in what Aunt Min would have called "companionable silence." Occasionally Fran pointed to a particularly striking tree, or Cora hummed one of the Stephen Foster songs she learned long before she learned she couldn't carry a tune. Dismayed by this deeply American reflex, she diverted herself by peering into windows of passing cars.

◦ ◦ ◦

"Why're you so jumpy?" Fran leaned over as her mother drove during the last hour before dark.

Cora had grown nervous as they approached Kansas. She would *have* to check in with Aunt Min from here. She had chosen Kansas because it was the middle. Because it was where her mother was born. Because she really should have called from West Virginia or Kentucky and could procrastinate no longer.

"Jumpy? What makes you say I'm jumpy?" She relaxed her grip on the steering wheel.

"You've eaten five sticks of gum since the last town, and you don't even like spearmint."

Cora laughed, aware of a soreness in her jaw.

"You tired of driving? I don't mind doing the final stretch."

"No, hon, that's sweet of you. But driving knocks out some of my kinks."

Fran could handle her mother sounding silly, Cora reflected. She wouldn't mix that up with mentally ill. Not even in Kansas.

"You need more exercise?" Fran persisted. "We could find a place with a pool."

"No, more like *emotional* kinks. Calling Aunt Min makes me anxious. It seems so definite. No, that's not it. I don't know . . . " Her voice trailed off.

Five minutes later . . . ten minutes . . . Cora couldn't tell, but she knew time had passed because the soft, mauve light had dimmed . . . Fran tried again. "I'll phone Aunt Min."

"That's not the point."

"What is?" Fran absently ran a hand over her crown of spikes.

Shaken, Cora was still caught in her own amazement that she had only recently considered Fran being related to Aunt Min—or to Ron, or George. Or Pop.

* * *

Cora poured herself a double scotch as the girl dialed Oregon. She watched the ice cubes melting as their call stretched over mountains and deserts across the continent. Generations passed before Fran said, "Hello Aunt Min?"

Cora held her breath. Would Aunt Min think it was her? No, she could hear Fran explaining.

"I'm your, well, your grand niece, Fran, Cora's daughter."

Cora closed her eyes. That was the crazy-making thing about family—you had so many identities, and you had to own all of them at once.

"We're really just calling to say hello, to say everything's on schedule, that we should arrive on Saturday. . . . Oh, OK, just a second. Yes, very nice to speak to you, too."

"Mom," Fran whispered, "she wants to talk to you." She put her hand over the receiver. "You didn't tell me she sounded so New York."

Cora shrugged, for she had never noticed Aunt Min's accent. New York? This was just the way Aunt Min sounded. She could hear Ericka Johnson and Carolyn Rogers teasing about her aunt's accent and asking after her mother. Was it true that she was in a hospital? What kind of hospital? Tell us, Cora. Tell us about your family.

"Aunt Min," Cora anchored herself with the words from childhood. Aunt Min would make it all right.

"Oh, Cora sweetheart, how nice to hear your voice. No, I didn't think Fran was you. She does have some of your alto. Beautiful kid, I bet."

"Well, you'll be able to decide that for yourself soon enough."

"Hon, I'd like to talk to you about that." Aunt Min sobered.

"Yes?" Cora sat down and stared at her fingernails, an old, nervous habit.

"I'm not sure it was smart of me to write. I mean I think we may be able to take care of things just fine as we are . . . "

"What's going on, Aunt Min? You can't fool me—what's bothering you?"

"Actually, your brother George called yesterday. And your Pop—with his stupid mouth—told him you were arriving to rescue him!"

"Idiot!" Cora looked around for a cigarette although she hadn't smoked in ten years and found, instead, her wary daughter listening between the lines.

"George certainly hasn't changed. Full of wild ideas. Told your father that it could be dangerous for you to return." Aunt Min coughed. "Oh, dear, such animosity in a family. I don't get it. I tried. I tried, but I couldn't take your mother's place."

"Calm down, Aunt Min. You know our family has always been drums and horns."

"But I'm responsible for you coming back."

Hundreds of miles till home. Was Kansas home already? Kansas, Colorado, Utah, Nevada, California, Oregon.

Her aunt persisted. "Cora, hon . . . "

"Don't worry, Aunt Min, I can take care of myself." Now why had she said that?

Eventually Aunt Min conceded, mostly, Cora suspected, because of the mounting telephone bill.

Fran studied her mother. "Problems at the Ponderosa?" Her light-heartedness was almost convincing.

"Just a little brotherly hate." Cora shrugged, taking her cue from Fran. Nothing bad could happen to her daughter, she reminded herself. "And when did you watch *Bonanza*? You're far too young."

"In school. It's Canadian-American culture. Lorne Greene was Canadian, remember?"

◦ ◦ ◦

The next morning Cora began the driving. She enjoyed their first hour the most—smelling the damp, grassy scents and watching the earth soften in new light. Within a few hours they would feel the dry snap of autumn, but now everything seemed gently permeable. Even as she basked in this pleasure, she felt nudges of guilt for she should be using this time to talk seriously with Fran. Next year, Fran might be on Broadway. At least Off Broadway. She vowed not to argue on this trip with Fran about her career. Enough old sores would be opened without that.

Questions raced through Cora's mind: Did Martha Graham continue speaking to her mother? Would Fran travel most of the year? Judging from this trip, she certainly had a talent for being in transit. What ever happened to her relationship with Megan? Cora had liked Megan better than Fran's other lesbian friends. In the last four years she had grown more comfortable with her daughter's sexuality. "Tolerant is different from comfortable," Fran had corrected her recently. This parent business was tough. (Was that why Mom had exited so early? Cora always thought it had more to do with her father's drinking.) Cora considered Fran's attitudes toward her own love affairs over the centuries. Obviously Fran was fond of Jacques. How could she not be? Jacques would have made a better mother. He had faith in the passage of time while Cora herself, defended against the imminent moment of disaster.

Ohhh Jacques, how she missed his steady presence. Cora ached thinking of weeks, months, without him. There would be letters. And calls. She would splurge and phone home tonight. Home: Toronto and Jacques and her desk and the garden. Home: Oregon and Pop and Aunt Min and her brothers.

Cora glanced at Fran, resting under orange eyeshades, concentrating on music from her Walkman. Such a contrast to her own overserious self at that age.

◦ ◦ ◦

Colorado. As Fran drove, Cora was free to consider a beauty she had never quite imagined. When she was growing up, Colorado meant skiing holidays for rich kids. The background for TV Westerns. The location of the Air Force Academy. She had never pictured the glory of these mountains. Long ago, she had forfeited the Rockies to Alberta. As Fran oohed and aahed at Colorado, Cora was vaguely distressed at her own sense of personal pride in American landscape.

She thought about Jacques on the phone last night, laughing at their circuitous route.

"Well, there was a lot Fran wanted to see," Cora had explained to her merry lover.

"Fran?"

"Well, OK, so maybe some of our delay is unconscious procrastinating, Sigmund. But this is a beautiful country. And the trip is giving me a chance to get to know my daughter."

"Who's criticizing? At most you could have saved two days going straight there. It's great you're looking around."

"I wish I were looking at you."

"I wish I were inside you."

"Ummm. Yes. I love you, Jacques."

The days took longer as they approached Utah. Was this because she was afraid of returning west? Was it due to a natural attrition of energy after eight days in an automobile? Chiropractors said sitting was the most unnatural posture. Cora fantasized cars with standing room, where you leaned back against a cushion and zoomed forward, scooter style. Whatever the cause of Cora's own ennui, Fran was getting tired too. The trip was beginning to feel like a marathon. Cora found herself looking forward to the next restaurant, lusting after chocolate cake and sweet iced tea. Even Fran was giving in, and although the diet hadn't yet distorted her professional figure, Cora felt a poignancy as she noticed two pimples emerge on her daughter's chin. What was this trip doing to them? The leisurely nights chatting over dinner had turned into short bites and a rush back to the motel for the evening TV movie. Two vital, intelligent women had been transformed into rag dolls by the ravages of Interstate 70.

○ ○ ○

Still, dawn in the desert was compensation for the days behind and before them. If she had overlooked Colorado as a girl, she had completely ignored Utah. Utah, Idaho, Iowa, she mixed up those vowel states. When Cora put her mind to Utah, she remembered the Morman Tabernacle Choir singing "O Tannenbaum" on the *Mitch Miller Show*. She also recalled tales about bearded men who kept four wives and believed Jesus had reappeared in Hawaii with Captain Cook. Truthfully she didn't know how much she remembered and how much she imagined, for Utah now seemed as foreign as Lagos or Buenos Aires.

Gold rocks shone against the bronze earth. She had not known such energy and spirit could come from arid land, raised as she was on a coastal provincialism about the sanctity of blue and green. She watched a turkey vulture fly near the rim of high rock, streaking a dark breath of shadow. On the ground, she saw cactus and wild, hairy shrubs; below them she conjured snakes and scorpions. Perhaps they could return to Canada this way for a close look at the desert? No, she stopped herself, not wanting to think about what might occur between now and then. She meditated on the wide sky and the surprisingly benevolent sun.

Cora heard the blinker before she felt Fran slowing down. Startled, she swiveled to find a hitchhiker running to catch up with them.

"You said we should pick up single females." Fran's voice was defiant.

Cora imagined the backseat crowded with one orangutan, one chimpanzee, one ape and one spider monkey—single widows from their extended family.

Of course she had said that. Of course she believed in sharing resources. Where would she have been without kind strangers when she was crossing Canada? She regarded the fresh-faced hitchhiker, who looked younger than Fran. There was plenty of room in the car and three days ago they had agreed to pick up women hitchhikers. Strange that it was in Utah that they encountered their first solitary female with a backpack. Perhaps she was running away from a suffocating polygamous marriage.

She slugged her pack into the rear seat, then slid, neatly, next to it. "Gee, thanks," she said, watching Fran's reflection in the rearview mirror. "I've been there for two hours and was beginning to worry."

"No problem," Fran grinned.

Cora studied her competent, reassuring daughter. Maybe Fran was hungry for the company of someone her own age. "Let me drive the next stretch, honey," she said.

Fran nodded gratefully.

They switched positions.

"Where are you going?" Cora asked, adjusting the rearview mirror.

"San Francisco." The young woman fished for her seatbelt.

Cora's heart sank. Nine hundred miles with a stranger in the backseat. There was so much she and Fran would never say to each other now.

Resignedly Cora steered the car back onto the road.

"My name is Fran. And this is Cora."

The young woman grinned. "Fran. Cora. I'm Cheryl. Pleased to meet you."

"On holiday?" Fran asked.

Conscious of her daughter's enthusiastic gregariousness, Cora felt chastened about the past day of weary silence, about her unasked questions. They would have time between San Francisco and Grandview, even if it meant being greedy about their car.

"Holiday?" Cheryl inquired. "Oh, vacation, no. I'm coming home from one. Actually, I'm going back to college, at Stanford. 'Holiday.' Are you Canadian or what?"

"Canadian," Fran smiled.

"Oh," said Cheryl. She attached her seatbelt and stared out the window. They chatted a little longer. Then their guest fell asleep.

The world was flat between Rowley Junction, Utah, and Wendover, Nevada. Cora felt they were in the West again as they climbed to Silver Zone Pass at 6,000 feet and Pequop Summit at 7,000. She loved the Nevada placenames—Wells, Deeth, Elko, Battle Mountain. Forty miles past Winnemucca, the map had shown an intriguing looking place called Rye Patch Reservoir, but she knew Fran wouldn't want to stop.

Cheryl sighed and stretched. "You in school, too?"

"I'm a dancer," Fran straightened her back.

"Oh, neat," Cheryl nodded. "And you, Cora?"

"I'm a journalist. Freelance. Mostly magazines."

"You writing an article about America?"

"Well, maybe. We'll see."

"I think that kind of freedom is outstanding." Cheryl unbuckled her seatbelt and sat forward. "To get paid to travel and write up your perceptions. I'd love to do that."

"Yes," agreed Cora. She turned the conversation back between the two younger women. "Fran will be returning to the States in a few months, to study dance in New York."

"My father lives in Manhattan." Cheryl yawned. "Terrific place. You know where you'll stay?"

"No." Fran shrugged. "Any suggestions?"

"Upper East Side is nice. Kind of quiet. My father likes it. I prefer Soho. It's tacky, but lively. People on the streets at all hours. Safe."

Cora remembered this route would take them through Oreana, Lovelock, Fernley and Sparks before they got to Reno. She concentrated on the scenery but found herself worrying about residual fallout from nuclear tests.

"Just make sure you find a place with good heating. The winters can kill you in New York."

Cora refrained from saying that New York got its winter wind from Canada and that Fran knew more about cold than she . . . why the defensiveness? About winter! For the first year in Toronto, she thought November was a cruel joke and kept waiting for life to warm up. She scoffed at people who stood on Yonge Street for an hour in the snow for a Woody Allen movie. Now, of course, she found herself doing all of it—waiting for the films, spending ten minutes scraping ice from her car windows, buying suitable underwear, shoveling snow off the front walk, going bonkers in March when the winter had stayed too goddamned long. On this dry October day in Nevada, she also remembered the gifts of Northern winter—sunny walks in the snow and the friendliness of people who offered to take your coat and served you a cup of coffee to celebrate your safe return to the inside world. Of course she would be back in Toronto for winter this year. Maybe she would even catch the last of autumn, depending how long Pop held on.

She concentrated on the girl. Terrible to revert to that word. Woman. The upper East Side apartment made sense when Cora looked closer at Cheryl's casual clothes: expensive hiking boots; new backpack; designer jeans; silk-screened T-shirt. She wondered why she was hitchhiking and ignored the vague sense of danger. Cheryl probably just wanted an adventure. Cora knew it was ridiculous to feel scared. What was really bugging her was jealousy—resentment at Cheryl's innocent intrusion.

"What are you studying at Stanford?" Fran asked.

"Well, I'm in mass communications—like your mother," she grinned.

"Wish my communications were more mass," Cora laughed. "I might make a better living at it."

"But I started out more on your turf," she tapped Fran on the shoulder. "Human movement. Thought I'd like to teach PE to young kids. You know, get them while they're young. Train them to appreciate their health. A kind of physical fitness evangelist."

"So why did you switch to mass communications?" Fran asked.

"Well, it was the nature of my fellow students. And a few of my profs, if you get the drift."

Cora rolled her eyes and tried to meditate on the scenery. They were approaching a small town.

"How many years do you have until graduation," Fran tried to detour the discussion.

But Cora was angry. "No, I don't catch your drift at all."

"You know, they were, um, dykes." Cheryl looked uncomfortable for the first time. "Perverts. I didn't want to associate with those wrong-way ladies, if you know what I mean."

"Got it." Cora slowed and turned into the town. She stopped in front of a bank. "Guess we'll let you off here."

"What?" Cheryl was genuinely confused.

"Your drift is becoming a bit of a draft." Cora shrugged.

"What, you mean to let me off here in the middle of the desert?" Cheryl blurted.

"Hardly the middle of the desert. The town must have 500 to 600 souls. Look, here's a bank. There's a diner. Over there's a public telephone. Ask Daddy to send a helicopter." Cora cut the engine. "It's a lot safer to disembark now than to travel any further with wrong-way ladies."

"You've got to be joking," Cheryl's jaw dropped.

Fran hopped from the car and removed Cheryl's backpack. "See, there's a Greyhound station. Must be a bus through here every three or four days. Meanwhile, enjoy the sights of Broomley, Nevada. I understand they have no trouble with the heating here."

Cora forced back her smile.

Cheryl had regained her wind. "Thanks for nothing." She stepped out with elaborate dignity. "This is really sicko. A mother-daughter team."

Cora turned on the ignition.

Fran could see her mother's hands shaking. "Want me to take over?"

"No, I need to ride out this aggravation." She gunned the engine. If she had been a better person, she would have tried to talk with the girl. Her temper, Pop's temper, had always got her into trouble.

"Thanks, Mom. That was hard to do."

"On the contrary. It was the easiest thing in the world." She smiled. "Never thought of my daughter as a wrong-way lady. It has a certain ring."

"More appealing than 'sicko.' " Fran grinned.

"Sicko," Cora repeated.

They burst out laughing.

❋ ❋ ❋

On their way to San Francisco—how could they come all this way and not visit San Francisco?—they passed through lush farmland. Truthfully, Cora had never thought about these miles of vegetable and fruit. Now odd facts from high school filtered through her mind. California is the garden of the West. California is the eighth largest economy in the world. California agribusiness pressed for the internment of Japanese Americans. California provides salad for 3 1/2 million people each night.

Indian summer in Northern California had to be one of the most benign of seasons: wide, blue skies, bright sun, golden hills. Cora wished the days were a little longer. When the sun closed at 7:00, she began to brood about Oregon. After the brief detour to San Francisco, they were traveling relentlessly northward. Cora considered her old California dream—the fantasy of graduate school, and after that, of a pleasant grown-up life below the border. Yes, this is where she would have lived if there had been a choice, if she hadn't had to go to Canada. But how could she be ungrateful about Toronto? Think of those long, late summer nights on the porch, sipping iced coffee with Jacques and talking soccer with Mr. Caputo. Think about the thrill of wildflowers in Algonquin Park during the late spring. And the melancholy of autumn. Think. Think. Still, the old dream tugged.

The further north they traveled, the darker it got. At the center of day they were shadowed by enormous sequoias. The sun set earlier. California was a large state, yet they were at the border and she knew it.

As they drove into Oregon, a strange thought formed in Cora's mind. Your friends are the muscles—supporting you through crises—but your family is the bones, the skeleton, framing all possibilities.

EIGHT

Summer, 1968
Oregon

Cora forced herself to eat shredded wheat. It was eleven o'clock. She *had* to
eat breakfast, then lunch, then dinner before she and Ralph . . . no, she
mustn't let herself *think* in too much detail. She surveyed the tiny kitchen of
the cluttered apartment she was sharing with Sara and Becky.

Coffee should get her going. Setting the kettle on the stove, she caught
her reflection in the kitchen window. What a big face. Aunt Min called it "an
expressive countenance," but she hated her own oversized features which exposed thoughts and feelings as her eyes grew enormous or her cheeks washed
bright red. She had never been good at secrets.

What was that burning smell? Oh, no, she had dropped the dishtowel
on top of the kettle. Shit. She doused the dishtowel in water and concentrated
on every step of the instant coffee preparation.

A little Dylan should help, so she switched on Sara's portable stereo.
Reclining on the couch with a three teaspoon dose of Yuban, she recalled sitting on the basement steps in Grandview, eavesdropping as George and his
boyfriends whispered beneath the strains of "Blue Suede Shoes." George, in
his own way, would understand what she was doing tonight, better than Ron.
George also bore a pulse which drove him to act. Look at the way he had
pulled army strings to extend his time in Vietnam. Certainly he would hate
her for *how* she had chosen to act. Well, he couldn't hate her any more than
he already did. She remembered the letter to Pop which he neatly carboned
(where did soldiers find carbon paper in Vietnam?) for her information. For
her information.

> *"I'm sorry to inform you, Pop, that your daughter has fallen in with the
> lunatic fringe. . . . "* There he was again, accusing her of being mad. *"I*

*can't call Cora my sister any more and I hope you'll also want to dis-
own her for the abominable . . . "*

Dylan wasn't helping. She flipped the album. "Hey, Mr. Tambourine
Man . . . " Better. But she needed to study for the Spenser midterm. That
would be the best alibi—acing a test the day after the fire. No one would suspect she had spent the night before incinerating draft files. She would say she
had been at the library . . .

Studying stains on their couch from the year's parties—wine, onion dip,
semen, guacamole, Pepsi—Cora knew they would not get back the cleaning deposit. Her mind wandered to tonight's wardrobe, smooth-soled shoes and dark
clothes. Yes, the jeans would be impossible to trace. She told herself not to fuss.

⁰ ⁰ ⁰

They drove silently through the moonless night. Cora ignored Ralph's
wheezing, concentrating on automotive purrs and rattles.

She thought about that time George had dared her to hold the garter
snake. She had understood it was harmless. Although he said it was a rattler,
she knew it was just a baby garter. Yet it took enormous willpower to extend
her hand. It took half a minute to open her eyes and look at the pathetic thing
wriggling in her palm. Why, if she *knew* that it couldn't hurt her, was it so hard
to hold? She should have shown more cool. Still, she had been wickedly pleased
when George had scoffed at Ron for not being able to touch the snake at all.

*The road was a ribbon of moonlight over the purple moor,
And the highwayman came riding, . . .*

"What're you thinking about?" Ralph asked.
"Alfred Noyes."
"*Mad Magazine?*"
"Not Alfred E. Newman. Alfred Noyes. A bad poet," she laughed
anxiously.
Ralph didn't respond.
Immediately her mind shifted to tactics. She checked to insure that
their kerosene cannister was standing upright on the floor behind them. She
held the matches and the fire extinguisher securely in a bag on her lap and
reviewed their plan for the hundredth time. Ralph would enter through the
window first, then help her. They would pull out each drawer and light one
after another. The files on the right as they entered would be most crucial.
They had an hour to destroy the four cabinets before a night watchman was
due. They'd be out in forty-five minutes, easy.

"It'll be fine." She surveyed the road, the uneven thread created by off-
kilter headlights. "Really, Ralph, we could finish in forty minutes." She
turned for reassurance and saw that his jaw was locked.

They parked two blocks away and walked briskly to the draft board office. She conjured other flames. Girl Scout camp-outs with ghost stories. The destruction of Chicago after Mrs. O'Leary's cow kicked over the lantern. The fires in Washington, D.C., after Martin Luther King was assasinated.

She would never forget that day in April she heard about King's death. She was sipping coffee at the bus station, waiting for her coach to Grandview. The young black waitress was in tears. Cora heard an old white woman at the counter whisper to her friend, "I was never a *fan*. He was too big for his boots. But to be shot in broad daylight. . . . What is this country coming to?"

"Who was shot?" Cora demanded.

No response. Perhaps she had been rude for interrupting.

The waitress looked straight through her with cold brown eyes. "Dr. King. They killed Martin Luther King in Memphis today."

When she stopped at home that afternoon—one of the last times she ever went home—she heard her father say the same words. "They killed Martin Luther King in Memphis today." His tone was different, but his cold blue eyes were also accusing.

She noticed she was walking ahead of Ralph and turned. "You OK?"

"Yes," he wheezed. His grey eyes were small and irritable. Nervously, she smoothed the gloves over her fingers.

She wanted to comfort him by confessing her own fears, but she was afraid he might explode on the spot. There they would be shouting at each other, with kerosene and matches and fire extinguisher five hundred yards from the draft board.

Sooner than she had expected, they reached the building. The climb looked harder than it had in daylight. Of course she had brought a flashlight, but they could hardly use that for the ascent. Ralph didn't reveal any trepidation. Without breaking his stride, he put one foot on the ledge, then another. Quickly, deftly, he scaled the building. His graceful movements made her wonder, momentarily, if he might be gay. She had never felt any sexual attraction to him, from him. She didn't know any homosexuals. Ridiculous thing to be thinking about now. She could hear him prying open the window. She looked up: his hand was extended.

Cora took a deep breath and was surprised by the ease with which she climbed from one sill to another. Grabbing his hand, she slipped through the window to a dark room reeking of stale cigarette smoke and typewriter ribbons.

"Oooops," she heard herself say, stupidly, then noticed something crash to the floor. A long wet patch of coffee crept down her leg. "Oh, shit."

"Forget it," he whispered, not so much to forgive or comfort her as reminding her to concentrate. "Here." He switched on his flashlight. "Is that better?"

"Umhmm," she nodded, still quivering from her clumsiness. What idiocy: playing insurgent when you can't even make your way across a room.

"Over here," he whispered again, focusing on their task. "This is the current file."

"Yes." Cora looked down as he held the flashlight. She could not resist flipping through the drawer for familiar names. She recognized a man from one of her classes and holding out his file, she dropped a dozen folders into a metal wastebasket. To make sure her classmate's file was destroyed, she used it for kindling, dropping it in the basket to ignite the others. Solemnly they watched the first batch twist, glow, turn to ash.

As Ralph reached in for the second group, she felt a twinge about her greed in going first. His wheezing increased. She averted her face from the thick plumes of smoke.

The next steel grey cabinet contained files of men who had been inducted during the previous two years. Was this action a sin or a prayer? Cora knew she could never pull George or Ron or Pop from that war.

The last time she had visited Pop was the weekend after Bobby Kennedy had been shot in Los Angeles. "Damn immigrants," he had spat. "Why we let those Arabs into the country is beyond me." Cora would have fought back, at least countered that his own parents were immigrants, /but she could see he was not in the mood for argument. She decided she wasn't in the mood either for she hadn't seen tears in Pop's eyes since Mom's funeral.

As the embers from Ralph's batch died, she studied a file in the next cabinet—medical history, school records—hardly enough evidence for the death penalty. Abruptly, she cleared the rest of the drawer. Lighting the basket now, she watched as oblivion first claimed thin, white paper before crumbling the heavier beige cardboard.

"Over here," he whispered. "This is the next bunch."

She followed swiftly with the basket, using a thick file as a hot pad against the burning metal. How did Ralph know so much about the office layout? Who had been his contact? She wouldn't ask the name, just as she knew Ralph would not reveal her identity. Respectful of Ralph's professionalism, she admonished herself to pay closer attention.

They continued to alternate their tasks, one steadying the wastebasket while the other dropped in files. She faced away from the fire when she wasn't doing the burning; Ralph's eyes always remained fixed on the job. She knew his mind wasn't wandering like hers, from old family arguments to newspaper reports of slash and burn agriculture. He was soberly single-minded. She thought about that silly column in *The Oregonian* claiming that people who used violent tactics were psychological cripples or loonies preparing for the Apocalypse. Concentrate, she reminded herself, and the anger momentarily steadied her.

Then she couldn't help coughing from the smoke.

"Almost finished," he said softly. "Just two more drawers."

"Oh, it's nothing." She noticed how the flames etched their shadows on the wall opposite: two mountains rising and falling, as if in an earthquake. Certainly her cough was nothing compared to his discomfort. Ralph could hardly breathe.

"Trouble is," he spoke as if he were addressing a distant crowd, "The papers won't give us more than eight or ten inches."

She shivered. Although she appreciated the significance of media coverage, she found it hard to think about that now. Her heart pumped faster with each file destroyed. What was their small invasion compared to the long-term campaign? Of course you had to think about publicity.

"Still, it's better than nothing," he sounded resigned. They finished the last two drawers without further conversation.

She faced toward the window and inhaled, surprising herself again with a raking cough. "That's it," she said, to take control, to congratulate each of them, to get Ralph's attention.

"Yes, well, umm," he stumbled. "I've been thinking I might just stay and finish it off."

"What do you mean?" She tempered her panic. "We agreed. Four cabinets. In and out in an hour. You know the security guard will be here in thirty minutes."

"No, I've got it all worked out," his voice was clear. Impenetrable. "You drive the car back to the library. It'll only take me another ten minutes. I'll finish in time; don't worry."

She stared at him.

He continued. "It'll look better if we don't show up at the library together. Don't forget to change your clothes in the car before you go to the reference room."

Slowly, she shook her head.

"It'll be fine," he insisted. "I've made up my mind."

"No," she stood firm. "It's too risky. What if the guard arrives early? Even if he comes on time, he'll smell smoke right away; they'll put out an alarm and pick you off the road." She caught her breath and coughed again.

"No," he declared, drawing a key from his pocket. "I drove Norm's car out here this afternoon. Parked it on a side street. I'll be on my way before any of that happens."

"You're crazy." She knew that he was crazy just as she knew he wasn't.

"I'm not going to get caught."

"I'm warning you, Ralph, I'm going."

As she walked to the window, another drawer opened with a heavy metal sigh.

"Ralph." She turned around.

His eyes were calm and steady in the orange light.

"Ralph," she whispered again.

"Go," he said.
Was he talking to her or to the fire?

Carefully, she climbed down the side of the building. They had talked about how you shouldn't leave traceable shreds of clothing. They had planned meticulously—buying jeans at the Salvation Army to insure anonymity in the forensics laboratory. They had timed their actions to the minute, had rehearsed the location of the files and their burning technique. Cora had found learning to use the fire extinguisher the hardest part. You needed to be strong and coordinated to work those things in an emergency. Was this an emergency? She was as angry with Ralph as she was worried about him. Of course, he was right that it would look better if they went to the library at different times. Shadowed by guilt at following his orders, she had always known he could be reckless.

Cora slipped into the car and started the engine. As she pressed the clutch, following Ralph's instructions about the stick shift (instructions he was giving her, he had said, in case something went wrong), she realized he had planned this from the beginning.

Suddenly a man's figure lurched toward the car. Small and thin like Ralph. She was relieved. On closer inspection she saw he was reeling, with a bottle in one hand. She pressed the lock buttons on both doors and switched on her headlights authoritatively. Finding first gear, she eased down the road.

The streets near campus were quiet during summer session. Pulling into the darkest road, she turned off the car lights and changed clothes. Ten o'clock, he *must* be finished now. He was precise, fastidious. Still, she would feel better when they spoke on the phone tomorrow. Shoving the jeans into a plastic sack, she gathered her notes on *The Fairie Queene* and snapped open the door.

A drunk man in dark clothes weaved toward her. Cora blinked, no, it was a jock wheeling his bicycle. She imagined that alcoholic downtown reaching into his breast pocket for a pen and registering her license plate number. Concentrate. She steered herself toward the reference room.

The high-ceiling chamber was uncommonly hot and close with the nervous smell of students cramming for exams. She found a seat near Sara, nodded and opened her notebook. She should have stayed with him because together they could have gutted the entire office in a few more minutes. What if he got hurt?

The guy across the aisle snapped his gum loudly. Christ. She tried to concentrate. Cora found the noise making her angrier and angrier. Her nerves shot, she headed for the drinking fountain. Remarkable how thirsty she was. She couldn't get enough of the tepid water. (Would Ralph remember to take the fire extinguisher? It would be so easy to trace to his rooming-house because of the serial number.)

"You all right?"

She heard a voice behind her. Her whole body stiffened and she forced herself to breathe slowly as she turned.

"Sara!" she concealed her alarm. "Hi. How's the studying?"

"Fine." Sara regarded her cautiously, almost closing her left eye in that thoughtful way of hers. "But you look as if you've seen a ghost and you smell like . . . you've been toking up." Her voice betrayed amused concern. "I thought you were above—or beyond—dope."

Cora found herself in the middle of an elaborate lie. "I stopped by a friend's house to borrow some notes and people were sitting around smoking pot, and I guess it stuck to my hair or something." She blanched as she realized that this completely blew the alibi that she and Ralph had concocted. Already, Sara looked suspicious.

"Are you . . . " Sara dropped the question and patted Cora's shoulder. "Well, in any case, are you coming back to the reference room to spend a little time with Eddie Spenser's fan club?"

Cora smiled wanly.

Sara took her friend's arm, gently steering Cora into the reference room.

Cora tried to concentrate. Book Two, Canto Ten.

The guy across the aisle was now sucking Junior Mints. Suddenly she felt faint with hunger, remembering that she had skipped dinner. Becky had planned barbequed ribs and chicken. Focus, she scolded herself. "Delia" is an anagram for "ideal." Ten-thirty, she checked her watch. He would be safely doing his homework now. And he would call her in the morning.

Book Two, Canto Eleven.

⋄ ⋄ ⋄

She woke at dawn, frantically trying to remember details of a nightmare about her mother. Only sadness and guilt lingered. Cora forced herself back below the surface. She needed sleep. Ralph wouldn't be calling until eight. Turning on her side, she conjured sunsets on the Grandview beach. One evening she had seen a little girl wearing a pink and blue sweater fishing off the rocks. . . . Maybe she should call Ralph. No, she would wake her own roommates and his as well. Relax, she practiced the breathing exercise. She didn't know the first thing about relaxing. Breathe in one-two-three-four. Hold it for eight counts. She rolled over on her stomach, trapped in an argument with Pop. Ridiculous. She would get up and read Book Two again.

"You're up early," Sara stumbled from the bedroom, rubbing her red eyes. "What an eager little beaver." Her face was suddenly invaded by yesterday's concern. "You are OK, aren't you, Cora?"

" 'Cora' spelled backwards is 'a rock,' " she answered. Secretly, she wondered if the missing *k* were a vital chromosome.

"What?" Sara asked, refilling Cora's cup with coffee.

"Nothing. I'm fine. Maybe you're just projecting your own Spenserian anxiety."

"Maybe I'm just being a good friend." Sara cleared her throat and walked into the living room.

"Reveling at 8:30 in the morning?" Becky appeared in her Grateful Dead T-shirt and pink striped underpants.

"Eight-thirty!" Cora stared at the phone.

Becky and Sara exchanged worried glances.

"The test isn't until ten o'clock," comforted Sara. "And it's only a midterm. What's got into you?"

"My period," Cora listened to her voice, which sounded perfectly normal. She escaped to the bathroom where in the mirror she was struck by how old she had become—lines circled her brown eyes and dregs of dark hair straggled over her rounded shoulders. Something was dreadfully wrong. Ralph would not be half an hour late. Maybe she should just wait in the apartment for the police to arrest her. What sense did it make to write a midterm when you would spend the rest of your life in jail? She pictured cops bursting into Professor Whitman's classroom.

o o o

Cora used all her willpower to concentrate on the exam. It wasn't a hard test. Somehow she had picked the right passages to study. At least she knew she wouldn't fail. She might be the first person to earn a Ph.D. in a federal penitentiary. Refusing to think about Ralph being hurt, she reminded herself that he was smart, calculating, an engineer, for Christsake. The worst possibility is that the guard would have arrived early and called the cops.

A tap on her shoulder. "Time, Miss Casey." Professor Whitman's voice. Professor Whitman's face. "Have you quite finished your meditation?"

"Yes, I mean I'm sorry." She fumbled to close her bluebook and handed it to the bearded man, who looked uncannily human despite his arch announcer voice.

"Thank you, sir." Her father's word, *sir*.

More alert now, Cora noticed Sara standing by the door, one hand on her hip, frowning.

She had promised to treat Sara to a cappuccino at Serimelli's before their noon class. Yes, she would carry off this pretense of normality. Let them arrest her in the coffee shop. She felt a small relief that she had not been apprehended during the test.

Professor Whitman was smiling indulgently. "Thank you, Miss Casey."

She blushed, realizing how much she liked being taken seriously as "Miss Casey."

The judge would call her Miss Casey.

Cora and Sara walked across campus fretting about the test, then fell into silence.

The atmosphere at Serimelli's was more than usually intense for a weekday morning. The coffee shop, which called itself "the only Italian cafe for thousands of miles," was always crowded, but today it was packed. People huddled over newspapers, concentrating despite the dissonant whines of steaming milk and the radio voice invoking "G-l-o-r-i-a."

Sara claimed a place at the large back table. As Cora carried two foaming cups across the room she noticed Sara buried in the town paper. Stalled in the aisle, Cora read the banner headline, "Man killed in draft arson." Blood drained from her face. The guard, no, no, hadn't Ralph used the goddamned extinguisher? Was he just too greedy; had he stayed a fraction too long and fucked up the whole thing by killing the security guard? She was swaying. Sara came forward to take the cups.

"I guess . . . you saw about . . . Ralph," her voice cracked.

"Ralph, yes, Ralph." Cora said numbly, staring at her roommate, astonished that the papers would be releasing suspects' names this early.

The cafe seemed obscenely mundane. Friends and classmates sat drinking orange juice, eating late breakfasts. In the corner, Becky stood flirting with an exchange student from Marseilles—probably the son of a multinational corporate murderer. Murder, she pictured herself standing before the judge. Everyone in the cafe seemed immature and trivial.

Sara opened out the newspaper between them.

"He was so young." Sara was in tears.

"Who?" Cora gripped the edge of the small, round table.

"Ralph. Imagine—dying at twenty-one."

◦ ◦ ◦

That Sunday, *The Oregonian* did a full page spread on "The Draftboard Pyre." "Authorities called it a professional job, almost obsessive in the precision with which it was executed." Ralph was dubbed "the radical monk" because of the suicide note he had left in his room earlier that evening. He tied the draft board arson to a larger struggle for self-determination in Southeast Asia. He claimed sole responsibility for the fire.

Sara looked up from the paper.

"Corey," she asked hesitantly, "you didn't know anything about this, did you?"

"No," Cora said flatly. "Nothing." She gazed across the room, seeing nothing. "Why do you ask?"

Sara looked stunned. "I don't know." She paused. "I guess the FBI will investigate."

Cora stared at Sara, wondering if she had ever seen her before.

"And you knew Ralph best. You and Henry Rhinehart."

"Henry Rhinehart?"

"They went to high school together. To some preppie academy."

"Oh, Ralph mentioned it once. Actually I never knew him that well."

"Good," Sara said with finality. "For once your innocence and naïveté will stand you in good stead."

Sara continued talking—chatting in that compulsive way of hers. Cora thought how, coming from a family of few words, she found Sara's ability to talk amazing and sometimes nerve-wracking. These days she was simply grateful for the chatter, which provided an emotional caulking between one disaster and the next.

* * *

The rest of the summer went by too slowly and too fast. Cora wove back and forth between mourning for her friend, gratitude for his absolving her and fury that he had appropriated the entire action for himself. At night she remembered thin lines on his wrists, old rumors of suicide attempts. She should have known. She should have talked with someone. But who? Who could she talk to then—or now? Cora began getting terribly sick at odd times of day and followed herbal remedies with patent medicines; still the vomiting would not stop. Who could she trust? What did she know?

News reports would interrupt her reading of "Epithalamion" and "Amoretti." Local police wanted to close the case, but the Bureau of Alcohol, Tobacco and Firearms was investigating. And the FBI was talking conspiracy. According to an *Oregonian* editorial, it couldn't have been a one-man job and since there had been a death—a possible homicide—there was no statute of limitations on the arson, and they could keep the case open forever. Ralph's family refused to accept the popular verdict of suicide. They gave interviews saying he was a brilliant boy, with everything to live for, and lobbied for a thorough investigation of the fire. Henry, who was described as the Northwest State University student who knew Ralph best, was quoted as saying, "He was a loner, but not a lunatic."

Even *The National Enquirer* got into the act—running a story about a night nurse named Rose White who saw a red-haired woman fleeing the scene of the fire. They reported the police had found strange bits of evidence on the sidewalk outside the draft office: a yellow rubber glove, duck feathers, a sterling silver thimble. However nobody believed *The National Enquirer*.

Cora's vomiting grew worse around finals. She now thought it was an emotional reaction and that she needed help. But what could she say at the student health center—"Excuse me, I'm suffering from post-arson syndrome"? No, she would just wait it out until the end of term and then take a short trip to clear her head, maybe to visit Aunt Helen in California.

* * *

Sara drove her friend to the Greyhound station. She was sorry she couldn't wait around for Cora's bus, but her family was coming up for a visit today. Cora urged Sara to hurry back to campus. She promised to send a postcard from the land of her dreams, San Francisco. She insisted that she'd be fine on her own.

Cora knew she *was* fine when she inquired at the counter if she could use the Round America Ticket to go North as well.

"Listen, lady," sighed the harassed clerk, wiping the black hair from her eyes, "*Round* means you can go in any direction you like."

III

NINE

Fall, 1988
Oregon

As Cora rode down Market Street with Fran, Grandview looked smaller.
Cora had expected that. The first time she returned from college, her bedroom had become tiny. Today, however, she was stunned by the immensity
of change. Gibson's Five-and-Dime had been taken over by Walgreen's
Drugs. The Mode O' Day Shop, where she had worked one high school summer, didn't even have the dignity of replacement. Through the dusty windows
she saw the mannequin they had called Florine standing naked on her blue
carpeted pedestal. If Cora had been driving, she wouldn't have been so distracted by these meaningless observations. Aunt Min had tried to prepare
her, had told her that most of the shopping was now done at the mall between
Grandview and Winston. Remembering this detail from Aunt Min's letter,
she understood that it had been intended as a warning.

"Anywhere else you want to go, Mom?" Fran's voice was indulgent.
"Your old high school? Your boyfriend's house?"

"No, no thanks," Cora responded distractedly. If Grandview felt foreign, it was also sufficiently familiar to make her uneasy. She imagined riding
through the Masai Mara past carcasses of scavanged animals—just enough of
them remaining to testify to the ruthlessness of change. Lighten up, she told
herself.

She switched off the tape, just as the narrator started the last chapter
of *Northanger Abbey*. She hadn't heard the last ten minutes of her book on
tape anyway, and she knew Fran only listened to humor her. "Just keep going along Market. We'll turn left for Aunt Min's at the light. We can't miss
the street."

Maybe coming home after twenty years was a little like dying, Cora
thought, as life flashed before her eyes. Not her whole life, simply the undone

deeds. She always planned to have written three or four books before she returned. She would be working tirelessly on a political campaign and only be able to tear herself away for two or three days. Of course she should be arriving in an airport limo from Portland, returning to give a lecture at a college or to accept an award from her high school, returning to forgive.

In reality, she was sneaking back, driven by a person who had been nonexistent (almost) twenty years before, riding on the last gasps of an old car, sitting in a body that creaked and sagged in humiliating ways. Alone, then, was how Cora felt as she and Fran arrived in Grandview. Such a strange sensation for someone surrounded by past and present demands.

The old blue clapboard house looked pretty much the same as when Aunt Min married John Earle over two decades before. However Aunt Min had installed bark in the front yard. "It's ever so much easier than tending a lawn," she had written to Cora.

"Looks familiar," she nodded to Fran. Then, forgetting how much of the story she had told her daughter, how much she had hidden and how much she assumed Fran had learned by osmosis, Cora explained, "Aunt Min moved here when she was married—that would have been the year I started college. John Earle was one of my father's bachelor friends. We used to invite him on Christmas. That's how he and Aunt Min got together. Their twins, Edie and Tommie, were born just before I went to Canada. He died, oh, I guess it was five years ago now."

Fran was more absorbed in the parking than in her mother's hectic reminiscing.

A woman stood at the front door, arms across her belly, shaking her head. This stranger's finely lined skin was drawn tight across her jawbones; her hair had turned gray. But the smile was the same. And the laugh!

"Cora, my Cora!"

The two hugged.

Cora found herself listening for reproach in Aunt Min's voice, but heard only pleasure and surprise. She was beginning to look familiar. Cora tried to stop recasting Min as the young aunt who had rescued her from orphanhood thirty-two years before and to see a woman in her late sixties who had had her own children. For a moment, Cora ignored the lines of blood and time, once again experiencing Aunt Min as a luminous source of energy.

"And this must be Fran, beautiful Fran!"

Cora was relieved to see Fran give herself over, accomodating the old woman. It was more than that: Fran went to her hungrily. Yes, it had been the right decision to visit Aunt Min before venturing to Pop's house on the other side of town.

"Hi there!" A voice from the hallway.

"Welcome." Another, throatier voice.

The speakers looked alike. Aunt Min's twins had worked hard to distinguish themselves—Edie with a Valley girl sort of confidence in her flowing blond hair and wool challis dress. Tommie, with punk determination in her shaved head and leather duds. It was clear that Edie was the bank teller and Tommie the community college student. They seemed more like alter egos than twins, perhaps linked in a deeper way than those sisters who dressed identically.

The house felt as familiar and strange as Aunt Min herself. Cora fondly regarded the battered leather ottoman on which she used to watch TV. Here was the music box Pop had brought back from Switzerland. How had a seaman found his way to Switzerland? The yellowing lace doilies on the arms of the easy chair had the same holes in them as when Cora was a kid, leading her to think that Edie and Tommie must have been more well-behaved than she and her brothers. From the kitchen, Cora detected the aromas of Aunt Min's famous gingersnaps and scones.

"Tea? Coffee? Or are you hungry enough to eat now? We've got tons of food for lunch."

"Coffee, thanks," Cora spoke automatically. She wasn't sure she wanted to commit herself to lunch here. She wasn't sure she might not turn around and drive straight for the border. If they raced due north they could make Canada in seven hours.

They did stay for lunch, then afternoon tea. Cora's attention constantly shifted. She was grateful that Edie, Tommie and Fran seemed to be getting on. And relieved to hear Aunt Min's voice filling the room on this damp day as it had filled the later years of her childhood. Cora was saddened by her Aunt's glaucoma, and wished that she could see both Fran and herself more fully. Cora felt an amorphous dread whenever Pop was mentioned, yet forced herself to absorb the grim details: The visits by a public health nurse. The steady progression of his illness. The sharpness of his mind. His resistance against a nursing home. George's and Ron's refusal to pay for the services of home visitors, "after all he gave them." Cora knew from the cold snap in Aunt Min's voice that she meant money. As much as she hated to face the truth about Pop's illness, she felt a stronger aversion to hearing news of her brothers.

On the surface, their stories were undramatic. Ron worked for a ship outfitting company in Portland as assistant manager. He and his wife Ally were deeply involved in the Church. George sold real estate, and Connie had a job at the Medford airport. They had become active members of the Republican party.

"How was the trip?" asked Edie as she poured a round of tea. "What part of America was the most interesting?"

"Washington," Cora and Fran answered in unison, then looked at each other with surprise.

"Don't you two disagree about anything?" Tommie looked mildly disgusted.

"Music," said Cora, wondering if her first assessment had been right. Maybe she didn't like Tommie better than Edie.

"Type *and* volume," Fran acceded. And books-on-tape. *Emma, Pride and Prejudice, Northanger Abbey*. Can you imagine doing Jane Austen all along I-70?"

"*Doing* Jane Austen?" Cora raised an eyebrow.

"See, you managed to start an argument," Edie shook her head. "And I bet they didn't fight their whole trip across the country."

"Not *exactly* true," smiled Cora.

Edie and Tommie were doing most of the talking now, for by midafternoon, Aunt Min was content to sit back and drink in family. "Sometimes I gave up on you *ever* coming back." She shook her head at one point. "So good to hear your voice. To hear *both* your voices." She nodded in Fran's direction.

"How come you stayed away so long?" Edie asked.

Aunt Min frowned. "I told you, she's been busy. Toronto is a long way from here. Another country. I didn't get up to visit her either."

Edie nodded absently and fiddled her hair into a ponytail. Cora noticed the family resemblance in her broad chin and wide eyes. Sometimes she thought her family had almost obscenely expressive faces. "*Non,*" she could hear Jacques scolding her, "it's wonderful that you're so open, that I can read what you're thinking."

"Really great meeting you after all this time," Tommie was saying again. "Seems crazy that we're first cousins and have never met. Of course we've known Ron and George for years, but this is different. It's different with women."

"Tommie is a budding feminist," Edie reported.

"She looks pretty much in full flower to me," Cora spoke evenly, ignoring her irritation with Edie, who after all, was just a kid, working in her first job, with miles of the world ahead of her.

"That's what George says," Edie continued. "He was surprised to hear you were arriving today."

Aunt Min regarded her sharply. "When did George call?"

"He didn't," she shrugged. "I called him. He promised to come up and talk at the county Young Republicans' dinner. You know," she turned to Fran, whose eyes were as wide as her mother's, "he won mulitiple decorations in Vietnam, your uncle."

Typical Casey exchange. Cora thought the "your uncle" sounded like a combination accusation and benediction. She was more Casey than Earle, this cousin. Cora insisted to herself that there was no menace in Edie's phone call, simply an adolescent ache for self-importance.

"I don't know much about my uncles," Fran shrugged non-commitally.

"Well, you should. They were *heroes*." Edie continued.

Tommie leaned forward. "I'm not sure you want to get Edie started on this. She's a regular Statue of Liberty."

Edie spoke over her sister. "It's a crime the way the vets were ignored. But next month there's going to be a big welcome-home parade. And George will be in the head car."

"What about Uncle Ron?"

Cora felt a blow to her solar plexis at the mention of "Uncle Ron." What had she done bringing Fran into this den of lunatic patriots? Did she have to sacrifice her daughter to save her father?

"He's marching with the Father's Brigade." Edie returned cryptically.

"Fathers?" Cora burst in.

"Yes," Tommie spoke in a more cautious voice. "Ron had a child over there. He and Ally are trying to adopt her."

"Another cousin we haven't met," Edie nodded conspiratorially to Fran. "Just like you. Well, not *just* like you because she's Oriental. Half-Oriental, I guess. But that doesn't matter."

° ° °

Cora saw only women on the beach. Women in their fifties through eighties. And dogs. That ugly dog looked like a pit bull. She should have asked Fran to switch off the minidocumentary about pit bulls on the motel TV last night. It never occurred to her that dogs could eat people alive. At least it hadn't occurred to her since she was five or six. And what good did it do to know these things? She breathed in the tart, salty air, to revive herself, to bring her home. However the present continued to interrupt her nostalgia. The blond dog running across the sand reminded her of a dingo or a coyote.

It was time to get in the car and drive up to Pop's house. She had been in Grandview five hours, had toured the main street, visted Aunt Min, left Fran with her new cousins, even bought her father a yellow chrysanthemum plant. Still, she was not ready to face him. Perhaps she was a coward. The beach had an inviolable hold.

Most of the women were alone or with dogs. She saw two friends gossiping. Sisters? She had never learned to identify sisters. As a child, she had walked this same shore tracking dreams amid malevolent tangles of seaweed and covert boulders, creating a constantly changing narrative of suspense. As a teenager, she had mused along the beach, noticing no one, no thing for hours, earnestly absorbed in profound universalities.

Cora had always walked just at water's edge. Often in Toronto she tried, unsuccessfully, to imagine Lake Ontario into an ocean. On Centre Island, surrounded by lake and stranded until the next ferry, it almost worked. Now with the Pacific Ocean on one side and pebbling sand on the other, she felt completely amphibious: a safe, comfortable identity, much more appealing than kinship with chimpanzees. Cora felt the *fact* of being over 90 percent water. She had come from the sea. She might return. She could walk into the water and never emerge. Even as she considered the logistics—rocks in her pocket, sleeping pills, sheer courage—she knew she could *not* give into the sea. This was an ocean her father had spent years overcoming.

Stones and shells: solid versus empty; opaque versus transluscent; heavy versus thin. She preferred to regard herself as a stone, glistening on the sand, taking light from the sun and gloss from the water, existing for itself. However the day in Grandview had left her feeling more like a shell. A half-shell, torn from its mooring—the membrane joint deteriorated—floating out to sea and lost forever. Now she was the beached half-shell, filled with salt-water. With sand. A child might come along and use her as a shovel, might rinse her off, put her in a pocket and take her home.

Near the water the sand was firm, perfect for walking because one's prints were soon erased in the waxing tide. Cora moved back a few steps and stood on a log in order to watch the birds. Gulls (which Cora had always found the most beautiful sea birds despite their commonness) flitted back from the waves like flirtatious young girls in satin shoes. How strange and wonderful to travel via tides and curves of wind.

Windsurfers. Scuba divers. Cora had often gone swimming here as a girl. Now people wore bodysuits, insulated against the unsympathetic Pacific waters. Cora didn't know if she approved of these unsightly attempts to con-quer nature. She watched a substantial old woman with a red cap and a blue wet suit, swimming alone.

⁎ ⁎ ⁎

Suddenly the shore felt colder. It really was time to get in the car and drive to Pop's. Cora remembered how you could never rely on the beach. When the sun dropped behind a cloud everything was impossibly grey—the sky was sapped of color—waiting. That waiting was the worst part of child-hood. How she had romanticized the beach over the years. In Toronto, on those days when either coast seemed centuries away, she used to remember bright, healing afternoons with the sparkling crush of waves. Yes, there had been plenty of wonderful walks. But, to be honest, the beach had always transformed with her mood. On the good days she wouldn't even think about sharks. On the bad days she would remember that terrible painting by Winslow Homer of the man alone on a sailboat, tossing among bloodied wa-ters. On the bad days she would find her eyes drifting over the waves for sleek rudders.

Of course she was right to let Fran see the town with Tommie and Edie. It would do her good to get away from maternal company for a while and be with people her own age. Cora shook her head. It wasn't fair to judge Edie after one afternoon. Everyone had been nervous. Even Aunt Min had seemed more relieved than disappointed when Cora said she would take a solitary walk along the beach.

An old man jogged by. Not much left of him, but he displayed most of what he had in a deep bronze. Must own a tanning lamp or a commuter pass to Hawaii; you'd never earn that color in Oregon. Well, who knew, maybe since we ripped a hole in the ozone layer, anything was possible. The jogger reminded her of Mr. Caputo, and she hoped the cold weather in Toronto wasn't being too hard on him. Funny that she would think of Mr. Caputo instead of Pop. But Pop was hard to associate with most men. God, Satan, John Milton, Stalin, maybe, but hardly most men.

The woman caught her attention. Handsome, fit. About her own age. Cora could tell because although she was slim, her bottom drooped and her face was slightly drawn. In spite of herself, Cora stared, and as they made eye contact, she recognized Sara Riley.

She had read about Sara several times in recent years. She had become a highly regarded feminist academic on the lecture circuit. In fact Cora had almost gone to hear her when she spoke at U of T. But the same thing that had stopped Cora from attending the talk, caused her to lower her eyes now. Instinctively, she pulled her knit hat further down, fixing her gaze in the distance.

"Corey?" The woman claimed her with a startled, uncertain voice.

Cora's shoulders stiffened as she paused. She breathed slowly through her mouth, to keep it occupied.

"Corey, is that you?" the woman spoke louder. "Excuse me," more formal now, but just as insistent, "are you . . . "

Another involuntary reflex: Cora stopped because you stopped when someone addressed you. No, it wasn't as simple as that, for she had spent years avoiding people in Canada. No, she shivered, she felt safe here in Grandview, hearing her old friend's voice.

"Sara!" Cora extended her hand. Was she more thrilled or frightened? "Amazing. How amazing to meet you on the beach."

"And you. Whatever became of you?" A brief look of distress crossed Sara's eyes. She seemed to be censoring herself, finding words to conceal her curiosity. "Well, here you are. After all this time. How wonderful."

"You're living here, in Grandview?" Cora rushed to ask before Sara could inquire about her. Of course she had her story planned; she was sure it would come out all right, but she felt more secure asking after Sara first.

"God, no, just here on R and R. I'm thoroughly depleted after a weekend conference in Portland. I gave the keynote and had to contend with a certain amount of, well, controversy is what I was going to say but more like jealousy actually. Academia is not the polite profession I once imagined."

"You're a sociologist now, aren't you?" Cora peered through Sara's composure to the tough, competitive Irish girl with whom she had grown up. Sara had been such a firebrand at college, always arguing with her about women's position. She found her stomach muscles relaxing now and her chest rising with fondness.

"Yes, but I do more feminist theory nowadays. Interdisciplinary stuff. No one stays in the same department any more. What I write is more cultural studies."

"I see your name everywhere." Cora paused, for this wasn't exactly true, and she was baffled by the impulse to flatter.

Sara blushed. "I've been lucky with my new collection."

Cora smiled, glad for her friend's success.

"I'm in a tizzy now because I just got invited to apply for a dean position. Of course I know it's a privileged tizzy. The pay is tempting, but I'm not sure I'll get my writing done. That's why I'm at the beach—to meditate on the pros and cons. Life is supposed to get easier after forty, but I find there are so many more choices, do you know what I mean? I feel terribly responsible about making the *right* choice. Culpable. It all goes back to Sister Mary Perfection in first grade."

Cora laughed affectionately. Despite their differences they were still Bishop Eagen School girls sharing the conviction that life should be settled by now and worried that it would *never* be settled because of some personal inadequacy.

"But look at you," Sara interrupted herself. "You look so *well*. Christ, it must be twenty years since I've seen you, since you went off to California on that damned bus." She paused, clearly deciding not to say something. "So how are you? And what are you doing here?"

Cora started with her father, although at no other time in her life would it be easier to start with Pop. "My father is very sick. He's dying of cancer." This directness made her nervous, as if she were giving him a sentence. "I've come to help out." She was suddenly aware of the gap between them—the caverns of time and separate options. Perhaps her link with Sara was silly and sentimental.

"Oh, I'm so sorry, Corey." Sara put a hand on her friend's shoulder, gently, hesitantly. "My mother died last year. This must be a very hard time."

"Yes," Cora said, for something to stem the tears. "Harder than I thought."

The two women watched the sun dropping, turning into a giant blood orange as it approached the horizon. It illumined overhead clouds, threading pink across the sky. Beneath, the water turned turquoise.

Sara checked her watch. Was she nervous, Cora wondered. Cora cleared her throat, as if to speak, but remained silent.

"I should run. Gotta get back to fix dinner. Richard and I take turns, and I'm up tonight. Say, I haven't even asked if you were with someone, if you had children. We'll have to get together. I mean it. Listen, here's my card.

Cards always feel pretentious, but sometimes they come in handy, like on the beach, when you don't have a Rolodex," she laughed anxiously.

The sun had left a carmine smear.

"Right," Cora smiled. "You can reach me through my Pop—Roy Casey, you remember. I'm sure he's listed."

∘ ∘ ∘

She *had* to get to Pop's house. She couldn't delay any longer. She had promised to come for dinner. Just ten more minutes, she told herself. She had already procrastinated unforgivably by taking that slow, slow route across the country. Ten more minutes.

The moon rested in a sly wink. Almost not there. Another day gone. Now a star. A wish? The ocean lapped continually. Cora was aware of it at odd intervals. Two old women passed. One walked with serene containment. The other moved her arms, wagged her head, talking rapidly. "Look," offered the quiet one. They both stopped instantaneously to regard the lunar sliver in the rosy dusk.

Several yards ahead, a man and woman stared out at the sea together, their bodies almost touching. Gulls lined the rail, facing away from the sun, squawking—for this was today's last shot at junk food before tourists abandoned the beach.

Cora knew she should get to her father's house. He always ate dinner early. Instead of turning into the parking lot, she walked down the pier between the men, women and kids. Alert to danger from eager anglers, she put on her sunglasses as protection and walked along. People approached their tasks with different degrees of seriousness. One man was straightening his catch on the pavement. Such a small amount. Was he soliciting sympathy? Two women talked volubly in Spanish as their poles arched into the water. A father in newish sports clothes was teaching his daughter how to reel. At the end of the pier, Cora rested, listening to the loud yawning boat horns. Down along the esplanade, the light house blinked green into the coral evening.

Turning around, she was struck by darkness as she walked away from the sunset into the night, wearing sunglasses. Still, she didn't want to remove the shades until she was safely past the anglers.

The fun house was blasting loud rock. Did it seem loud only because it wasn't her music? Four girls sauntered on the ballustrade—two wearing black patent shoes. She imagined herself among them in those pumps she and Sara wore in the tenth grade. If only she had saved her clothes, Fran could use them now. The girls were all wearing calf-length dresses and had pulled their hair into ponytails. Edie, Tommie, Fran, the Funsters: this is what young women looked like now. *This* is what she had wanted to discuss with Sara: *now* and *then*. But her disorienation seemed so narcissistic. She hurried toward the fun house, leaving night to the girls.

Over the entrance was an ominous sign: "The establishment regrets that it cannot provide first aid or medical care to people injured on the beach. They should proceed straight to the police office on the corner of Fourth and Birch Streets."

Inside the fun house a dozen teenage boys were playing video machines. A bald man sat in a teller's cage, snapping his gum and arranging coins in neat piles.

She purchased four fifty-cent tokens.

On the right was a miniature golf game in which you scored points into the Eiffel Tower, Big Ben, the Washington Monument. She was irritated with herself for being distressed by the absence of Canadian icons. Did she really think Americans would pitch half a dollar at a bust of Louis Riel or a miniature of the Toronto Dominion Towers? Her anger was out of all proportion, she understood this. She thought about the simplicity with which she had slipped across the border—as if she hadn't been separated for two decades, as if she always could have returned. No, she slammed her tokens down on the pinball machine and fled the fun house.

She needed air. Cora trudged in the dim light toward the car. Fran. Pop. Jacques. Aunt Min. Could she keep them all in her life? She considered Sara's job offer, which she had made sound like a marriage proposal. In a way that's what it was. Everyone engaged in serial monogamy nowadays—with editors, institutions, lovers. But what about people you left along the way? The reality was, you didn't leave them. They were always with you—directing the construction of your new relationships. Maybe that's why Mom recycled Aunt Helen's outfits into doll clothes to confound the insidious continuum.

Stars intruded. Lyra, Scutum, Sagitarius? Cora scrambled for the constellations Jacques had taught her. Normally, sighting and naming the stars would calm her, but tonight she felt agitated about her distance from Canada. She would call home later. Jacques would be waiting.

Edie bothered her. She had wanted to like Aunt Min's daughters. But there was *something* about Edie. Something about the way she had mentioned George. Something sexual. Cora's breath caught, and she found herself staring into a chasm. No, she exaggerated her older brother's evil. After all, he was just a Tory realtor. How she would have laughed at that twenty years ago. Now she was surprised at the sadness she felt that despite his grand dreams of playing major league ball, he wound up in Medford selling houses.

Like George, Pop had always lived largest in imagination. It's true that he was often brutal, drunk, abusive. But Pop hadn't killed Mom. He hadn't declared war on Vietnam. And now he was simply an old man, a dying man. She shivered, reason too frail against memory, and forced herself to get into the car.

TEN

Fall, 1988
Oregon

Driving up the old gravel road, Cora realized she should have changed clothes. Pop hated jeans and it would not have been that much of a compromise to wear a good pair of slacks. She should also have phoned to say she'd be a little late for dinner. For people with time on their hands, planning was important. You watched TV. You worked a crossword. You filled the time before *it* filled *you* with fear or despair. She inherited this determined temperament from her father. Would she also get his cancer? She had often wondered how to break the code of those genes, to know where to thank and where to blame him.

Aubrey Drive was not much more built up than when she left. Pop had bought here thirty years before because he had reckoned that he could sell the place for a decent profit when the street had become a popular housing tract. Then they would move closer to the beach. However the neighborhood was never fully settled because wind was so bad on this part of the hill.

Turning the corner, she saw their old house. Home, meatloaf dinners, Christmases, late nights reading under the blanket. Cora's eyes blurred with tears as she surveyed the large picture window shielded by new venetian blinds. She glanced down the length of the house until she saw her old room, also closed to the street by white blinds. But behind them, a lamp was lit. Was he doing something there—clearing it out in anticipation of her return—or cluttering it up to keep her from taking too much for granted? Suddenly something disturbed her: the lawn had been replaced by juniper. Putrid juniper and venetian blinds—maybe he had got them at a two-for-one sale.

As she parked the car, she noticed a slat in the living room blinds shift. This one gesture articulated what she had known—that she had the leverage now. For all his rage, for all their history, he was dependent on the prodigal

89

daughter. As much as she once howled over his decision to disown her, she did not want this terrifying new power. Cora got out of the car, hoping he was not still watching for she didn't know how much she could cope with his wanting. She forced herself to look down to the ocean. It's all right, she whispered to young Cora and to herself now. It's going to be all right.

The dog began barking as she walked up the driveway. She pictured their golden retriever mutt, Tenk, but realized Tenk must be dead now. How had George felt about that? He had always been the kindest to Tenk. She remembered the day her older brother found the scraggly dog, suffering badly from hunger and fleas. This high-pitched barking was the work of a smaller animal.

Cora lifted the anchor doorknocker which was tarnished beyond its brass, and rapped firmly.

"Coming," a familiar voice argued back.

She had time to smooth down her hair and straighten the collar outside her bulky sweater. Pop had always liked white blouses.

He looked older.

His once jet black hair had gone completely white. Even when she left, he had been greying. Still, she had persisted in picturing him as the slim, handsome man in the wedding pictures, as a man younger and gentler than she had ever known. She saw his jaw had filled out in the last twenty years—a buttress against the outside world. The face was a jumble of bleached boulders. The blue eyes pulsed, as he squinted in recognition or in pain, half-hiding behind his wrinkled lids. The cheeks ran to jowl, and his ears were like tiny wings.

What did he see? The voice betrayed nothing as he said curtly, "Come in. It's cold out there." More order than invitation, and she relaxed at the familiarity of this.

"Hi, Pop," she said.

He patted her shoulder with one large, hairy hand.

Her eyes filled with tears again.

"Coffee?" he offered, walking into the kitchen before she could answer.

She sat on the old couch scanning the room for childhood memories. The rug and most of the furniture were the same. Pop had bought a new black Naugahyde recliner chair. There were the Ganesh and the Buddha ornaments he had collected in India, but where was the miniature mosque?

He returned with two mugs of black coffee.

Momentarily, she wondered if he had put something poisonous in her cup. He kept his eyes on her. Even when the dog—she had observed it was a pathetic little blond cocker spaniel—jumped all over him, he pushed her away, his attention fixed on his daughter.

She sipped the coffee. "How are you feeling?" she finally managed.

"OK for an old man." He aimed for a Cary Grant cockiness.

It was up to him to talk about the cancer, she had resolved. He was hiding the disease well in this big tortoise of a body. And it looked as if the hair had grown back completely since the chemotherapy. Had they been lying to her? Did they lure her into a trap?

"How are you?" His voice was low, thick.

"Fine," she said cautiously. Then suddenly conscious of how far she had traveled, how little time they had, she added, "It's good to see you."

"Yes." He nodded and patted his thigh for the dog to come.

She wished she weren't so tongue-tied. This was an important moment, she told herself. Still, she was paralyzed. She was glad she had asked Fran to spend this first evening at Aunt Min's.

He stared out the window.

"The cancer isn't as bad as the arthritis. I mean it doesn't restrict me as much—not yet. It doesn't hurt as much as the diverticulitis." He described a horrifying series of ailments he had suffered since retiring three years before.

◦ ◦ ◦

He talked with impressive endurance for two hours. He had not said anything directly welcoming her. There had been no real acknowledgment of their twenty-year estrangement. He was filling her in as if she had been on a long trip. He spoke with the same intensity about his limp, Tenk's death, Ron's marriage, the new septic tank. She knew this was his way of taking her back.

Her attention flagged as her hunger increased. Well past dinner time they were still sipping coffee that had simmered all day. He had told her not to bring groceries, that the larder was packed. She was beginning to doubt this.

"How about some supper?" Cora listened to her voice for the right tone. How much coaxing? She was talking as if to a child, yet it was clear that he needed to be taken care of, even that he wanted to be taken care of. The trick was finding the right tone.

He seemed distracted by something on the street and stared out the window instead of answering her. Cora went into the kitchen to investigate culinary possibilities.

"Hey," he shouted, in a foiling-the-intruder voice.

"Yes," she reported back to the living room. He had turned on the TV and now switched down the volume with his remote control device.

"We'll go to Runnymede's for a barbequed chicken."

A life of Sunday dinners filled her gut. She pictured a phalanx of fluffy, white creatures parading across the carpet.

"To celebrate your homecoming."

She shook herself, annoyed at how pleased his words made her, yet pleased all the same. "Are you sure you're well enough?"

"I'm not dead yet," he interrupted, amused as always when he held the trump card. "Come on, Follie, that's a good dog."

They took his car—because it was nearer, because he would feel more in control this way. She insisted on getting behind the wheel. He was too tired to drive, perhaps too tired altogether for this expedition. Pride was their fuel as she backed down the driveway.

Silence between them, they drove through the neon dark town. She smelled piss. Was it the dog's? Was Pop incontinent? The quiet was broken by his loud wheezing, a bellowed sound that made her think of Ralph at the draft office. Pop lit a cigarette. She breathed in the burning paper and acrid tobacco.

"Park here," he pointed to the blue disabled strip on the curb. Taken aback, she was about to argue with him who never honored other people's needs, when she realized he was, in fact, disabled, that he had a white certificate with a red wheelchair clipped to the sun visor. His frail claim on accommodation terrified her. Despite his bulk, the blustering boss was disintegrating. In his last days, Roy Casey had won the right to park by the supermarket door.

He grabbed a shopping cart, leaning on it for support, barging his way past more reflective shoppers in the natural foods section and a young guy mesmerized by the spice rack.

"Evening, Mr. Casey." a freckled youth greeted him from behind the rotating chickens. He continued to varnish them thoroughly with a pungent, brick-colored sauce.

"Hello, Johnny. We'll take a plump one. The best you've got. You owe me, you know, after that stringy thing you pawned off on me last time. It must have jogged here all the way from Vermont."

"Yes, Mr. Casey." He regarded his customer with a blend of timidity and admiration. How often she had sensed that same look in her own eyes.

Johnny held up four chickens before his customer stopped shaking his head in disgust. Finally there was a barely visible nod of approval.

Cora accepted the chicken from the grateful clerk. Her impatient father sighed and shoved the shopping cart along without saying good-bye to Johnny.

Follie barked wildly as they approached the car. "Ah, down, you dumb mutt." He rapped her roughly across the nose.

Cora tried to remember how to shift the car into reverse, but was overwhelmed by Follie's yapping, Pop's heavy breathing and the aromas of piss and barbequed chicken.

Concentrate, she told herself.

"Women drivers!" he shouted.

But his touch was gentle as he guided her hand back across the gear shift.

They ate on TV trays in the living room. Cora noticed that his face had softened over the evening, that his eyes had grown less cold. Pop was now regarding her with complete recognition.

He wore his old Omega watch, with the black face and gold hands, one of his most prized bargains, still resilient after years of circumnavigating his furry wrist. She always loved this watch—the first one she had ever seen. Mom never wore a watch and refused to put a wall clock in the kitchen. All her life, Cora had looked for his Omega on other men's wrists.

He caught her gaze and grinned. "Still ticks."

"Yes." She smiled, then suddenly embarrassed and remembering it was autumn, she asked, "So who do you think will win the pennant?" It was either this or the election, and baseball might be a tamer topic.

"It's not called the pennant any more," he spoke with generous, instructive tolerance. "It's the league playoffs . . . "

She concentrated on the lesson but was distracted and saddened by his swishing, clicking dentures. He used to have such a fine, precise voice. Aunt Min always said he should be on stage. Tonight Cora occasionally found that to understand, she had to study his lips.

This reminded her of problems she had following the refugees she tutored in Toronto. The technical difficulties were different, of course, but the barriers were of the same magnitude. She couldn't imagine telling Pop about her volunteer English tutoring or her abortion counseling downtown in the clinic next door to the Right-to-Death offices. She wondered how much she could tell him about Jacques and her journalism. Jacques said she exaggerated her father's bullheadedness. Cora tried to explain what it was like to grow in a house surrounded by quicksand.

"But the Giants don't have a prayer." He was unsnapping a third beer.

A few years ago, he would have said "chance" instead of "prayer." Had he returned to the Church?

"Say," he interrupted himself, consulting the gold hands on the black face, "if you're really interested, the sports is on CNN right now."

"Sure," she said, noticing that he had finished the entire meal. He collected another beer and waddled back to the living room. Steadying himself on one arm of the recliner, he carefully dropped into the seat, causing the release of air in a loud shhhh. At this cue, Follie ran over and lay beside the ottoman.

Cora smiled at the man and dog watching the Yankees versus the Athletics. She had always hated the Yankees if for no other reason than they seemed to win constantly. The nasal sportscaster bothered her. She picked up a copy of *The Oregonian* and delved into a story about the dissolution of the Rajneeshees.

The television continued to drone. Her attention was caught by a shiny red photo album on the side table. Mom had always kept their photos in shoeboxes at the bottom of the linen closet. One day, she had promised, they would buy an album and organize the pictures. But they never got around to it. After she died, they continued to deposit their photos from school and camp into shoeboxes. Aunt Min also vowed to sort out the snapshots, but Cora guessed that the overflowing boxes daunted her. She stared at the album now, gleaming, new, and recalled a teenage daydream—that one afternoon she would find her mother alive, sitting in the livingroom puzzling over the order of two black-and-white photos, a leather album open on her lap.

"So who did this?" Cora inquired.

He looked up from his game, focusing his eyes, and betraying the slightest surprise in finding her there. "What?" he asked blankly.

Joe Isuzu was wisecracking from the front seat of a silver sedan. Pop's attention momentarily strayed back to the commercial. "I love this guy."

"Who did the photo album?"

"Oh, that. Oh, what's-her-Ally did that a year or two ago. She's a great one for projects, that girl."

"Ally," Cora bit her lip as she leafed through the first couple of pages. Why should she be annoyed, jealous? What a nice thing for her to do. A good way to learn about the family. And useful therapy for someone coping with the disorder of the Casey clan.

Cora was pleased to see Ally had started with a photo of Mom—one of Cora's own favorites—sitting in the backyard stitching a quilt. Then there were pictures of Mom and Pop on their honeymoon—Mom with those wide white shorts, white top and a gardenia behind her ear. Pop standing next to her, tall, thin, barely able to contain his glee.

She flipped through pictures of George, with his curly black mop of hair, which Mom must not have cut until he was three or four. Lots of pictures of George here; perhaps it was always that way with first children. Then one of herself—a sour-looking, round baby sitting in a basin on the picnic table—she was relieved and grateful that she had been included. Then a page of Ron, running in polka-dot suspendered shorts across the back lawn with the ducks. She hadn't thought about those ducks in years.

Cora was annoyed that Ally had got so much out of sequence—her First Communion before George's Confirmation. Pictures of the house in Torrence mixed up with photos of the Grandview garden. But her irritation was petty. How was Ally to know? Maybe Cora was simply displacing her own guilt, knowing that as the girl in the family, the photo album should have been her task. She regarded Pop watching TV and wondered if he had bothered to look at Ally's album.

She paused at the photo of herself and Sara at high school graduation, both looking so mature under that makeup and hairspray, yet petrified about the world ahead. She flushed thinking about bumping into Sara on the beach today. Well, *she* had done fine in the world. Had the two girls changed much by their first year in college, she wondered. But she couldn't find any evidence. As she flipped ahead, Cora saw no more photos of herself. Had Pop destroyed the college pictures? Had Ally ommitted them out of deference to Pop? She did know that she had sent snapshots, had brought them home on holidays. She choked back her irrational tears and remembered a great picture of her and Sara hanging over the railing of their college apartment, smoking Gauloises.

The next pages contained photos of George entering the service. Then some shots of him and his buddies in Vietnam: sweaty, tired-looking men sitting outside a tent drinking beer. Photos of his duty in Germany. He looked cold here—bundled in a sheepskin jacket and cap. The album switched back to Oregon. George and Connie's wedding. Cora had known Connie slightly from when the older girl had clerked in her uncle's drug store. George holding what must be a real estate license. Hey, what happened to Amber? Perhaps as a woman of taste, Ally had decided that there would be only one spouse per person in the official family archive. Connie rocking a sweet-looking baby. Connie clasping the hand of a blond boy, while holding a swaddled infant. George, Connie and two toddlers in front of a small colonial-style house in Medford.

Ron looked ill, posing in uniform at the Grandview post office with Pop and Tenk. Cora remembered that Aunt Min had explained he had spent six months going back and forth to the veterans' hospital for some joint disorder. She wondered if Ron, like his father, had earned a warrior's limp. He did look different—more changed than George—heavier, tired, perhaps a little more confident of himself. Too bad he had dropped his GI college tuition. He would have been a generous, kind teacher, yet she guessed Aunt Min was right—the strain might prove too much for him. Now, here was a livelier Ron in tuxedo, standing next to his bride, who was smaller than Cora had imagined, at Saint Leo's Church. And here was George again, a few years older, slightly looped, dangling an empty champagne glass.

The last photo showed Pop, George, his sons, and Ron: the red-cheeked Casey men standing tough together in front of the old brick church.

Then a dozen empty pages: clear plastic over black paper. Had Ally given up? Started her own album? Did she regard these blank pages as some kind of memorial to her or her mother, the disappearing women?

"Nice job," Cora looked first to the humming television, then to her father. Pop was sound asleep. She, too, felt completely exhausted.

Awakened by a loud snap, she opened her eyes to see him sitting beside her on the couch, holding out a can of beer.

"No, thanks." She sat up, blinking.

"You must be tired after your long trip," he said.

She was crying—at his attentiveness, at the predictable vacancy of their evening, at her utter fatigue. She checked her watch. Fran and Aunt Min wouldn't be worried yet; she said she might not be back until eleven. He wiped the tears, as if they were sleep, from her eyes.

"Your room's all set." He slurred his words. The combination of alcohol and dentures made him almost incomprehensible.

This was his way of forgiving her. There would be no direct acknowledgment. No absolution. No gratitude. She was his daughter again. This was as it should be, as it always should have been. As far as her forgiving him—it would never occur to Pop. She knew that's what she was doing the moment they crossed the border. If she had needed catharsis, she should have been born to a different family.

Cora did not want to turn down his invitation, but she could not stay tonight. "I, I have to get back to Aunt Min's. She's expecting me. I'll bring my bags over tomorrow. But if I don't get back there soon tonight, she'll worry."

"Ah, take a load off your feet." He was concentrating carefully. "Give her a call, that's what phones are for."

"But Fran, my daughter," she began, noticing her anger. What had he asked her about herself? Was she supposed to assume that Aunt Min had filled him in over the years, during the last week? Or did he think she had been frozen in time for two decades?

"Min mentioned that I have a granddaughter." His eyes softened.

"I'll bring her to meet you tomorrow," she offered.

He peered ahead, his broad face reddening along the jawline.

She stared back, conscious that her chin would always be a little smaller than his.

"All right, Follie," he cajoled the dog sweetly, as if they were alone. "Come on girl," he struggled to his feet.

Cora stood uneasily and stared at the full can of beer he had opened for her. She recalled the smell of piss in the car.

He shuffled toward the hallway and just as he reached it, he tripped. Cora rushed forward, but too late to prevent his crashing to the floor.

"Oh, Pop."

Propped on his elbows, he tried to catch his breath.

"Are you OK, Pop?"

"Yeah, yeah, nothing busted," he managed, recovering his dignity. Lifting himself painfully against the wall, he took her arm.

"You suppose you could help an old man to his bunk?"

"Sure," she answered gratefully.

Pop dressed down to his boxer shorts and T-shirt and climbed into bed. He pulled up the threadbare Star-of-Bethelehem quilt. Running her hand along the traditional pattern, she marveled at the orderliness of Mom's mind. Mrs. Larsen had been right, she was an intelligent, talented woman. Cora, herself, had always been hopeless at sewing and felt pathetic every time she paid for a pair of slacks to be hemmed. How touching that he would keep the quilt all these years, for it offered no substantial insulation.

She sat in the bedside chair for a long time, comfortable in their silence.

"You won't let them take me, will you?" he demanded.

Startled, she couldn't catch herself before she asked, "Who?"

"The boys," his voice was thin and anxious. "They want me in a convalescent hospital. I need to stay here. At home."

"No, I won't let them take you."

Reaching for her hand, he shut his eyes.

She sat beside her father until he fell asleep.

ELEVEN

Summer, 1951
Oregon

It all began serenely enough with the whole family enjoying a warm Sunday in the back yard. Mom was mending dungarees in the wicker chair. Ron was playing marbles. Cora was working a new jigsaw puzzle from Aunt Min. Pop lay on the newly mown grass with his eyes closed. Suddenly George was climbing to the roof of the garage, carrying their two pet ducks in the large picnic basket.

"George, get down from there, you stupid ass." Pop's voice boomed across the backyard, across several backyards. From his language and the brief slur in the word *stupid*, Cora knew to expect trouble.

Her first instinct was to go to her room and lock the door, but she found herself watching carefully. Mom jumped up, dropping needle and thread and dungarees. She shouted in a high, frail voice, "No, Roy, no."

Pop started up the ladder to the roof.

Cora's eyes followed the rungs to the top where she saw George holding a squawking duck.

The afternoon grew white and empty.

She became conscious of a pathetic beeping at her feet. Here was Gemmy, Ron's pet duck, dragging a bloodied, broken wing across the grass. Snowy feathers marked a trail from where she had landed.

Ron backed up against the garage, wailing.

"If you ruin another one, I'll wring your neck," Pop was huffing up the ladder.

"But you said ducks could fly," George spoke to someone, anyone, before he released the second bird, his own pet, Corky, to its destiny with gravity.

"Oh, Christ, " Pop bellowed louder, clambering down the ladder to retrieve the second bird. "What the *hell's* wrong with your son? He's a nine year old maniac."

99

Cora's first thought was that George's action made sense. How else could he prove Pop was wrong? He couldn't possibly get into more trouble for two ducks than for one. Her tall, skinny older brother stood on the roof, hands on his hips and a half-satisfied smile on his face.

"Christ!" Pop was yelling as the duck hit the grass.

Mom threw up her hands in despair, emitting a noise that sounded curiously like Corky as he landed. She gathered the first bird in her arms and began to repair its wing with, Cora felt sure, the same stitch she had been using on the dungarees.

For Mom, who always imagined the worst, this disaster seemed reassuring. Pop kept his promise to lick George good. But George seemed gratified, as if he had proven beyond a doubt that their birds could never fly the coop.

Spring–Fall, 1952

Mom invented the bus ticket game on a rainy Saturday. Soon Cora and Ron were playing it two or three times a week. Whenever they got off the bus, they would inspect Mom's booty. Sometimes she would have ten or twelve of the square, white transfers, "Munroe County Transport," these were the first words Cora learned to read. Gradually, she and Ron became bold enough to request the tickets themselves. A few drivers were mean. They would shake their heads and say tickets weren't for reuse. But most drivers were charmed. "Twins?" they were asked more than once. Ron would beam while Cora would try to sound mature, "No. I'm five. He's my *younger* brother."

"Oh, very sorry, miss," one driver had responded, managing an extra handful of tickets in recompense.

Mom showed them how to turn over the chairs, in a neat row on the dining-room rug. One of them would perch on the crossbar between the legs. The other would drive the bus, standing to indicate authority.

"Why don't you just sit on the chairs like normal people?" George condescended to inquire one afternoon.

"Because it wouldn't look like a bus that way," Ron answered immediately.

George shook his head in exaggerated irritation. "You're getting as screwy as your sister."

"George, do I hear you arguing in there?" Mom called from the kitchen.

He answered, walking off to his room, "They let me off at the wrong stop."

In the complexity of their game, Cora and Ron forgot about George. They had to switch positions to keep it fair. She would drive. He would drive. The driver got to collect all the tickets.

They played happily that year until Pop came home from sea. Pop didn't see the logic of turning chairs upside down, of continuing to collect *new tickets*. There were shoeboxes full of transfers, why did they constantly need new ones?

"Clutter!" he exploded after two days of bus driver. "I come home from four grueling months on the ship and find the place littered with paper."

The game was canceled until he shipped out again. Then, over the next months, they launched into refinements—a flowered lady's hat for the passenger and a green visored cap for the driver. They traded hats with the same equanimity with which they switched roles. By then, they had collected hundreds of tickets.

Pop returned home again and slept for a week. When he woke from his hibernation, as Mom called it, they were in the living room, Ron wearing the bonnet and Cora the visor.

"Louise!" he shouted, staring at his offspring.

She ran in from the kitchen, pulling off her yellow rubber gloves, panic covering her eyes as she surveyed her raging husband and two bewildered children.

"Yes dear." She composed her face. "What is it?"

"What is it?!" he yelled. "All over again the house is topsy-turvy with chairs and little pieces of," he bent down to retrieve a stub, gulping air as he reclaimed his height, "with tiny bus tickets!"

Cora stared at their mother, uncertain how to defend her, unclear how she was going to protect them.

"Bus tickets!" he exploded again.

Ron leapt up to explain. "It's OK, Pop, they gave them to us . . . " His voice lost shape, rising and falling erratically as some words emerged too slowly and others too fast. "It's OK."

"It's *not OK*, you insolent little . . . "

Cora closed her eyes, but she could see it all from behind tight lids as Ron collapsed hard into a passenger seat, breaking the joint of the chair. The broad-brimmed, veiled hat tilted foolishly to one side as he tried to right himself.

"Christ almighty, the good dining room chairs," Pop cried, "Christ almighty, woman, what-kind-of-children-are-you-raising?"

In spite of herself, Cora opened an eye and regarded her mother. Mom stood there, tears steaming down her face, sucking on the rubber thumb of one glove.

Spring, 1953

Cora cuddled up to her mother on the big bus seat, as they rode to Coos Bay to meet Pop. It was a cold, drizzling April morning, and Cora asked Saint Christopher to guide the bus driver.

"Don't worry," her mother leaned over. "We'll be safe. This guy looks like he knows the road blindfolded."

Cora flushed, unnerved by how easy it was to read her mind. Could Sister Augustine tell what she was thinking in class? Well, she would only have four school days this week to worry about Sister Augustine. Mom had said whoever won the coin flip could go on the trip. At first her brothers were mad that she got to go. Then Aunt Min agreed to take them to the circus. Truth was, if she had a choice between a trip with her mother and the circus, she'd choose the trip every time. She wished her father wasn't gone for months at a stretch. Rain pinged against the window. The sky was a vacant gray.

She looked over to find Mom intently watching the fog-softened land-scape. Cora thought she had the prettiest mother in the world—with her rich red hair and green eyes, her slim figure and rosy skin. What she admired most was Mom's graceful spirit, her almost delicate way of walking and talking.

"Tell me that story about you being a singer, again?" Cora pleaded.

She rolled her eyes. "I would think you knew it by heart. Why don't you tell me?"

Cora sat up to her full height. "There you were on stage, singing in front of thousands of people when Pop walked in and fell in love with you."

"Well, there weren't thousands of people at the USO and you could hardly call our makeshift platform a stage, but, yes, that's more . . . or less . . . the way it happened."

"Now, the other part."

"OK, and what knocked me off my feet was that he sent me two roses every day that next week."

"One red and one white," Cora recalled.

"Passion and loyalty." Mom smiled.

"So romantic," Cora beamed.

She looked with fond amusement at her daughter. "Yes, that's the word for your father, *romantic*."

"And then Pop left the base to fight the Japs . . . "

"The Japanese, dear, I think it's better to call them the Japanese."

"Then you came out West to meet his ship at the end of the war. Just like we're doing now."

"That's it." Mom opened a roll of butterscotch Lifesavers.

Cora took one, closed her eyes and imagined sunshine as she sucked on it.

As a reward for these good thoughts, the sun did come out as they were watching Pop's ship dock. She and her mother stood on the pier, craning their necks up at the large white ship, inhaling the salt air and basking in the early spring warmth, waiting, waiting. Waiting for the man to drop the gangplank. Waiting for officials with notebooks to climb aboard. Waiting for crates and pipes to be discharged from the hold. Cora observed very carefully, so she could recite the events to Pop and show that she had been paying attention. Waiting as five, ten, twenty men walked ashore. Finally there he was, clean-shaven, freshly dressed, limping slightly and carrying a green paper funnel.

He grinned as his women rushed toward him. First he gave his wife a grizzly bear hug, grunting, snorting, laughing. Then he picked up Cora and twirled her around. "My little princess," he shouted for all the men on the dock to hear. Mom looked on, smiling and crying at the same time.

Since he had to be back aboard in two hours, they only went as far as the coffee shop at the end of the pier.

"Here, you guys wait at this outside table," Pop instructed. "I'll get us coffee and, what'll it be, Cora, a dry martini or a Coke?"

"Oh," she giggled, confused momentarily by his joke. "Coke, Pop, a Coke with ice."

When he opened the door to the cafe, they could hear Frankie Laine crooning from the juke box. Cora noticed Mom beaming at the gray water. Embarrassed by this intimate moment, she switched her attention to the mysterious green paper funnel. As she lifted it, Pop emerged with a tray.

"Hang on there, let me serve the ladies' drinks first." With excruciating slowness, he set down one cup, then the other, then a tall glass of frosty Coke.

Cora distracted herself by thinking of the last present he brought her— a pink satin quilt from France—a "doovit" he called it, the sounds of that word discomfiting her slightly. The quilt was a reward for her kindergarten report card. He had called her his "bright dolly," cheerfully, yet with a note of resignation. She would never be one of the boys.

Pop eased himself into a chair. "Now, let's see what's in here." He untaped one side of the funnel and pulled out a pipe-cleaner daisy for Cora. She thought the small, furry flower was more beautiful than a real one. He helped her attach it to a buttonhole in her sweater.

"Not too many florists between Oakland and Coos Bay." He shrugged.

Mom was laughing as she drank the bitter-smelling black coffee.

"And for my glorious wife," he reached into the funnel, "Tatah!" He handed her two pipe-cleaner roses, one red and one white.

She was smiling and crying again.

Fall, 1953

Cora and George were walking home from Mass in the drizzle. The rains always began in October. By the time Cora was six, she knew they would live under water for over half the year. She held out her tongue to catch the drops.

"Don't do that; you look like a goofball," George jabbed her shoulder with his elbow.

Cora crossed her eyes in an effort to conceal the hurt. She concentrated on smelling the deep, sour, musky secrets opening in the moisture. This was fairy weather, she knew, for Aunt Min said fairies favored soft days.

"Where are we going?" Cora asked. Not until they had been walking for ten minutes did she notice they weren't heading home. She disguised her panic as curiosity. "Where are we going?"

"To China," he answered matter-of-factly. "I'm taking you to China."

She stared at him. He squinted back. She would not believe he had turned Oriental. She did believe, though, that her brother would kidnap her to China. George, the bully, and Ron, the wimp, that's what Pop called her brothers.

"No," she said evenly. "Mom will be mad."

He shrugged, walking faster. Cora had no choice but to follow. Completely lost, she studied the wide street lined with enormous houses set far back from the sidewalk. The white mansion on the right seemed to have three garages.

"No," her quavering was uncontrollable now. "Stop. Please stop." Suddenly she realized that she didn't care about Mom. *She* didn't want to go to China. It had nothing to do with anyone but herself. China was full of pagans. She didn't belong in China. Yet her mysterious brother was powerful enough to take them there, to keep them there, where they did not belong. Cora did her best not to weep. "No!!!" she screamed.

Someone parted the curtains in a large, gray house.

"You're nuts!" He tried to calm her down and shut her up. Putting his hand over her mouth, he said, "Come back to earth. Don't you recognize this street? Sherry lives over there."

Cora, like her mother, was bad at directions. Pop teased saying that they didn't pay attention to where they were going, but there was so much else to see.

"In that green house," he laughed.

It wasn't fair. They had only been to Sherry's once and that had been nighttime. She was jealous of the cute girl in George's class and this strange feeling overshadowed her panic at being called "nuts."

George often called her nuts. When she woke from a bad dream screaming, he sometimes comforted his silly, nutty sister. He let her crawl into his bed for the rest of the night. Nuts. She was nuts to worry about Father Manley's threats of damnation. She was nuts to pay attention when Pop was drunk. Nuts to tattle when George skipped school. Nuts to worry about Mom when she went to the hospital.

"You're acting like a *freak*," he laughed. "But I won't tell no one if you don't tell about the China trip."

He lightly cuffed her chin.

Winter, 1954

"Roy, Roy, please stop, Roy."

Usually it was her mother's voice that first alerted Cora to the fights. They *were* fights, even if Pop were the only person using his hands. Mom sounded like that skinny woman on "Beulah."

"No, Roy, that's enough. You'll hurt him."

Twack. Twack. The sound of the belt was cold and hot.

"Roy, he's only a . . . "

Twack. Twack.

"Ow!"

George wasn't too proud to shout. He never wept, yet he could yell bloody murder, particularly when his father used the buckle end of the belt.

Cora would run to the opposite side of the house when she heard her mother screaming. Mom's protests were louder than Pop's cursing, the crack of the leather or even George's screams.

Once, returning from the back yard, she stumbled upon a scene with all three of them huddled in a corner of the kitchen. Her first image was glue—it felt as if someone were pouring together bodies in rapid movement and sound: "Twack—Oh, no, Roy, Ow—you rotten—Twack—Roy—Bloody rude—Ow—No, Roy, no . . . "

George would be sent to bed without dinner. Sometimes he wouldn't surface for days. What amazed Cora was that within a month or even a few weeks, George would brag to her about committing the same misdemeanor, and often as not, he would be caught and whipped again.

Ron was whipped too, but usually for the opposite reason—because he had backed out of a chore or failed at school. Ron's beatings were less dramatic for he caved in so easily, screeching at the top of his lungs for Pop to "Please stop! Please stop!" Disgusted with his weeping son, Pop would shake his head and send Ron away.

Cora reckoned Ron was smarter than George because he was never badly hurt. Never, for instance, did they have to take Ron to the hospital—as they had taken George, for a broken elbow and a fractured ankle—after Pop's scoldings. The closest Ron had come to real disaster was when he got his thumb stuck in a bowling ball, and that, as Pop said, was his own doing.

Yet there was something admirable in the way George stood up to their father. He wore his split lips and black eyes like medals, badges of a secret order about which he never answered the nuns' concerned questions. Cora simply stayed out of Pop's way when he was drinking. He never did beat her. She lived in terror that he might and in disappointment that he didn't.

Spring, 1955

"Someone's shot George in the head with an arrow."

Her first thought—for which ever after she felt guilty—was, How exotic. George had all the drama in the family. Imagine going around with a staff and feather sticking out of your forehead.

Then she panicked, realizing that he could have been hit in the temple. She remembered the softness of that place between her brother's brown eye and his pink ear. Mom had warned them against poking each other there. George might be badly hurt, dying. Cora raced through the house, wailing after her wounded brother.

Pop was already on the scene. (Why was Pop always there when excitement happened? He would be gone for quiet months at a time, then with his return life would erupt.) Pop was screaming at Mrs. Franco, asking what kind of mother would let her imbecile son run around like Robin Hood, shooting twentieth-century bystanders?

Mom winced, more horrified by Pop's attempt at humor than by his volume.

Mrs. Franco held both sides of her thick neck, rocking from right to left, moaning, "Jesus, Mary and Joseph."

"I'll give you Jesus, Mary and Joseph." Pop's voice grew stronger. "I'll give you a law suit. I'll give you a jail cell. I'll send you straight back to . . . "

"Roy, Roy," Mom called as she knelt on the grass, holding George's hand. "The boy's all right. It's just a scratch on his forehead."

Cora was relieved though disappointed.

George writhed on the front lawn, groaning for all he was worth.

Pop's volume increased as neighbors rushed over from their yards. "There are laws, you know . . . "

"Roy, Roy," Mom pleaded. "The boy's all right."

Late spring, 1955

"Did you see what happened?" Mr. Nowicki asked Mrs. MacLeod. He pointed to the broken gate in front of Cora's house.

Cora rushed past them, carting groceries. However, the rest of the conversation was too brief to avoid.

"Did you see," Mr. Nowicki persisted, to Mrs. MacLeod's poker face. "That someone was swinging on Mr. Casey's gate last night, blind drunk."

"I saw." Mrs. MacLeod whispered with certainty. "I saw. It was Mr. Casey, himself."

Summer, 1955

Mom went away for good when Cora was almost eight. Oh, no one said it was for good, although they said it would *be good* for everyone and that she would be *good as new* in a couple of months. After all, the hospital had helped before. This new experimental program was subsidized and used all the latest procedures.

Pop wasn't lying when he said it would be a few months. Although he knew it might take several years for her to recover, he also knew that months were as long as years to children and that years were unimaginable. People often said he was an insensitive man, but he understood about pain. That's why, Cora told herself, he drank too much. Only once in a while.

Cora made Mom a different card each week, which Aunt Min mailed religiously. Cora could talk with Aunt Min as she could talk with no one else in the family, and after Aunt Min moved in, life seemed to improve. When Mom came back, life would be perfect. Cora was sure she could persuade Aunt Min to stay.

Fall, 1955

"So how was school today?" Pop sat across the dining-room table licking the perimeter of a chocolate mint cookie.

Cora was glad Pop was on leave. At least she was glad in the afternoons, because he never started drinking until the six o'clock news. He was usually interested in school—particularly in hearing about history or geography class or about Sister Clara, who came from Clifden at the same time his parents had immigrated.

"Ron was punished by Sister Patrick today." What had made her say it? Cora had resolved not to tattle. It was none of her business that her little brother had *screamed out* in frustration during arithmetic. It was none of her business that stony Sister Patrick had shaken her head, explaining that he would have to learn to control his temper.

"None of my business," she told Lisa Stark, whose younger sister Marie was in Ron's class. "Nothing to do with *me*."

Yet the story had distracted her all afternoon, to the point that she almost failed her own math exam. Why did they have to pick on poor Ron?

None of the Casey's had been good at math except Mom, who was a whiz at fine detail of any kind. Cora herself had barely squeezed by last year with a $C-$ from Sister Patrick. But she had never thought about crying.

Cora studied her long face in the dining-room mirror behind Pop; her jaw jutted slightly.

"What for, what did he do?" Pop demanded.

"For sassing, I guess," Cora's voice faded. She wished she had kept silent. She wished it had never happened. Now she was confusing her keeping silent with his sassing. Well, that wasn't *crazy*, was it?

How much of things happening was people knowing about them? Of course Cora and Ron couldn't play bus driver forever; they had to grow up. But school separated them irrevocably. That she was a year ahead of him didn't help. When he finally started school, she saw what everybody saw: he

was a frightened, whiny, bespectacled little boy. A creep, they said. At home
Ron was often sick to his stomach. He couldn't eat vegetables and wasn't partial to meat. When they had lamb, Aunt Min told him it was pork so he would
eat it. He did love hot dogs. Come to think of it, what he liked was all pig.
Good thing he never read *Charlotte's Web*, or he might have starved. Was he
for or against pigs?

Cora also tried to remember the strong points: he was a kind, gentle boy,
whom all the neighbors hired to mind their pets when they went on vacation.
She tried to protect him the way Aunt Min told her to. But she didn't really
believe he was so delicate and uncoordinated and afraid for if she did believe
this she would have to acknowledge the fear was also in her. She would never
be as vulnerable as he. Did that make her more cowardly or smarter or both?

Pop leaned forward, his chocolate mint breath rousing her. "So what
the hell did he do this time?"

Before Cora could take a second cookie, Pop was clearing the table. Although she was hungry—for she had been unable to eat her lunch after Lisa's
story—she knew better than to challenge Pop right now. "He got angry," she
answered evenly, "at the math problems."

"That boy will have to grow up," Pop's voice was firm.

The next morning Cora and Ron walked to school together as usual.
When they reached the highway, he turned to her, more hurt than angry.
"Why'd you do it?" His blue eyes were soft and large. "Why'd you tattle?"

"I don't know." The words rushed from her, "I'm sorry. I shouldn't have
done it."

He peered at her, then shrugged.

Her tears dried immediately. She was frightened, yet exhilarated. She
understood that she was not a good person.

Summer, 1957

"Hey, Georgie Boy, Georgie Boy, Georgie Boy." The catcher wooed her
brother as he stood on the mound. Expectantly Cora and Ron sat in the
stands, watching George plan his strategy, dramatically circle his arm and deliver the ball across the plate smack between the batter's waist and knees.

"Steerike!" called the umpire, who was really Connie Taper's uncle, the
druggist. "Strike two!"

"One more strike and the Chargers would win the season. Could he do
it? Cora thought back to that article in the paper, " . . . talented, handsome
kid with a good chance of making it to the Portland Beavers and maybe even
the majors." Of course her tall, dark, handsome, talented brother could do it.

"Kid doesn't have it in him," sneered a man behind Cora and Ron. She
turned to see the father of the Pioneers' short stop pointing at her big brother

and talking more loudly. "Kid'll never make it. Doesn't have the *nerve* to be a pitcher, do you kid?"

She felt heat rise to her face and glanced at Ron, who looked angry and a little frightened.

"Hey, kid, one more." The man smelled of beer and his foot was tapping heavily on the bleacher.

George kept his gaze on the plate. Cora noticed his left eye—the one that had required five stitches after the last fight with Pop—drooping badly.

The man continued heckling, "Can you do it, kid, can you do it?"

Why didn't one of the adults *do something?* Surely it wasn't fair to let a big man heckle a kid.

Her action involved no forethought. Afterwards, she didn't exactly remember doing it. But she knew it must have been *her* elbow which knocked the giant bottle of Coke off the top of the cooler and onto the foot of the loud man. It took some time for the commotion to die down, for him to stop cursing and to limp off to his car.

The game resumed. Hushed silence ripened the hot afternoon as Georgie Boy delivered his third and final strike.

TWELVE

Winter, 1955–56
Oregon

"Nothing wrong with Louise's mind; it takes intelligence to stitch like that."
Mrs. Larsen spoke with sticky anger.

"Shhh," Aunt Min was firm. "The children will hear you."

Cora paused at the fridge where she was pouring Kool Aid. She understood that they were talking about her Christmas present. Mom had sent dolls' clothes from the hospital. She wasn't supposed to know about the gift. But this was all Mom sewed any more.

Cora quietly closed the refrigerator. Eavesdropping was the only way you learned anything in this house. She liked Mrs. Larsen for saying her mother was intelligent. Cora had always believed that. Maybe now they would let her out of that place. This was the thing Mrs. Larsen didn't seem to know: Mom hated being here, away from her children.

The dolls' clothes first appeared four years before. Aunt Helen from San Francisco always sent up her old outfits for dress-ups. Aunt Helen wasn't a real aunt like Aunt Min, but rather a girlhood friend of Mom's from Kansas. Now that she was a secretary for a large insurance company, she "went through" lots of clothes, mostly tailored dresses and light woolen suits. All the outfits had plenty of wear left, Mom would tsk-tsk. Once Aunt Helen sent a pale pink silk nightie and a purple satin ball gown. Aunt Helen was the same size as Cora's mother. But she would never have *thought* about trying on the clothes because Pop would not tolerate a wife of his wearing hand-me-downs. So they all went for Cora's dress-ups or for the dolls' wardrobe.

Cora remembered the first Christmas she awoke to find Rosemary sitting among the presents. Initially, she had thought it was George's bad joke—putting her favorite old doll under the tree and hiding her real Christmas presents. Would there be a bag of coal next to Rosemary? Then she realized the doll wore a new blue lambswool coat and under that a black taffeta dress. On the other side of the tree sat her Dutch doll in an elegant red velvet robe trimmed with white ribbon.

Every birthday and Christmas after that Mom created new doll fashions. She never sewed clothes for herself or her family. Although Aunt Min behaved as if this were strange, Cora thought it made perfect sense. You couldn't hand-stitch real clothes, and Mom never looked at the machine any more. Besides, she and George and Ron didn't need clothes; they wore school uniforms.

❀ ❀ ❀

It was a cold, rainy day and Cora knew something was happening be-cause Aunt Min had sent Ron and herself to play at Mrs. Miller's house. Cora often helped their pretty young neighbor by looking after her two babies while Mrs. Miller was fixing dinner. Never before had she been "sent" to Mrs. Miller's house, and she didn't like it. Ron seemed indifferent.

Something must have happened because Aunt Min had been on the phone all morning trying to reach Pop, who was just about to arrive in or de-part from Seoul. Normally, you would never try to reach Pop. Like a hurri-cane, you contended with him as he blew into town: negotiating the tension when his arrival was forecast; the chaos during his visit, the calm afterward, the assessment of damage. Anyway, no one would think of *inviting* Pop home. Cora knew she shouldn't consider her father's return a visit. This was, after all, *his* home. He paid the bills. If anything, *they* were the visitors. Sometimes, depending on his mood, she felt they might be evicted any minute. All the more reason not to phone around the world looking for him. But that's what Aunt Min was doing. "Go on up to Mrs. Miller's," she said. Children were too noisy to be around long-distance phone calls.

Cora loved Mrs. Miller's blue walls. Unlike their own home cluttered with lumpy, mismatched furniture, Mrs. Miller's house was sparely ap-pointed with Danish Modern. Awaiting just the right chairs, the rec room re-mained half-empty. Cora respected this kind of patience.

Mrs. Miller was especially friendly today. She had baked Ron's favorite Toll House cookies and she played canasta with Cora. Cora was worried that little Donna and Bobbie would feel left out. After all, *they* were the babies. She didn't exactly like all this attention, for she was used to being acknowl-edged as a responsible eight-year-old. Today she read sympathy into Mrs. Miller's smiles and cardgames and cookies. By four o'clock, Cora couldn't bear it any longer.

"I need to go home now," she informed Mrs. Miller politely.

"Don't worry, your aunt said she'd come get you later."

"I need to help with supper. It's four o'clock." Cora nodded at the round wall clock, lest Mrs. Miller forget she was old enough to tell the time.

"We thought it might be fun to have a TV dinner here. I've got Swan-son's turkey and roast beef."

Cora pitied the nervousness in Mrs. Miller's voice. "No, thank you," she answered patiently. "We don't eat TV dinners." She spoke more rapidly now, creating momentum for escape. "And I really have to go home. Thank you for the cookies." She reached out for Ron's hand, which he obediently gave. "Thank you for your hospitality."

It was Mom's voice—courteous, but with a note of unstated criticism.

As they made their way across the yard, Cora felt very tired. It wasn't far, but her legs moved in slow motion, as if the damp of the last month had rusted her bones. A rain shower had just ended, so she knew they should make a run for it before another started. Ron had terrible chest trouble; surely he would get bronchitis. She must take care of her younger brother. Still, she found herself standing in a puddle of sunlight—halfway between the two houses. Sun lit up the palm of her hand, revealing a riotous sequence of lines. Horrified, she imagined herself an old woman. Older than Aunt Min, older than Sister Ann.

"Come on, hurry up."

Ron was from calling five feet away. His eyes looked wider behind the new dark-rimmed glasses.

Why couldn't he simply run into the house by himself? She knew why, just as she knew she would feel betrayed if he did. For the first time in her life, Cora saw how the safe boundaries of family are drawn between suffocation and desertion.

Yet she could not move. Determindedly she stood in the sun as it soaked through the thick cotton of her blue pants and sweater. She felt heat first on her calves, then on her thighs, then on the upper part of her body—chest and shoulders. This was the warmest she had felt for months. Momentarily she wondered if she might fall asleep, for what else was the purpose of stillness? Never a second wasted, Aunt Min would tease her affectionately. The sun was coating her cheek now and the whole left side of her head. She considered the possibility of simply staying to savor the smell of pine trees, the squabbling of jays. Her eyes and mouth opened involuntarily at the same time.

"OK, Ron, let's go in."

The house felt strangely quiet for four o'clock. Involuntarily they headed for the living room. The kitchen was cool and damp with none of the usual signs of life. Two plates waded in the sink, with the remains of egg salad sandwiches. Crust and lettuce, Cora noticed, George must be home. She shivered as they approached the parlor.

All curtains were drawn. After a moment, Cora focused on Aunt Min sitting on the couch, staring straight ahead at the ochre wallpaper she kept threatening to change. Cora heard a loud snap and turned to see George cracking his knuckles.

Snap. Snap.

Like branches in a fireplace.

Ron began to scream for no reason. For every reason.

"Come here, child." Aunt Min opened her arms.

Cora watched Ron race to her.

Cora proceeded toward the center of the room and sat on the marble coffee table Pop had brought back from Greece. She had never sat on the table because Aunt Min was always scolding her brothers for doing so. Cora waited. Aunt Min said nothing. Both her eyes were closed now. She rocked Ron silently.

Snap. George's knuckles were the only sound in the room. Cora couldn't even hear herself breathing. She knew she shouldn't ask anything because the questions might make her responsible for answers. Slowly she formed words in her mind. She opened her mouth.

George interrupted with disgust. "She croaked herself."

No, Cora wanted to stop him.

George stood. "Your mother." He looked from Cora to Ron. Ron stared in horror. Cora lowered her eyes. "She finally hanged herself in that looney bin." Snap. He left the room cracking his knuckles.

◦ ◦ ◦

The day Mom died, they found a miniature communion dress—perhaps a bridal gown—in her hospital room. A week later, a fourth-class package arrived from Aunt Helen. Aunt Min shook her head as she handed it to Cora. Cora, who had that week grown beyond dolls and dress-ups, said they should give the clothes to the Saint Vincent de Paul Society. Aunt Min almost contained her surprise as she nodded approval.

◦ ◦ ◦

Crystal White's mother said Cora lived in "an old fashioned house which suited her old fashioned name." Aunt Min asked, "Whatever does the woman mean?" But Cora knew Crystal's mother was right. They had a front porch with a swing. Chickens and ducks in the backyard. A sunroom. A cool basement. Cora decided their house had been imported from Kansas. She identified with Dorothy in *The Wizard of Oz*, another motherless girl with midwestern connections.

Yes, Cora said, the Caseys had an old-fashioned home, except that it had a disappearing mother who went dead. "Died," Aunt Min winced, correcting Cora's grammar. She never contradicted the disappearing part. Aunt Min was that tied to the eighth commandment. Cora knew it had been her mother's choice to leave. Death was something she *did*, not something that was done to her. Something she did with that delicate macramé cord.

◦ ◦ ◦

They would be allowed to attend the funeral mass but not the actual interment. Aunt Min had called the mother of Ron's rich friend, Donny Montrose, and asked if she might look after them later that afternoon.

Donny's mother would come to the service. Aunt Min thought this was generous, but Cora didn't see the point. Mrs. Montrose didn't know Mom. Hardly anyone knew Mom, who had never quite developed the knack of making friends on the West Coast. So it would be a small gathering—just the children, Pop, Aunt Min, Mrs. Montrose, Mrs. Larsen and a couple of Aunt Min's friends from the Altar Society. Uncle Bernie planned to fly down from North Dakota, but there had been a snow storm. Snow storm! Pop exploded as if Uncle Bernie had created the weather. Cora could hear Pop thinking that if he could make it from Korea for Christsake—everything he had done in the last year had been done for Christsake—Bernie could make it down from North Dakota, which was in the same country for Christsake. He had phoned when Pop and Aunt Min were at the florist. His voice full of panic and relief, he had informed Cora that although he couldn't come, he was sending mass cards.

◦ ◦ ◦

"Let us pray," said Father Ferrier.

They knelt. The familiarity of the Latin "Simon Says" exercises—Stand up. Sit down. Kneel. Come forward for Communion. Kneel again—was comforting to Cora. She listened for the asynchronic way her father knelt—first the right leg, then the slightly stiff left leg hitting the kneeler. Normally on Sundays she got embarrassed as everyone in their pew was disturbed by the second thump of his left knee. She knew she should be proud of his World War II wound, a mark of courage and of history.

Now she would contemplate her mother's soul. Mom must have gone straight to heaven. Surely that hospital would have been purgatory enough. Cora had a hard time thinking of Mom's soul without feeling enormous pain about her missing body. The girl's chest felt bruised on the inside. Perhaps the pain was polio—God punishing her for not paying attention.

God could be very strict. She was reminded of that when she heard Aunt Min explaining to Mrs. Larsen that she had had to beg for a mass and that the priest had finally relented because a crazy person should not be held responsible for suicide.

Crazy person! She had ached to defend her mother, but she didn't want to ruin Mom's chances for a mass. Or were they Aunt Min's chances? The mass seemed to matter to Pop too, and he kept muttering satisfaction about a burial in hallowed ground. Of course Cora and Ron wouldn't get to see her being buried. But that was OK with Cora because this way she didn't have to completely believe she was dead. She wouldn't tell anyone—especially George—about this strategy.

"*Agnus Dei, qui tollis peccata mundi . . .* "

They followed the priest.

George was staring at the stained glass window. What a jerk. At his mother's funeral he daydreamed out the window. No, Cora looked closer—he was crying, sucking in the sides of his cheeks. This shocked her because

George had made all those jokes about looney bins and had finally refused to visit Mom in the hospital. "Croaked herself," she could hear the words, would continue to hear them at odd, painful moments. As quickly as her rage swelled, it shrank into a hard, tight new hurt: George's hurt. George had known their mother longest. And, Cora admitted as she watched the juvenile delinquent snivel at the windows, it was always George whom Mom loved best.

Tears straggled across the broken veins of Pop's nose, down the relentless jaw, all the way to the red birthmark under his right ear. She had never seen her father cry. She felt none of the alarm she experienced with George's tears; rather she was comforted by this indisputable evidence that he had loved her mother. Despite his complaints, his sarcasm, he had, at least once, loved her mother.

"It is hard when a dear one leaves us so young."

Cora blinked as if the priest had been dropped from the sky.

"It is tragic when innocent children are deprived of a mother."

Were they innocent?

"It is incomprehensible when a man loses his wife."

Maybe Pop lost her. Maybe if he had stayed home . . .

"But we can turn to faith. Faith in Jesus. By doing this we are reunited with Louise for she is in a better place . . . "

Cora agreed. Maybe she didn't believe Mom had died or gone to heaven. But any place was better than that looney bin.

Aunt Min's face held a more complicated story. Behind red lids, her eyes revealed shock, reprieve and perhaps a little envy. Cora remembered a conversation she had overheard last summer. At first, Aunt Min confessed to Mrs. Larsen, she had mistrusted her sister-in-law. Although Louise's family was as poor as the Caseys, they had pretensions. Didn't Louise's brother grow up to be a priest? And didn't Louise herself complete two years of high school before quitting to support her mother and younger sisters? But if Louise initially seemed too full of airs for Roy, Min learned it was the opposite. Roy grew into a powerful, prideful man. As the years passed, the two women became good friends. Min tried to hold up her sister-in-law through Roy's absences through his drinking. Now Cora watched her aunt carefully drying her tears. She would be strong while her brother wept. She would hold together his family as she had not been able to hold up his wife. If she cried, it would be silently, in the dark house which her friend had forfeited and willed to her. Aunt Min's face contained a certain wonder, Cora thought, and perhaps an admiration.

° ° °

"This way, children," Mrs. Montrose shepherded Cora and Ron across the church parking lot.

Cora stood her ground, eyes fastened on George, Pop and Aunt Min as they climbed into the funeral director's car. She did not want to go with them and watch the gruesome burial. All the same she didn't like Mrs. Montrose's tone. She didn't like being a child. Cora hated the fact that on this sad, scarey day she was being carted off by a stranger.

Unwilling to be dismissed as petulant, she waved slowly at the black car with windows tinted like sunglasses. Faith was required to believe the whole family would be returned to her at the end of the day. This was a whole family, just smaller than before. She was grateful Aunt Min had joined them. She wouldn't want to be the only girl.

Donny Montrose stood at his door, greeted Ron briskly and nodded to her. Soon the boys were engrossed in a game of catch; there were only two mitts. Mrs. Montrose encouraged them to play something that would include her—Monopoly, Parcheesi, Chutes and Ladders—but Ron said these games were sissy. Cora watched victory overtake his face as he realized that today, of all days, he did not need her. Because she could not bear to admit how much she needed him this afternoon, she shrugged and said it was OK. She was happy to look at the Montroses' library, which she knew contained the *World Book Encyclopedia*, like the one at school. She loved reading the encyclopedia.

"OK," Mrs. M. conceded, "I've got a dinner party tonight. As long as you're sure you'd *like* to read in the library."

"May I help?" Cora felt back in her milieu. She had once assisted Mrs. Miller in preparing a dinner party, dicing the carrots and celery perfectly.

"Oh, no, I don't think so." Mrs. Montrose stumbled, "I'll be fine."

Mrs. Montrose looked at her as if she were contaminated. She had been careful to say "May I" instead of "Can I." This was Cora's cue to go.

"May I look at the books then?" She opened her hands in what she hoped was a natural gesture, but one which would allow Mrs. Montrose to see how clean she was. She would leave no smudges on the encyclopedia. She put on what Aunt Min called her "pretty face" for Mrs. Montrose.

"Of course, dear," the woman relaxed. "That sounds like the perfect solution."

Cora padded into the study, struck by the insulating beauty of the dark green rug. When she grew up, she would have a study. Precocious, Aunt Min called her. Had Mom been precocious, too? She pulled out the *L* volume in honor of Louise and found an overstuffed chair. Labor Day. Lacewing. Lacrosse. She skipped the names—Lafayette, Lagrange—because she wanted to learn about *things*. Things you needed to know. Cora was tempted to continue reading about Mary Lamb, who for some reason had caught her eye, but she wasn't in the mood today. Lambeth Palace. Lamian War. Lammas Days. Lamp. So much to learn about something as common as a lamp. "The lamp," she imagined her mother saying.

Her mind was filled with Mom—resting on the sunporch in that old-fashioned house of theirs—with a cup of tea and the dictionary. Mom read the dictionary for fun.

"You learn that there's so much you don't know." Cora had overheard Mom explaining to Aunt Min.

Cora had been next door in the kitchen, but she pictured Aunt Min's face, her curly head shaking as she parried fondly, "And there's so much you don't *need* to know."

"Hey, little girl!" A tall, freckled man entered the room. "Isn't this a gloomy thing for a person to be doing on a beautiful Saturday?"

The man had the same husky frame as Donny. She blinked as he turned on an overhead light, taken aback by her own annoyance. After all, this was his house, probably his chair. Still, she did not care for the offhand greeting. If she wasn't going to pursue Mary Lamb, she certainly didn't want to be interrupted by a live person.

"Hush, Tom. She's enjoying herself," Mrs. Montrose whispered from the hallway. The voice lowered further, "At least she's keeping busy."

"But she should be out in the fresh air. She should come down to the stable with the boys and me."

Cora didn't like being called "she." It was so impersonal, something they would call a patient. Also, it was impolite not to use a person's name. "She's the cat's mother," Aunt Min would say.

"Lamprey" was a new kind of fish. Cora concentrated on the details. She heard herself speak to the page. "If it's all the same to you, I'd rather continue reading."

They whispered to each other with concern.

She chose her blasphemous words carefully, then looked up. "I'm having a good time."

IV

THIRTEEN

Fall, 1988
Oregon

"Glorious morning," Fran sucked in her breath and looked closely out the car window.

"You OK?" Cora's voice was neutral.

"Of course. All I said was 'glorious morning.' The question is 'Are *you* OK?' "

"Will you really find your way up to Pop's house if I drop you at the beach?"

"I'll be *fine*. If I don't get some exercise after Aunt Min's home cooking, I'll burst my leotards. Besides, it'll be good to have some quiet time to think. Edie and Tommie are a real trip. All that arguing! Makes me grateful I don't have sibs."

Cora swallowed and broke into a smile—at her maternal neurosis, at her even-tempered daughter, at the travel poster Oregon day. Ahead, the beach gleamed under full sun. She pulled into a parking spot. They sat, staring at the horizon, at pyrotechnic waves. Sandpipers gaggled along the seaweed-scattered shoreline. A boy and his father raised a windsock in the air.

Fran spoke quietly, "I guess this is my stop." In response to her mother's worried expression, she added impatiently, "Yes, I know—the house is up that road, six blocks on the left, fifth one in from the corner."

Cora grinned, cuffing Fran lightly on the ear.

Fran unlatched the door, then flew to the beach as Cora watched.

Pop's blinds were drawn again. Cora rang the bell, nervously fingering the key she hadn't thrown away in twenty years. No point standing on ceremony. Pop could be lying in bed, unable to get up. On the other hand, he could be leaning behind the peephole, staring sadistically as she waited.

"Keep your shirt on. I'm *coming*."

Relieved, she nevertheless shrank back a step, then stood tall, remembering what she could about posture from her dancer daughter.

When he opened the door, sun bleached his great gray head into the white hallway. He was breathing heavily, propping himself against the sill, for opening the door had been both a victory and a defeat. He was a hundred years older than last night, and closer to the truth.

"Well, come in; you waiting for an invitation?"

Yes, she thought. "Good morning," she said.

He took some time closing the door. So as not to embarrass him by lingering, she walked into the kitchen for coffee. On the counter were open bottles of vodka and tomato juice and the empty glass which had contained his hair-of-the-dog. Cora mused about the years it took first to admit and then to detach from his drinking. She washed her hands and proceeded to brew Folger's drip coffee as she hadn't done since being banished from her father's house.

"Make it good and strong," he called from the living room.

She noticed that the television was on, had been on, since she arrived and recognized the ancient game show, *Jeopardy*. She rummaged around the refrigerator in search of breakfast food.

"Don't worry about breakfast," he called out over his shoulder. "Come in here and keep an old man company."

"In a sec." She poured coffee and arranged it on a metal tray with the sugar bowl and cream pitcher. Actually, she remembered he drank black coffee with two sugars, but she didn't care for the way he was taking her for granted.

Her remorse was immediate as he leaned forward, trembling, to stir the sugar cubes into the muddy mug.

Follie wagged furiously at his movement, making pathetic, mewling sounds, just short of the bark which would get her sent to the cold garage. "Down Follie," he said. "That's it. Easy girl."

Cora discovered herself pleased that her father had chosen a female dog. She sipped the bitter coffee, filled with tenderness for this man who had never had an easy time in the mornings.

He stared at the TV, watching tiny shutters lift over the question boxes. "Good coffee."

She knew he was doing his best. Together they watched the show until the commercial.

"Fran—my daughter—will be coming by about noon," she said, heart in her throat.

"That's nice." He lifted his eyes from the screen.

At first she worried he might bug her about Fran's father. But he hadn't asked a thing. Maybe he thought it was Jacques. Or maybe he thought she'd been married and divorced. "Happens in the best of families" is what Aunt Min had said about Fran being born without an official father. This seemed to confirm what Cora had guessed to be the truth about George's "premature" birth as well as the precipitous marriage of Pop's own parents. The understanding relieved her and made her nervous about how much of her future was already predetermined by family.

"Your granddaughter looks a little like you." She was conscious of flirting with her father, of acting girlish since she had arrived yesterday. Here she was offering an even younger woman.

Now he was absorbed in *Dragnet*. Cora followed a while, then turned to her novel, then flipped through yesterday's newspaper, then leaned back and stared at her father. She thought whimsically of Jacques doing his *Vipassanah* sittings. Jacques would transform the big bear into Buddha.

Reaching into her purse, she found Jacques's letter, which she had only had the chance to skim quickly at Aunt Min's last night. Just seeing her lover's easy, even handwriting filled Cora with pleasure and well-being.

> . . . . *Oh, I miss you, what can I say, chérie. Never thought I would lie in bed waiting for those endless questions, but I do every night. The upstairs room is unbearably empty, so I've taken to sleeping on the living room couch. At least there I have your clutter of books and files around me. You know, you never really straightened up after that Central American piece, so I imagine that you'll be back any minute from the store.*

Cora grinned at Jacques's tolerance. Deep longing swept through her body. How lucky she was to have this man in her life. She wished she could introduce him to Aunt Min.

> *Speaking of the Central American article, it's causing quite a little stir. Arthur phoned yesterday to say it was mentioned in Parliament. He says he's had the biggest rash of letters since you did that piece on the Free Trade proposal. Wanted to know when his muckraker was coming home.*

Home. Cora savored the feeling of Canada as home and the knowledge of the new self she had become there. She was Cora Casey, journalist. Cora *chérie,* lover of Jacques. She was "Oh, Mom," mother of Fran. She had to be careful not to lose herself here below the border. She had to remember she would return home.

> *Mr. Caputo also asks after you. He dropped by yesterday with four pages of leaves he had pressed, saying how much you loved the red*

maple in his front yard. Really, Cora, if you stay down there too long, I think your Toronto fans are going to send the RCMP after you.

When the doorbell rang, Cora checked her watch, surprised it was already eleven o'clock. Still, this was an hour early for Fran. Pop didn't raise his eyes from the TV. Follie began to bark loudly. He rapped the dog once across the nose, then she slumped down beside the ottoman.

Through the peephole she discovered her younger brother shifting his weight from one foot to the other. Her first thought was how much he looked like Fran—the deep red hair, the high cheek bones, the grey-blue eyes. Then there was that nervous movement of his head, inimitably Ron.

"Ron." She opened the door. "Ron." She extended her hand to curb an impulse to hug him.

Awkwardly, he took her hand. "You seem startled to see me," he said with affection, annoyance.

"A little." She would not give him much.

"*He* didn't tell you I was coming?" he spoke louder to get Pop's attention.

Together they regarded the old man watching television. She shook her head, too depleted to speak, saving herself against the next surprise. Resist the fear, she reminded herself she was an adult now. They couldn't harm her. She lived in another country. She had a new family with Jacques and Fran. She had almost earned a degree in yoga. Looking at Ron, she was caught in the perennial web of wary attachment.

Finally Pop spoke. Rather, he cleared his throat authoritatively.

They turned.

"Are you two going to stand there all day, heating up the front porch?"

They both shrugged, laughing.

"Coffee?" she offered.

"Yes, black."

"I remember." She smiled.

"Ran into a lot of traffic coming down from Portland," Ron said to no one in particular. "Otherwise, I would have been here on time."

"On time?" She steadied her hand as she poured the steaming coffee.

"Yeah, Pop said you and George would be here by ten. Say, where is the big guy?"

Cora started to sit on the couch next to Ron, then abruptly moved to the green brocade chair. It had been Mom's favorite; she could see people still honored that because it was the least worn piece of furniture.

"George?" she managed.

Ron looked blank.

She was tracing the raised threads of the brocade with her index finger.

They turned to their father.

"Don't look *there*, you asshole," he was instructing Jack Webb.

Ron filled in. "Well, it's a long haul from Medford. Maybe he and Connie stopped for breakfast." He paused, a vagueness crossing his face. "So how are you, sister?"

Cora told herself not to think about George. One brother at a time.

"Fine," she answered; she wanted him to know that the last two decades of her life had turned out fine.

"And you?"

He blinked and sipped his coffee.

Cora was touched by how dramatically he had aged. She had grey hairs and wrinkles too, but Ron was her *younger* brother and he looked a little lost in this middle-aged face. He had gained a lot of weight. Still, there was that billboard smile testifying his braces had been worth the effort.

"Oh," his voice gained strength. "I've been out making merry in the galaxy," he said with what was an unmistakable twinkle.

Cora looked over to Pop, who had fallen asleep. Did she dare turn down the TV volume? Phil Donahue was interviewing four men who had tried to prevent their wives from having abortions.

"Life was rocky for a while," Ron continued, undisturbed by the glaring television and Pop's snoring and her own amazement.

In fact, Cora thought, Ron sounded as if he were on TV.

"Then I met Ally, that's my wife, at a Growth for Joy conference. I had never gone to anything like that, but I was feeling desperate. It was a last ditch attempt before, I don't know, suicide or something."

Cora winced.

"Ally was going through a lot, too. Her husband had been killed in 'Nam the year before. Her daughter had died of cystic fibrosis. She was having a tough time hanging on to work. It's difficult to believe all this now because Ally is such an organizer, such a basically "up" person, but she seemed to be at the end of her rope, too. Well, we landed in the same give-and-take session, and as our group leader said, we decided to take the ropes and make a braid."

Cora's eyes widened.

"That was fifteen years ago—exactly fifteen years—because we'll be celebrating our fifteenth anniversary in April. We got married in the church. That was a big part of my recovery, returning to the sacraments as someone who was openly choosing them. I now understand why despair is the greatest sin."

Cora recalled that rainy day when she and Ron were forced to visit their neighbor. She heard Aunt Min's frantic calls to Seoul. She remembered her own unequivocal understanding about the way Mom had died.

"Cora, Corey," Pop slurred his words. He opened his eyes halfway. "Could you make more coffee?"

"Yes," she bounced up, guiltily grateful for escape.

From the kitchen she listened to the Donahue Show: the image in her mind was decades old: Pop and the boys watching baseball while she and Aunt Min fixed Sunday dinner. How she had ached, then, to be her father's ally over her brothers. Now she could detect this realliance even in the uncomfortable way the two men avoided eye contact. Yet, it was all too late. She had wanted strength as well as love from her father. Pop, in aligning with Cora, required these things *from her*.

Ron followed his sister into the kitchen. "Then the most wonderful miracle occurred last year. Our little Jennifer was returned to us."

"Jennifer?" Cora blanched. "Oh, Ally's daughter. I thought she had *died* of cystic fibrosis."

"She did." His voice betrayed that familiar aggravation at being confused.

She concentrated on measuring the coffee, a messy business because Pop's yellow plastic scoop was cracked. Brown grains sucked along the rims of her fingernails.

"Jennifer is *my* daughter. Well, Ally's too, because she'll be adopting her. A child I fathered in Vietnam." His voice was muted.

"Her name is Jennifer?" Cora asked.

"Well, her birth mother calls her Kieu. But I've been writing to her as Jennifer."

"Her 'birth mother' put her in an orphanage?" Cora stopped fiddling with the pot in order to concentrate on Ron's story. "No," he was angry now, "she lives with her, with her, with Linh. But Linh has finally agreed it will be better for Jennifer to come to the States for an education, for a chance . . . "

The doorbell rang. George. Cora wasn't ready yet for George. She would never be ready for George. Ridiculous panic for a forty-year-old woman. George had no power over her any more. She watched Ron hurry to the door. Then she turned away, resolving to be calm, steadied by the flame under the coffee. She reached into the cupboard for another mug. This one, like the others, was ringed with greasy fingerprints.

"Hi, I'm Fran." Cora heard the person at the door. "And you must be Ron. You kind of look like the picture Mom has—only different. The glasses are different."

Ron stood, mesmerized.

"Fran, welcome," she rushed into the living room. "Now that you've met Uncle Ron" (had she actually said that?) "let me introduce you to your grandfather."

He turned regally toward his descendants from the black recliner, head bobbing slightly, as if nodding in some internal conversation. Cora, who had not noticed she was gripping Fran's shoulders, became aware of this as her daughter gently detached herself and stepped toward the old man.

Aghast, Cora was afraid Fran might kiss Pop, an act so demonstrative it could crack the glazing that held them together. But Fran, choreographer of the emotional moment, made a perfect move as she bent down to caress the eager dog. "There, there, Follie. That's her name, isn't it?" she inquired of her infatuated grandfather, "Follie?"

"That's her name, Fran, welcome." He ran one finger along her brush of red hair. "Just like your mother, a rebel, I see."

Cora sat on the couch, savoring the extraordinary scene, too caught up in the visuals to hear all the words. She imagined playing foursquare, bouncing the ball back to each of them. The tension in Ron's face dissolved as he and Pop teased this exotic young creature who was somehow related to them. Even Follie dropped her guard, lying quietly by Pop's feet.

Cora grew more conscious of family resemblances. Through all the same traits that claimed Fran as her daughter—the large eyes, the tough jaw, the big bones, she was also quite obviously Pop's granddaughter. Once again she noticed Fran's similarity to Ron. Even the long nose, which she attributed to Fran's anonymous father, could be seen in Ron.

She stared at her black coffee, nauseated by shiny, oily blobs on the surface. When she looked up, Fran had metamorphosed into a doll under the Christmas tree, dressed in a purple and orange pinafore designed by Mom.

Shaking away the horror movie fantasy, Cora walked into the kitchen to make a fresh brew, thinking the Caseys drank coffee the way other people drank water.

Now they were teasing Fran about her accent. It was always hard to tell if Pop were teasing or criticizing. Standing in the kitchen doorway, Cora listened.

"Why do you say 'eh' after every sentence? Makes you sound like a tinker."

"Bothers you, eh?" Fran grinned.

"It's a *different* accent." Ron tried to be helpful. "More like the English."

"Well, we can't have Limeys in this house," Pop retorted.

He can't control her, Cora thought, that's what's getting him. Did Fran sense Pop's anxiety? She wondered at herself for taking it all so seriously. He was an old man whose color had already turned to ash. Couldn't she simply let go, allow him his petulance? No, she knew in some inflexible and brave corner of herself, she couldn't make that bargain.

"You may call me a Canuck," Fran was still grinning, "but never a Limey."

Cora was relieved to hear the boundaries established by everyone. Fran was very much her own person. She poured herself a cup of coffee and returned to the front room.

"Did George phone?" Ron asked his father.

"No," the old man's shoulders stiffened. "I haven't heard from your brother in a long time."

Had Pop forgotten? Was Ron lying about their conversation? If so, how did he know she would be here at ten? The horror movie reeled on.

"Oh, yeah," Ron stumbled, "George was coming through Grandview this weekend on his way to Portland—for some kind of political meeting." He spoke more rhythmically now, as if the words had lost their individual textures.

Pop turned back to a rerun of "The Honeymooners."

"He thought we should all talk about Pop," Ron faced Cora. "He needs more care than he can get at home. Dover Memorial is a world-class convalescent place." He blushed. "I mean, they've got a very concerned staff of nurses. Remember Lucille Emory, from high school? She's head nurse. He'd get the best care."

Cora couldn't believe he was talking as if Pop weren't in the room. "Ron!"

She heard another voice, low, almost inaudible. From the television? No, to the television. Pop was addressing Audrey Meadows. Cora always suspected he had a crush on Audrey. "You raise them. You put a roof over their heads. You send them through high school. Then they grow up . . . " he paused.

Cora wondered if he were distracted by the program. No, he was catching his breath.

Cora, Ron and Fran continued eavesdropping.

"And then," he told Art Carney, "they turn on you. Want to lock you up in a little white room with tubes attached to your body, attached to flashing lights and ringing bells so that when you go out, it will be like Christmas at Macy's."

Why had she always assumed she inherited her imagination from Mom?

Ron tried again. "It's safer there. Who knows what kind of nurse we could get to stay with him here. And the cost of equipment. The insurance would never cover it."

"But he had money saved. And this house—after he's gone you'll sell it for a good price." Now she was talking about him in the third person.

"That's all right for you to say. Your daughter is grown up. But George and I have kids in school. We're counting on that small inheritance."

She couldn't believe her ears, yet she knew it was pointless to do anything but enter the argument on his terms. "Still—this house—you'd get $60,000 or $65,000 for this place."

Ron lowered his voice. "Pop signed the house over to us ten years ago. And, well, George has already taken out a second mortgage."

"What?"

"He's in real estate. He knows what he's doing. Some investment south of the border. I try to stay clear of these things since I was never very good with money."

"But it's Pop's money." How could they go on talking about him like this, as if he weren't there? "Surely he can cash in his investment to take care of Pop the way he wants."

"Well, I'm not sure."

"What do you mean?" She came to. " 'South of the border?' "

Ron shrugged, reminding her how he would fade into the walls as a small boy—his complexion infinitely more subtle than the coloring of others in the family. She remembered Pop's terrible beatings.

He was cracking his fingers in that horrible way of George's.

"Argentinian beef? Or an investment further north?"

Pop was talking to the TV again. "A man comes to rely on his children. It's natural. It's the way things work the world over." He coughed, a loud hacking from deep in his bowels.

"See." Ron confronted her.

"Oh, for Christ's sake, Ron." She rushed to Pop, risking his wrath. "Pop, Pop, is there anything I can do for you?"

"Medicine's in the bedroom. Just help me to my feet and I'll find the pills."

"They better be humdingers," her claim on nostalgia fell flat.

After Pop retired, Cora, Ron and Fran sat staring at the TV a while. The noon newscaster was interviewing local mayoral candidates.

"OK," Ron said finally. "I'll talk to George. I'll see what I can do."

She drew a long breath. "Thank you."

They witnessed a commercial for Bayer aspirin.

"You think we can still expect George any minute?" She held her panic in check. She would not run away, although she considered sending Fran back to the safety of Aunt Min's.

"George, oh, no, he said if he didn't make it by noon, he probably wouldn't come today."

Typical of her older brother to hold them hostage with his ambiguity. She was getting angrier and angrier, but she knew better than to criticize him in front of Ron.

"He'll call me at the motel when he gets to Grandview. We can all get together tomorrow," he finished the beer, setting the can on the table next to Pop's lounger.

"Bye, Sis." He walked up to Fran and chucked her on the shoulder. "Bye, niece."

"See ya, Ron," Fran said.

As the door closed, Fran returned to the TV.

Cora knew she should speak, cry, moan, at least turn off the television.

"You OK, Mom?"

Cora looked up.

"You want to talk?"

"No," she abruptly marshaled her forces. "I need to get some air. Let's take a spin down to the supermarket and see if we can find some healthy food for this house."

"Inspired idea." Fran clicked off the TV.

Cora shivered, imagining Fran switching off her mother's life support system twenty to thirty years in the future.

She tiptoed to the bedroom, where her father lay wide awake staring at the ceiling. He was awake, wasn't he?

"Yeah?" he said.

"Fran and I are going to the market. Is there anything you want?"

He was silent. Then, "What?"

"Anything you want from the market?" she raised her voice.

"Ron gone?"

"Yes. He'll be back tomorrow."

"Tomorrow." He peered at, through, the ceiling. "Here, Follie," he patted the bed and the dog crawled closer. "No, nothing from the market today."

She watched the feeling of betrayal cloud his eyes and flatten his lips. She was, after all, just the girl. He knew she was useless just as she knew she was essential, and she tasted the old, mad violence of so many years ago.

FOURTEEN ✳

Summer, 1956
Oregon

Cora hated the new house almost as much as she hated the new town. Grandview, what a silly name for this dinky coastal village. But, Pop said, the house was a real buy, and they all needed a change of scene. The long ranchish house had none of the charming mystery of their old-fashioned home in Torrence. It was plain and cold, and one room led to another as if they were railroad cars except for the small bedrooms at the end of the house which fanned in discreetly separate directions. Cora's room was a cramped cell papered in pink. She would fix that as soon as she earned enough money for paint. The closet was almost as big as the room itself and in it was a window that wouldn't lock. Every night, pine branches rubbed against the pane in an odd arhythmic motion. She knew it was silly to be scared of a tree.

The family spent a lot of time together since they had no friends in Grandview. "Throws us back on ourselves," said Aunt Min, and Cora couldn't tell if she meant Mom's death or the moving or maybe both because they were related and Aunt Min was given to sweeping statements nowadays. She also sang a lot. Cora began to notice she was much younger than Mom—and kind of pretty if she would lose a little weight. So while Cora hated leaving Torrence and couldn't wait to leave Grandview, she did like the family times.

George taught Ron and Cora how to play poker and took them down to the beach when he was training Tenk to retrieve driftwood. Sometimes Pop would come. He seemed to be drinking less.

Pop would always join them for TV. During the Republican and Democratic conventions, the whole family laughed at Pop's jokes safely directed at the Communist Stevenson. Everyone cheered as Ike walked out on stage, holding hands with Mamie. Clark Gable was interviewed, explaining the reasons the country was safe with President Eisenhower.

131

They also watched *The Stuart Erwin Show, Amos and Andy, Milton Berle, Beulah, I Remember Mama, Ernie Kovacs* and Cora's favorite, *Red Skelton*. The television drew them together, requiring silence and bestowing a form of peace. Cora would glance across the room to find Ron and George in such repose that she hardly recognized them. Pop was there too, his distinctive face wonderfully handsome when he laughed. Here in the cozy dimness of the living room with everyone nibbling cold roast potatoes on Sunday evenings or popcorn on Friday nights, life was filled with sweetness.

Fall, 1956

Then Ron had to go and break his arm. The week after Pop returned to sea, Ron fell out of an oak tree in the town park. At first Cora didn't believe it because Ron didn't climb trees. She didn't think he had ever *considered* climbing a tree. But there was Aunt Min's note on the kitchen table saying she had gone to the hospital with Ron and for Cora not to worry, to have some cookies and settle down to her homework.

That night supper was excruciating. George regarded their brother with a mixture of incredulity and disdain. Ron didn't seem to mind the equivocal nature of this attention. Aunt Min served his favorite pork chops and cut his meat in small cubes so he wouldn't choke.

"Run through that one more time," demanded George, his mouth half-full of potatoes. "They dared you to climb the tree and then you didn't know how to get down?"

"Yeah." Ron pushed his glasses back on his nose with the one good hand. "It was simple. Getting up was no problem. There was this rope ladder. Then once I was there—once I threw the football back to them—they took the ladder and I wasn't . . . "

"Simple all right." George stroked the mutt's neck, "You really are *simple*."

Ron's face looked as if it might crack as he held back the indignation, fear, hurt and anger of this terrible Monday on the third week of school in horrible Grandview, Oregon.

"Bully!" Cora heard her own voice scratch across the room. "Can't you leave him alone either?"

"Jerks!" George swallowed the last of his pork chop, pushed away the dog and threw his napkin on the table. "I live with a bunch of jerks—a wimp brother, a cuckoo sister and a drunk father!"

"Enough, boy." Aunt Min's voice was low. "I think we've had enough, and it might be wise to enjoy your apple pie outside in the warm evening air."

Cora prayed that George would not talk back to Aunt Min. She didn't know why this frightened her so. She didn't know why George had exploded as he had. But she did know she was mad at Ron for causing all this.

She resolved to meditate on his good points. He didn't have George's violent temper. He wasn't a busybody. He wasn't grasping. While her older brother expressed his desires with swashbuckling confidence, her younger brother silently mooned after absences. Ron was a ghost who invisibly determined the atmosphere of a whole room.

At school, Ron won the sympathy of the nuns, most girls and the better-behaved boys. The kids responsible for Ron's fall were punished by their families, but they paraded brazenly around the playground. Cora was distressed to learn that one of the perpetrators (a word she had learned from Perry Mason) was Mike Riley, brother of Sara Riley, the girl she was eyeing as a possible friend.

Spring, 1957

The new pack of cards appeared on the kitchen table while Aunt Min was out shopping. The first thing Cora noticed was the rich, red color, then the intricate pattern, like on those flying carpets from Turkey.

George shuffled the deck noisily and warned Cora not to pick up her cards until he had dealt a complete hand. When she did, she was astonished by the array of bosoms and bottoms. Vivid, blonde women and brunette beauties. She was fixed on the breasts. She could hardly remember Mom's breasts—maybe she had seen them once or twice in a store dressing room—and recalled them as small, modest, rather discouraged.

By contrast, the women on these cards had playful, perky bosoms. Cora thought of balloons filled with succulent air. She wanted to reach into the ten of diamonds and touch the tender pinks and purples. Yes, Cora looked closer, purple nipples.

"Don't let your eyes fall out." George was gruff.

She blushed as she arranged the cards, and couldn't remember if they were playing pinochle or canasta.

"Haven't you ever seen real women before?" he asked.

Cora bit her bottom lip. So this is what she would look like in five? ten years? She imagined her own chest, which was boring and flat, similar to Ron's from what she could remember of their baths together. They each had two pink buttons the color of strawberry milkshakes made without sufficient strawberry. It horrified and thrilled her that one day she would be this different from her brothers.

From her younger brother. For certainly George was already different with his funny tart smells and the black hairs under his arms.

"Your play," he called to her.

"I know," she concentrated. "Don't rush me."

◦ ◦ ◦

Sister Eleanor was the best part of Grandview, although Cora didn't think that at first. Sister Eleanor didn't act like a nun. She had such a loud voice. While Sister Jane at the old school sympathized with Cora's "home situation," Sister Eleanor seemed to taunt her.

"What do you mean you were too busy to write more?" She watched carefully, as if this were Cora, rather than herself, talking. "You've just got started here. This is interesting—what you've done so far."

And when Cora did do extra work, it was never enough. She earned respectable B's but never the A's she got at the first school. Sara Riley always got A's.

Cora spent several nights crying and several afternoons complaining to Aunt Min, "It isn't fair."

"Why, no, it does seem strange, your grades going down." Aunt Min was clearly at a loss. "Would you like me to visit Sister Eleanor?"

"No," Cora realized as she said it, she wanted to straighten this out, herself. That term, as Cora worked harder and harder, inching her way from B to B+ to A-, she found herself enjoying school.

One afternoon, Sara Riley invited her to go shopping.

Cora began to lose weight. Even George commented on her lighter way of being.

"So what happened to my morose sister?" he asked.

She surprised them both by laughing, "Disappeared, I guess."

In Current Events class Sister asked them to name the prelate seeking sanctuary in the U.S. Embassy in Budapest.

Cora raised her hand. "Cardinal Min-zin-sky."

"A single hand?" Sister shook her head and paused.

Cora was sure she got it right, because she had heard Pop rant at the TV all week. Still, she grew anxious.

"First of all, it's a shame only one person in the entire class is awake to what's going on in the world. And second, Cora is right—although she could use a little help on her Hungarian pronunciation. Tell us, Cora, how do you know the answer?"

"My father," she spoke before thinking. "My father makes us watch the news at night. I mean I like the news. I mean, I . . . "

"A lucky girl," Sister Eleanor pronounced, "to be in a family so conscious of current events."

Cora blushed, surprised and pleased to be praised for her family. She was glad she hadn't mentioned the part about Pop shouting back at the TV. These people wouldn't understand. Sister Eleanor was right, she was lucky to have her family, especially her father.

By June, Cora had won an *A* from Sister Eleanor. And Sara Riley had become her best friend.

◦   ◦   ◦

Her first memory of the basement was the train set. Other things happened there: the washing of clothes, the storage of winter boots and summer beach gear, the birth of kittens, the invasion of raccoons. Cora loved this dark world with its mysterious damp smells, but the basement was George's domain, the place he ran his trains.

Occasionally he would invite his brother and sister to watch the long Lionel set chug along the track, past the papier-mâché mountains and houses and around the dangerous curves. She would hold her breath, praying it would not fall off the track, for when it did, George swore in a voice that sounded like Pop's. When the train built up enough momentum, it would emit a long stream of sulfuric smoke.

As George grew older, he preferred to be alone. They would have to tiptoe past his territory on the way to the laundry. The basement became George's sanctuary after Pop's strappings. Following one of these beatings and a trip to the hospital to stitch up his right hand, Cora crept halfway down the basement steps to find her brother clenching his teeth and smashing his good fist against the wall as the train sped around and around.

George made new friends in Grandview and invited *them* to play with the trains. When Cora heard the boys' deep voices droning along the front walk, she would run to her room and try to read. But she could feel the trains going around and around. Sometimes she could hear the whistle blow.

◦   ◦   ◦

When George was fourteen, he won a Victrola selling subscriptions to *The Grandview Chronicle*. At first, he kept the Victrola in the livingroom where Pop would play dusty Irish tunes and Aunt Min would listen to her hymns. That Easter, they all received records. Her favorite was "How Much Is That Doggie In The Window?" George was partial to "The Naughty Lady from Shady Lane." When Pop left for sea, George took the record player downstairs.

Every day after school, and sometimes during school if the guys could sneak in while Aunt Min was shopping, they would sit on the beat-up old couch and listen to Fats Domino, Buddy Holly, Frankie Lane, Chubby Checker and the King himself. Elvis became Cora's new favorite.

She would crouch at the head of the stairs, listening to "You Ain't Nothin' But A Hound Dog" or "Love Me Tender," careful not to breathe too loudly. She closed her eyes and imagined the record circling like the train, around and around. She wondered what the boys were doing as they listened. Did they lounge on the couch? Did they ever dance with each other the way girls did?

Summer, 1958

Cora dreamt about a normal American family vacation. Sara's parents took her to Vancouver Island every year. Karen and her sisters always went to visit their grandparents in Idaho. Usually Pop was at sea in the summer or too beat to vacation. Miraculously, when Cora was in seventh grade, the boss offered Pop his California cabin for two weeks. Pop had always dreamt of living in California.

A week prior to departure, Cora's excitement peaked. She had never understood hope bordered so closely on terror—and she prayed each night that nothing would hamper their trip. It looked as if God were answering her prayers.

She woke with the sun on Monday morning, unable to go back to sleep although they weren't scheduled to leave until nine o'clock. So she tiptoed downstairs for some orange juice. Sitting at the chipped oak table in the pinkening kitchen, she sipped the sweet yellow liquid, tasting exquisite anticipation.

Suddenly the quiet was broken by shuffling in the driveway. A burglar? Aunt Min had warned Pop against packing their car the night before—what with the spate of robberies this last month, which most people were blaming on the young people who camped along the beach. Cora was frozen to the red chair. The orange juice reduced to acid in her stomach. Her ears began to ring so badly she could hardly hear the person moving around outside. Guilt-stricken, she realized that theft was one contingency she hadn't prayed about; she had covered only accidents, weather, earthquakes and changes of mind.

What else could she do now? It was useless to sit glued by terror to a rickety kitchen chair. At least she could alert the rest of the family. Maybe they could salvage the things inside the car if not the suitcases strapped to the roof. Despite her fear, Cora stood up, creeped to the window and parted the flowered curtains slightly with her index finger.

He was on the opposite side of the Plymouth, testing the knots holding their suitcases. His face was concealed, but Cora identified Pop by his stubby brown slippers and by the paisley arm of his recently brought-from-India bathrobe. She stood there, reluctant to release the curtain, smiling broadly at her wonderful father.

* * *

Captain Ford's cabin was a quarter mile off the highway, burrowed at the end of a dirt road. Cora was interested to see the house on stilts, surrounded by trees. Whereas the object of their location in Oregon was to see as far away as possible, Captain Ford kept his family in hiding.

Tenk was first into the cabin, barking rapidly and sniffing everywhere. Eucalyptus, Sequoia and mildew: the cabin smelled idyllically rustic. George suggested Lysol, but Cora said they wouldn't sell that kind of product in small local shops. Ron immediately fell in love with the gigantic 1940s radio, delighted by the friendly facelike dial.

"No television," Aunt Min observed approvingly. "Throws a family back on itself."

Pop frowned as he surveyed the sleeping logistics. "Four beds. Ford said there were five. Well, I guess you and Corey can have the big one, Min."

Aunt Min smiled agreement. Cora wondered what it would be like to sleep all night next to her aunt's lavender skin.

The days sped as they swam, shopped, cooked, played cards and listened to baseball games on the radio. Cora appreciated everything except the baseball. But it was easy enough to slip away and read *Seventeen* magazine or one of her library books. The first part of *My Ántonia* was a little slow, then she got into it. She would lounge on the lumpy double bed and look across the large, open room at George, Aunt Min, Ron and Pop, eating pie, absorbed in the game. It reminded her of movies about World War II on the homefront; she felt almost perfectly happy.

Why couldn't she feel completely content? She recalled scenes of five years before—she and the boys and Pop watching Jackie Gleason while Mom sat in the dining room under the lamp, sewing. She still cried thinking of Mom in that hazy yellow light.

The school counselor said Cora's nervousness was related to her mother's death. Perhaps she hadn't given herself time to mourn? Cora nodded, how could she explain that she had had enough to cope with from the *live* members of her family? Meanwhile, she ignored the vague reappearances Mom made in a day. Cora would watch her cooking dinner to the accompaniment of the radio news. She would recall painful trips to the hospital—the first months Mom pretending nothing was wrong, that she was simply on vacation, then Mom growing very, very quiet. During the last couple of visits, she didn't seem to recognize people. Cora knew enough not to reveal these apparitions to the school counselor. Eventually she understood Mom would go away entirely or come back as her old self, just materialize one night at the dining-room table.

The Russian River beach was very different from their shore at home. Initially Cora was disappointed. But, she reflected, you *could* swim here as you couldn't really swim in the ocean. You could float for hours and hours in the cool—not cold—water under the hot sun. By the end of their first week she discovered a new passion for swimming. It bothered her to see Ron imprisoned on his towel because he hated the way the gravel cut into his feet.

"Come on in, Ron," Cora urged her younger brother as he sat on the shore reading comics.

"Who wants to play with a girl?" he demanded.

She knew he was just taking out his unhappiness on her, so she tried again, "We never get a chance to dive in Grandview."

"Who wants to be seen with my fat sister?" he asked, almost immediately remorseful when he caught the pain in her face.

Was she fat? She had been filling out lately, and this bathing suit gripped her miserably around the thighs. She wanted to bury herself in the gravel. Each step toward her green striped towel seemed an eternity. She would begin dieting today.

Instead, she got sick. Afterward, Cora reckoned she had been sick for days. She remembered being exhausted and losing her balance several times—walking into the car door once; bumping into the lifeguard's chair another day. But she was such a clod that none of the family noticed.

When the pain scorched her ear in the middle of the night, she was sure she was dreaming. No, she opened her eyes and considered the dim cabin. There was the popcorn bowl in the middle of the table. To the left, she observed the huddled shape of George under piles of blankets. Funny how he always felt the cold so much. From the far corner, she could hear Pop's snoring—long, slow, even little growls, with the exception of an occasional embarrassing gurgle. And next to her lay Aunt Min in her checked flannel nightgown, smelling of Listerine mouthwash and lavender soap.

The pain in Cora's right ear was almost unbearable, so intense that it was interesting—halfway between a sharp wound and a dull ache. Normally, she avoided aspirin because she was frightened of becoming a drug addict. Tonight there was no choice. She managed to take the pills and climb back into bed without waking anyone. However the pain didn't abate, and she couldn't sleep for the rest of the night.

When Pop brought Cora back from Dr. Salveson's office, Aunt Min set her up with pillows and a jug of orange juice and a selection of new magazines.

"Doctor said she could have gone deaf if we waited much longer." Pop shook his head. Cora couldn't tell if he were talking to Aunt Min, the general citizenry of Santa Katrina or herself.

"She'll be fine now," Aunt Min said soothingly.

"Why the hell didn't you say something *before*?" he demanded, "why'd you wait until it was a medical emergency?"

Cora didn't want to admit that she hadn't really noticed the pain. After all, she was seriously ill. If she hadn't noticed it, perhaps she was crazy. She knew Pop did not want a crazy daughter. "I guess I thought it would go away."

"Just another tough Casey," Pop winked at Aunt Min. Cora was touched by this rare moment of affection between brother and sister. Aunt Min smiled in a way which did not locate her wisdom in assent or dissent.

That afternoon, when Pop and the boys returned from town, Pop dropped the brown drug store sack on her bed. He went into the kitchen for a glass of water and returned, shaking his head. "When the druggist gave me the prescription he said, 'Your little girl must be pretty sick because these are humdingers.'" Pop handed Cora the water and opened the plastic vial, picking out two enormous green and brown capsules. "Impressive, huh?"

Cora nodded, inordinately proud of the stir her illness was creating. Bravely she swallowed one large pill, then the other.

"Humdinger of a price too." He was addressing the world at large again. "Twelve dollars and ninety-five cents for twenty-one capsules."

She tensed for Pop was unpredictable about money.

He reached over, mussing her hair affectionately. "I've got one humdinger of a daughter."

"You can say that again," muttered George from the sofabed where he was studying *Sports Illustrated*.

Summer, 1960
California

The second and last vacation was in California, leading Cora to speculate that the direction of pleasure was always downward. They drove the McNulty's camper trailer, Pop having done a brilliant job of convincing Mr. McNulty that one kept one's vehicle in shape through extensive highway use. Mrs. McNulty had always sympathized with the unfortunate motherless Casey children, thus charity outweighed her fears about Mr. Casey's alcoholic driving. Aunt Min couldn't make the holiday. Cora guessed that this had to do in equal parts with her memories of their last "humdinger of a vacation," as everyone called it, and with her hopes of getting to know Mr. Earle. Cora was not happy about being the only female on the trip and hence the shopper, cook and housekeeper.

Not only did Pop luck into the McNulty's camper, but he also managed to borrow Ted Doyle's box at Chavez Ravine for a week. Her father had always prided himself on successful friends, and this summer they were cashing in.

Cora knew she was an asset the night Pop took Ted Doyle and his wife Dorothy to dinner by way of thanking them for the baseball tickets. The boys stayed home in the trailer; Pop couldn't afford dinner for six.

When they arrived at the Santa Monica apartment, Dorothy Doyle was flitting around after Be-Be, their Brazilian parrot, who had escaped his cage. Quickly Mr. Doyle shut the French doors so Be-Be wouldn't head out to sea. Cora wondered if he could make it back to Rio alone. Perhaps he would find a friendly Canadian goose along the way to guide him. The view of the Pacific through the spotless glass of the French doors was dazzling. The Doyle's ocean was different from the one she knew in Oregon. Gentler, more tropical. Cora watched the exotic bird fly around and around the coral pink living room. She thought Mrs. Doyle, a heavy woman in a bright green and red muumuu, looked like her parrot. Did she want to go to Rio too?

Ted Doyle took everything in stride, serving Pop a martini and Cora a Shirley Temple, benevolently preparing his wife a double Scotch once the bird was firmly reinstated in his white metal cage.

Cora understood that her role was to accompany Mrs. Doyle through the evening while Pop and Mr. Doyle talked ships and baseball. As it turned out, she didn't have to strain for conversation because Mrs. Doyle loved to talk—in a spontaneous colorful way about movie stars, hairdressers, astrology, cafes. This seemed a very L.A. discussion, enough to make Cora think the family should have exited Highway 101 at San Francisco. None of these uncharitable thoughts were perceptible to Mrs. Doyle—who pronounced her "a little charmer" over dessert and liqueurs.

Pop nodded fondly. "I have a humdinger of a daughter."

Now that the baseball seats were completely paid off, Pop had a terrific time. The boys eagerly argued stolen bases and RBIs over breakfast. George hoped to pitch for the Dodgers one day. Unfortunately, Cora was beginning to find baseball a slow, uneventful game. Maybe she was too serious, as George had often told her. "Gee, Cora, why does everything have to have a *point?*"

She patiently, if unenthusiastically, attended the first two games, but when Pop took them to the third—a doubleheader—she couldn't bear it. What was happening to her vacation? During the first inning, she stared at the iridescent grass, silently reviewing her life in sports.

She hated the dull thudding of football on TV every winter Sunday. More than that, however, she detested the shrill hollowness of bowling tournaments, watching the heavy ball approach the pins. In spite of herself, she always wound up wondering at the labor involved in waxing the hardwood lanes. Did women arrive with mops and bottles of Pledge in the middle of the night between the drunken evening bowlers and the fanatical breakfast bowlers? She found bowling mildly frightening because the pins reminded her of female figures. She tried not to think about the forceful movement of the solid ball thrust along the shiny long lane toward the shapely pins. Maybe she was having a hormone fit, as George would call it, but most sports seemed to be about men knocking balls into holes—golf, basketball, billiards.

Vividly, she remembered the Floyd Patterson–Ingemar Johanssen championship bout, rooting for Patterson against her father. Although her arms ached weekly from poundings by George or Ron, she believed these professional fighters were tougher. She considered them immune to pain, until their skin broke and the blood gushed. Afterward, Cora felt ashamed of her small complicity in Patterson's victory.

Baseball was more pacific of course—slow and leaden. She tried to shake her mood. Pop was feeling great. He bought everyone Coke and frankfurters. She loved the taste of Gulden's mustard mixed with relish and ketchup.

"Disgusto," George sniffed. "it looks like a garbage disposal. You can't even *see* the hot dog."

She shrugged, her mouth full, eyes on the game, *willing* something to happen but knowing that the explosive flavors on her hot dog would constitute the day's excitement.

"Ah, leave your sister alone and enjoy the game," Pop said. His temper grew more brittle during the next hitless hour and three more bottles of beer.

During the eighth inning, she pulled a book from her shoulder bag. She hadn't planned to read. The library book happened to be there, and she was going out of her mind from boredom. It was a great novel—*Maude Martha* by Gwendolyn Brooks—and quickly she was engrossed. Cora read unnoticed, until the intermission between games when she put the book away and got more hot dogs with her brothers.

The second game was even slower, and soon she returned to Brooks. However, she had more trouble concentrating because the man seated behind them was listening to Vin Scully announce each play on his transistor radio. She shut out this new form of insanity but grew furious when the man began to argue back with Scully. She meditated on the more significant tribulations of Maude Martha.

Pop didn't discover her until the third inning. "What the *hell* is she doing?" she asked George.

"Reading." George cracked his knuckles and kept his eyes on the field.

Cora employed all her willpower not to look up.

"What's she doing that for?"

No one replied.

"What the hell's she doing that for?" Angrier now, Pop repeated the question so loudly that Vin Scully's fan leaned forward.

Quavering, Ron answered, "Probably she's bored."

"Bored!" Pop boomed, now addressing her directly. "Do you have any idea how much money seats at Chavez Ravine *cost* young lady?"

She stared at the page number: 123. One-two-three, she counted to herself. One-two-three.

"Well, *answer* me."

"Yes, sir." She nodded, imagining Be-Be flying south along the coast of Central America.

"Then I want to see you enjoying this privilege. Do you know how many kids would love to be in your place?"

Cora looked at her father, for the first time experiencing her pity for him virtually unrefined by fear. The fear was small enough and the pity not great enough so that she responded, "I'd rather read my book."

Southern California sun is not kind to Irish complexion: rage cast deep purple scars across her father's forehead and on either side of his nose. He took a swig of beer and swerved back toward her.

A loud crack ripped through the ball park.

Cora knew she would always be grateful to Wally Moon for his heroic home run in the third inning, which boosted the morale of the Dodgers and their passionate fans. The game moved swiftly after that—the Dodgers scoring five more runs before the ninth inning and Don Drysdale striking out one Giant after another. Pop kept pace, downing a bottle an inning. She was relieved when he let George drive back to the trailer park. Cora finished *Maude Martha* the next morning while Pop was sleeping in.

FIFTEEN

Fall, 1961
Oregon

Cora pleaded with her father for a month not to send her to public school. Why couldn't she attend Holy Names Academy with her friends?

"How do they expect a man to afford that tuition?" Pop demanded. "Why do they need so much, to send the nuns to the Vatican in the summer?"

Cora watched her brothers leave the dinner table, clearly bored with the familiar argument. Aunt Min had a date with Mr. Earle.

Cora drew a breath and tried again. "But Pop, I got a scholarship, and if that isn't enought, I can work afternoons, well, late afternoons and weekends."

"You'll work anyway," Pop exclaimed. "Do you have any idea what clothes cost now? As for that scholarship, young lady, I told you—the Caseys don't accept charity."

"It's not charity, Pop." Cora stared at the orange rug, one of Mom's worst purchases. Why had Pop lugged the hideous thing to Grandview? "I *earned* the scholarship."

"Young lady," he began, pushing himself away from the table.

She knew she had lost because formality was his last stage before explosion. She lowered her head.

His voice softened. "Young lady, the way you earn money is to work for it. Besides, if public school was good enough for your older brother, it's good enough for you. I didn't go past the sixth grade and I did OK, didn't I?"

She was proud of her father. She nodded.

"Believe me, honey, you don't need fancy. A diploma from a public school is a valuable thing."

George's electrical school was right in the next county—only fifteen miles up the coast, twenty-five minutes away at most. George came home

every night. Cora kept telling herself it was going to be all right. She had
thought it foolish of him to quit high school. He told her he *had* finished just
not graduated. He liked the Electrical Academy. Wiring and repair work
would be steady while he practiced for the Portland Beavers and then for the
majors. She knew better than to argue with her big brother.

After the first month, he came home later and later. Tenk lay by the
front door, waiting. Cora never fell asleep until she heard the latch click and
knew he was back safe. Now she felt terrible for all her bad thoughts about
her older brother. He really was a good person. Hadn't he brought that ten
dollars he found on the beach to the police station? Wasn't he the only one
who took responsibility for Tenk, well, until recently? Everyone thought her
brother had a great sense of humor, and now that he was teasing her less, she
had to admit he could be very funny. He had a wonderful ability to be friendly
and confident but still to let his shyness show through. He looked real cool
these days with his hair slicked back and the bottom of his jeans rolled into
pale cuffs. Aunt Min said he had a chip on his shoulder, and he thought he
was God's gift. Cora knew George continued to have nightmares about their
mother's death. He showed his kindness to Cora in little ways—such as driving her to class the first week in public school and warning her about which
teachers to avoid.

° ° °

Grandview High School consisted of a line of tacky modern structures
set on the farthest hill in town. Cora missed Bishop Eagen's cozy brick building and, she thought she'd never say this, the sight of younger kids. Here she
was in the first year class and for the only time in her school life alone without either her older or younger brother. A handful of kids had transferred
from Bishop Eagen, including Sara Riley, but most of Grandview's students
were old friends from the public grade school. They greeted one another in
the hallway and stared at her coldly. Cora had a hard time climbing the hill
to school from the bus stop. She told Aunt Min that she thought she might
have a heart attack. Aunt Min raised one eyebrow and asked if she weren't
exaggerating?

Cora disliked a lot of things about public education. Although the place
was fifty years newer than Bishop Eagen School, it was messy, shabby and
dirty. The first thing she noticed was how much paper they wasted. At Bishop
Eagen, students were instructed to always "write on the other side" and most
of their supply was used to begin with—the faulty mimeos from Kelly's Ce-
ment or the out-of-date invoices from Perilli's Furniture.

She missed the old blue and brown uniforms and realized she didn't
have the most basic fashion sense. You weren't supposed to wear prints with
stripes. You had to watch out for clashing colors. You *never* wore green on
Thursday. The nuns always said the uniforms hid distinctions, and Cora could
now see what they meant when she studied Michelle Anderson's camel cash-

mere mix-and-match sweater set. The line was also painfully visible between the kids who took the bus and those who drove their own cars. "Driving their own cars in *high school?*" Aunt Min had declared. Cora began to perceive the all wise Aunt Min as "*une peu naïve,*" to use one of Sara's favorite expressions.

The rules at Grandview High—where there were rules—were much more lax. Flexible, she told herself, for she tried to be positive. The flexible faculty didn't take life as seriously as the nuns. Cora could smell cigarette smoke as she walked by the staff room. Sometimes teachers stood in the hallways talking and laughing. They didn't seem to care if you were a couple of minutes tardy to class—tardy, they smiled at this word from another century—or even occasionally a day late with an assignment. Sara Riley and most of the other Bishop Eagen transfers loved the new informality.

One thing Cora *did* like was the variety of students. She was tentative, but curious, about the few Japanese, Chinese and Jewish kids. Her first week at Grandview she realized what she had never noticed in nine years of Catholic school—that her Bishop Eagen classmates had been all white and most of them had been Irish or Italian or Polish. Perhaps she had never noticed the uniformity because the teachers were always telling them how different *they* were from the rest of the town, how they should behave carefully while wearing their high school uniforms out in the dangerous world of non-Catholics.

◦ ◦ ◦

George made a whole new crowd of friends at his course—guys from towns up and down the coast. He was a natural with his hands, "definitely the best repairman on the floor," he revealed during one of his rare dinners at home. Most evenings he grabbed a pizza with the guys and went bowling. Sometimes his friends would come over late Saturday morning to shoot baskets in the back yard.

Aunt Min fixed them lemonade and gingerbread cake, arranging refreshments on the picnic table for when they were ready to take a break. Cora noticed that her aunt wanted to be hospitable but not obtrusive, lest they resist her ministrations. This was much the same way Aunt Min behaved toward Pop.

Cora was also pleased to see George bring home his friends. Sometimes she would now admit, she saw the Electrical Academy as George's first step out of the house. She wasn't ready for that. She knew, in the abstract, that they would all grow up—she knew that once she was able to dismiss Sister Madeline's admonitions about building a bomb shelter in the back yard—but she wasn't quite ready at fourteen to grow up. She kept waiting for something to happen, maybe something as small as all of them watching TV together one more time, before they went their separate ways. Cora was disturbed that when she brought new friends to the house, she heard herself saying, "I live with my aunt and my brothers" or "my father and my brothers" or "my father and my aunt," but never remembered to include them all in one sentence.

Therefore, when on one Saturday morning, George and his friends were shooting baskets; Ron was watching cartoons; Aunt Min was baking gingerbread, and Pop was due in from the ship within hours, she should have been happy.

Thump. Thump. Cora listened to the guys dribbling. *Guy,* it was such a funny word—meaning someone between boy and man (That's where George was, closer to the man. He had always been closer to the man.) She didn't care for the word *guy;* it had an ugly, spitting sound. She much preferred the word *fellow,* which her cute English teacher, Mr. Ferris from Canada, used. Fellow was much more musical. It made her think of a thin blond juggler dancing along a ridge of hills.

Thump. Thump.

She pictured them guarding each other against the basket. Plonk. Whissh. She recalled that silly cheer from school: "And the score goes up another notch . . . " what was the rest of it? She was not concentrating. She'd have to shut the door.

Cora set down *Portrait of the Artist as a Young Man* and ambled out to the patio. She noticed patient, obedient Tenk, lying beneath the picnic table, watching George adoringly. The game was going hot and heavy: two husky fellows played against George and his short, able ally. Cora took the handle of the patio door, yanking it shut firmly and quickly so that it wouldn't flip off the track.

George's teammate turned and demanded, "Hey, who's that? You didn't tell me there were beautiful girls in this house, George."

Cora couldn't stop blushing, but she knew enough to step further back inside. She considered her new blue striped pedal pushers, which did fit her rather well. Straining to hear the fellows, she was oddly pleased by the force of George's reply.

"Take off that smirk or I'll knock it off."

Cora hovered in the doorway between the sunporch and the hall.

"Leave my little sister alone."

Spring, 1962

Cora decided to become a new person at Grandview High. If you had to move, you might as well maximize the opportunities. So she sat down on her bed one Saturday and thought about all the changes she wanted to make.

She wanted to do better in classes. She wanted to be less shy. She wanted to be more organized, more adventurous, more fashionable, more sensitive to other people. Her strategies included joining clubs, getting active in class government, attending all sports, studying in the library rather than at home and sleeping an hour less each day.

Cora kept her plan secret because, despite its ingenuity and ambition, the scheme was simply geared to making her a normal teenager and she was embarrassed that so much thought had to go into it. She didn't admit that one of the necessary consequences was spending less time with her family. But she did think about the fact that if she kept herself this busy, she *had* to lose weight.

Cora lay back on her bed, savoring the fact that Sara was still her best friend. Saturdays after work she met Sara at the Milk Barn for cocoa. When Sara didn't have a date, she would often bring another girl, and they would all go to the movies together.

One night, as she walked to the Milk Barn, Cora thought about how she was beginning to enjoy Grandview High. It had been so helpful to know Sara amidst the sea of non-Catholics. Of course Sara *had wanted* to attend public school—had demanded her father's permission as a point of principle. After all, she argued, how was she going to learn about the world with such a homogenized education? Cora, who had never used the word *homogenized* for anything besides dairy products and who would never think of arguing with her father as much as Sara did with hers, was very impressed. Dr. Riley, far from being angry, had to admit his daughter had a point and eventually agreed to let her attend Grandview. Cora was later amazed when Sara admitted "the real reason I wanted to go to Public school was that I couldn't face four years of Latin." Cora was astonished on every level. She loved Latin and was abashed to hear Sara lying to her father. Cora was beginning to understand what adults meant when they said she herself was such a good girl. How tedious she must appear to other people.

This evening she spotted Sara and Margaret turning into the Milk Barn. They seemed to know fashion by osmosis. Sara wore pretty black pumps, textured stockings, a tartan skirt and a deep red shell blending in with her plaid. Margaret also wore pumps. Her handsome Logan green corduroy jumper was accented by a white Peter Pan collared blouse and a circle pin. Cora looked down at her own scuffed loafers. At least she was wearing the new blue shirtwaist dress she and Aunt Min had bought at Compton's discount basement in Portland. When Cora had seen the dress on the rack, she immediately thought it was something *Sara* would wear.

Cora felt grateful to Sara for much more than fashion sense. Sara was the one who had explained about college prep courses. She didn't follow Sara exactly. She took more French and English and less math. But she had watched Sara's choices carefully.

Cora held back a minute before she walked into the Milk Barn. The two girls were completely absorbed in their talking and laughing. She felt a touch of jealousy and fear. Would she ever look—or feel—that *normal*? What nonsense. She was not only normal, she was on the honor roll and had just been elected—with a little advice and lobbying from Sara and Margaret—to the student council. Cora puffed out her hair, readjusted her shoulder bag and quickened her pace.

"Hi, Cora. Great to see you."

"Hi, Corey."

Cora told herself their welcome was sincere. Sincerity was another new concept for Cora. So many people this year had written in her autograph book, "to a very sincere girl" that she had had to reflect that this was one gift she had inherited from her family. They were sincere. They might have a lot of other problems, but there was no doubting their sincerity.

"Nice dress," Margaret said as Cora slid into the booth. "The color's perfect on you."

Cora beamed.

"Yeah," Sara smiled. "Wish I'd seen it first."

Gretel shuffled over and served Cora's hot chocolate. Cora felt sorry for the old woman, having to work at her age, but she seemed to enjoy it enough and remembered everyone's order. Yes, Cora noticed, she had administered the usual double squirt of whipped cream.

"Don't know how you eat that stuff and stay so thin," Sara pretended to be affronted.

Cora contentedly sipped the hot, sweet, steamy cocoa.

"So it's either, *The Americanization of Emily* or *Pillow Talk*," said Margaret. "Which movie do you prefer, Cora, break the tie."

"Oh, I don't know." Cora felt cowardly; she didn't want to disappoint either girl.

"Come on," said Sara, "aren't you up for a good Doris Day—Rock Hudson romance?"

The three girls burst into a fit of giggles.

"How about a sophisticated war movie?" cajoled Margaret.

Cora hated Doris Day movies, but now that she knew who wanted which film, it was an even harder choice. She dug out a coin. "I don't really care. Why don't we flip?"

"They're at it again," Margaret nudged Sara with her elbow.

"So they are," Sara whispered, feigning shock.

"Who?" Cora asked. "What?"

"That cheap girl Amber, who works at the donut shop, you know?"

Cora didn't.

"You know, the fast one with the streaked hair and the short skirts." Margaret persisted.

"I don't eat donuts."

"Well, she came to town a couple of months ago, and word is she's, uh, shall we say, 'accompanied' most of the local greaser guys," explained Margaret.

Margaret and Sara giggled.

"There she is, two booths behind you, and she's been necking with that guy since we came in." Margaret added.

Cora turned, studying the backs of two heads. She was sure she'd never seen the girl, but the greaser guy was her brother George.

She looked at Sara, who couldn't meet her glance. Margaret didn't know George, but Sara did. Hadn't she recognized him?

Cora rubbed the quarter between her fingers. *"The Americanization of Emily,"* she said evenly. "The truth is, I'd rather see *The Americanization of Emily.*"

Fall–Winter, 1962–63

When Ron won the clarinet in the Saint Leo's raffle, they all thought it was a good joke, even Ron, who had pinned his hopes on the three-speed bicycle. Mrs. Macguire, the donor of the clarinet, through the generosity of her brother's musical instruments firm in Boston, assured Pop it was top-of-the-line. For a while, there was a rumor that Libby Polanski, who won the bike, might be willing to trade. But Ron fell in love with the clarinet.

At first he tried learning at home, through a teach-yourself manual Aunt Min checked out of the library. But the noise drove Pop nuts. Ron cleared out a space in the garage; by winter that grew too cold and damp.

A whole new chapter of Ron's life began when he enrolled in Band class.

The night Ron announced the new class at dinner, Cora held her breath because only the dippiest kids played in the school band. On the other hand, she had never seen her younger brother so excited.

"Band?" declared Pop. "How can you be in a band, when you can't even play five notes."

"They teach you. That's the point of being in school." Ron grinned.

Cora rolled her eyes, impressed by Ron who didn't usually talk back to Pop.

"Give the boy a chance," Aunt Min mediated, also smiling.

"Well, I guess if it doesn't cost anything." Pop grunted and returned to his mashed potatoes.

Cora noticed Ron lick his lower lip, a habit he had developed in the last month.

The band did change Ron's life. For one thing, he had to be up at 6 A.M. to make the early-morning Music class. He developed a whole new set of friends, people who embarrassed Cora a little, although she knew she had no right to feel this. In his first year of high school, he made the front row of the marching band and appeared in full uniform at all games.

"Who's that cute one on the end?" Lizzie, the new girl from Idaho, asked at the third home game.

Sara peered intently, a habit she had retained despite acquiring a pair of contact lenses the previous semester. "That's Ron. That's Corey's brother."

"Really, Corey?" asked Lizzie.

"Really," Cora enjoyed the pride in her voice.

As she sat back to watch the second half of the game, Cora thought about how everything in her family was changing. People seemed happy enough, though George was off with that girl Amber most evenings. Aunt Min was dating Mr. Earle, and Pop was at sea a lot, sailing to Southeast Asia. Ron lived and breathed the band. She, herself, was busy with her job, her studies and hanging out with Sara.

After the game—a smashing victory for Grandview High—Lizzie asked Cora if she could meet her brother.

○ ○ ○

When George brought his wife Amber home, everyone tried to fit in. From the first day, Cora could see Amber was trying. Intention counted for a lot in their family, so much so that Cora sometimes confused what she had *meant* to do with what she actually did.

Amber also didn't have any sisters and had always wanted one, so they spent a lot of time together. Cora was proud of this friendship with a girl four years older than herself. She was grateful to Amber for something they didn't speak about: with a wife and child, George would never get drafted.

No one ever said, "The baby is due in six months," when the newlyweds returned from their honeymoon, but Cora could see by Amber's girth that the kid would arrive sooner rather than later. Everyone looked forward to August.

Cora understood this would change things and was pleased with overcoming her petty jealousy of Amber. She hoped the marriage—as rushed as it was—would soften Pop's attitude toward George. Pop was going to be a grandpa.

Amber began to spend more and more time at the house. She said their small apartment was boring, that sometimes she felt so confined she feared she might explode. (Cora had nightmares for a week about her little nephew—she knew it would be a boy—splattered on the tasteful beige walls of the modern flat.) Often Amber came alone because George was working overtime to pay his new bills. Sometimes they watched TV, but usually they played pinochle. Cora sat at the dining room table for hours that summer with Amber, Aunt Min and Ron drinking Kool Aid and playing cards.

○ ○ ○

Amber disappeared after the miscarriage. George refused to answer his phone for a week. One afternoon Cora couldn't stand it any more. She cut school after lunch and went to his apartment.

Cora knocked and waited. Someone was home; she could hear the Beach Boys. She knocked again. Finally, a hand parted the curtain. George stared out.

"Let me in," she said firmly.

Several moments later, she heard him fumbling with the security chain. As he opened the door, the balcony was flooded with the stench of smoke and beer and with a loud, energetic chorus of "California Girls."

"Whaddaya want?" He stared at her, red-eyed.

"I want to know how you are."

"Mind your own business."

"They say you haven't shown up at the shop in days."

"What's it to you?"

If he thought he was intimidating her, he was crazy. She was just getting angry.

"Hey, over there," a woman called across the courtyard. "will you shut your door or turn off that fool music."

"Old horse ass," George spluttered back.

Cora pushed him inside. "You're my brother." She shut the door behind them. "That's what it is to me." She coughed at the thick smoke. The room was littered with Dairy Queen bags and beer bottles. And the Beach Boys rattled on.

George collapsed in an armchair, taking a swig of beer. "Make yourself at home," he said, somewhere between hopelessness and sarcasm.

Cora turned down the music; she knew better than to switch it off. "Have you had any more luck finding Amber?"

He stared back with hostility, cracking his knuckles. As he reached for his beer, he knocked it and watched the foam sink into the carpet. Cora and Ron had helped lay that carpet two months before.

"Are you OK?" she asked him.

Tears streamed down his cheeks; his shoulders heaved with silent sobs.

Cora wished he wouldn't do this. She wished he would do *anything* but this. She kept her eyes on the framed photo of Don Drysdale hanging over the nest of TV trays.

"She went to her mother's in Eugene," he sniffed. "She's been there the whole time. Says she's never coming back."

Cora sat on the arm of his chair and rubbed her brother's shoulder. "Oh, she'll get over it. It's a rough thing to lose a baby. But that doesn't mean she can't have another. A lot of women lose babies." She had spent three evenings this week in the library reading about miscarriages.

"She wants a divorce." His voice was colder now, but still shakey.

"Oh, George," soothed Cora, furious at Amber. "She'll get over that. People have extreme reactions at a time like this."

She thought how her brother was an innocent, good man who could never understand why people didn't behave the way he thought they should.

He was weeping again. "I didn't mean to hit her. It only happened a couple of times. Things have been tight at work lately. The weather's been hell, and I don't know. But I didn't mean it. And I don't think it could have affected the baby. I'm sure it didn't. No matter what Amber says."

Cora stepped back to her chair and waited for him to finish. Of course he was right. Amber must be exaggerating. George had a temper, but, well, of course Amber must be exaggerating.

He continued to sob.

The rug had completely absorbed the beer, leaving a dark brownish stain.

"Listen George, it'll work out. But you can't face something like this on your own. Why don't you come home a while. There's plenty of room. We all miss you. Tenk has been broken-hearted since you left."

George looked at her doubtfully. "I don't know, Cora." He lit a Marlboro and took a long drag. "Maybe. Home. Maybe."

SIXTEEN ✳

Fall, 1988
Oregon

This cold, bitter day was a crazy time to walk along the beach. Besides, he would be expecting her to move in this morning. Probably he was hung over again, waiting for his coffee. But it was thrilling to have the beach so close, as irresistible as a lover in the next room. And Cora needed to compose herself, to recover from the dream.

Sun streaked through the wind. Her cheeks felt alternately hot and cold. Gleaming from the sand were arrowheads. Cora knew that if she picked them up they would lose their sheen, turning into rocks and shards of flint. The beach was also littered with tiny white feathers and strings of seaweed—the spinach linguini kind as well as the amber whips which looked like medieval torture instruments.

The dream came back to her. She had been a soldier in ancient Europe, leading her troops to battle. Joan of Arc? Men were following her. Men were fighting her. The king or count or leader was, of course, a man. She had blond hair, so she couldn't have been Joan of Arc, could she? Exhausted, wounded, petrified, she kept on fighting. Then she woke. Strange. The only pleasant part of the dream was that she had been seven feet tall.

Two male joggers loped past. One wore earphones. The other carried weights in his hands. Each made her feel slothful in a different way. In the distance were a couple of people made androgynous by voluminous parkas. They raised a purple and orange dragon kite high, high on the wind. The waves were stupendous, drawing up a fierce breath and suddenly breaking madly against the rocks. She stood watching—again and again and again they crashed—until the world was simply too cold. She could not afford to catch the flu, so she turned to the car, wind full on her back.

As Cora parked in front of Pop's house, Follie began to bark. Good dog, she smiled, recalling the mock arguments she and Jacques used to have about dogs and cats. Cora—who had been brought up on loyal, if not particularly obedient, pups—longed to have a dog around the house. Jacques threw up his hands and argued that cats were much smarter, more interesting animals. As far as Cora could see, cats just sat around licking themselves and being waited upon. As far as Jacques could see, dogs just yapped a lot.

"Down girl," Cora called through the door, as she banged the knocker.

"It's open," Pop growled.

She took a long breath and walked in. Setting down her suitcase, she thought about the family moving here over thirty years ago, about being disowned by Pop ten years later and about how this frail, tough old man would be the one to leave her this time.

He nodded to her, then turned down the television with the remote control gun. She was touched by his gesture.

"Coffee's in the kitchen," he looked at her inquisitively.

"Sorry, I'm late. I-I-I . . . " There was no excuse, but the truth was better than nothing. "I went for a walk on the beach."

"Thought so," he nodded, turning up the volume.

The kitchen stank of beer and reheated coffee. She cleared away empty brown bottles, dumped the contents of the coffee pot and began again.

When Cora returned to the living room he was napping. Gently, she set down two cups of coffee and switched off the television. Silence woke him.

"Hey, hey, what's the idea?" He was back on the ship, arguing across the gangplank with the third mate.

Her heart pounded. How easily her strength and independence disappeared at the sound of his voice. Since she had returned to Oregon, she had begun to feel the old fears, to say the old words. Now she reminded herself that she had raised a child alone for fourteen years, that she had chosen Fran's schools and nursed her through her illnesses and held back letting her make almost all the mistakes she wanted to make. Cora reminded herself she was at least as much a mother as a daughter. She was an adult now and he could not harm her in the old ways.

"Sorry." She blushed.

He seemed to be waiting for her to say more.

"I thought you'd rest better without the TV."

"Old man's prerogative to snooze." He reached for his cup. "Fresh. Guess what I made you wasn't good enough."

"Well, it *was* a bit recycled. 'Cowboy coffee,' I remember you used to call it."

"Hmmm," he grunted with pleasure at the brew or her company or an old memory.

Just then she saw herself in him: the cantankerous idealism; the disbelief at other people's irrational behavior; the aching for an accomplice. As much as she had fought him all these years, she resembled her father more closely than either of her brothers did.

"So where's my cute granddaughter? You leave her on the beach again today?"

"No, Pop, she's gone exploring with her cousins."

"A sweet girl, Fran, but she could use a little fashion advice. Maybe from Edie."

"Edie? Don't you think she's a little, uh, well *conventional* looking?"

"No. I think she's darling. Very feminine. She's got all the boys at that bank where she works twisted around her little finger."

"Yes," Cora said evenly.

"I like that Edie. A regular little film star, I tell her. But the other one is so sour and tough—like something out of a prison movie."

"I don't know." Cora smiled. Of course the first real talks they would have after twenty years would be disagreements. She would tread carefully. "I think Tommie has a character of her own. And I understand she's doing really well at the community college."

"Tommie! What kind of name is that for a girl? Min gave her a perfectly nice name—Tamara—why did she have to change it to Tommie? Sounds like some kind of pervert if you ask me."

Cora took a long draught of coffee and counted. One thing at a time, she told herself. "Tommie's very bright."

"Too smart for her own good," he snapped. Follie looked up at the sharpness in his tone. He put his hand on the dog's head and pushed her down to the floor.

Cora changed the topic. "Did Ron say when he was coming by today?"

"No." Her father shifted his weight in an attempt to get comfortable. "No, he's not coming back for a few days. Went to visit George in Medford."

"Medford? I thought George was coming here." She tried to control her ridiculously quavering voice.

"He was. He is. I don't know, damn it. Nobody tells me anything any more." He was breathing so hard his face was red.

"OK, Pop, OK." She went over to comfort him but could get no further than collecting his cup.

"Refill?"

"Naw, I think I'll lie down a while. Didn't get much sleep last night."

"Sure," she said, disappointed and relieved. How much time did they have left together? How much of it would he sleep through?

"You don't mind hanging around while an old man rests, do you? It would be a comfort to me to know you're here. There's always the TV—noise won't bother me. Good Kirk Douglas movie on this morning."

"Don't worry." She stopped herself from saying she had brought something to read. "I'll be fine. You want some help into the bedroom?"

"No. Naw, I hope they'll shoot me before I get to that stage."

She used all her willpower to stay on the couch as he struggled out of his chair. Follie waited until he reached the hallway, then padded after her master.

Cora sat staring out the picture window. Fog was lifting at the beach. She thought about the orange and purple dragon and the industrious joggers. How the population had changed over the years. As a child she had frequently sat in this chair, watching the beach and monitoring the waves as if securing an anchor. This view was the single constancy in her life. She loved the very unpacific ocean and the hills of dark green trees. How did it happen that she was the one who had been banished? How did it happen that she, who never intended to be a caretaker, wound up raising a child and now tending a father? Jacques said she was so surprised by her life because she didn't know her powers. But she didn't understand this just as she didn't understand those people who told her it was brave to fight against the war, brave to go to Canada. Well, perhaps choice was more subtle than she had imagined; perhaps it was more constructed by character than by will.

She supposed she was a loving daughter—though that never meant the unequivocal loyalty they both would have preferred. Granted, she admired her father, who had pulled himself out of poverty in Manhattan and made a new life here. He had found a good job and a wife, and together they had created a family. As he said often enough, they had created a better life for their children. Yet, what was that beyond vanity? If you didn't have children you wouldn't have to construct their "better life." Indeed, Cora suspected that it was the other way around—if you decided to have children it was so you could stake out a better future for yourself.

Here again emerged the questions of imagination and possibility. He did what men did in those days. He married and reproduced and supported his family. He could be considered heroic—in his patience with Mom and responsibility to his children. Some men ran away from their families. Becky's father had skipped the state to avoid child support. It's true that in many ways he had never grown up—had never learned to control his temper or his drinking and had usually put his own needs first—but in some ways he had done better than most men.

Cora picked up Ally's photo album again. She was curious about the way her sister-in-law had ordered the adult photos. One section on George. One on Ron. And this next section on Pop. Maybe Ally was also puzzled by how their family fit together.

Anyway, here was Pop—fifteen years ago?—painting the back bedroom. He looked aggravated, tired, in charge. And here was Pop puttering in the backyard, nursing his ferns. Cora turned the page to a photo of him sitting between baby Edie and baby Tommie, darling little girls. (She had to admit Tommie was a little sullen. Maybe Pop was right about her.) Here was Pop at Mom's grave: Aunt Min stood stiffly to one side, holding a pot of coral geraniums. Cora paused, thinking she had promised Fran they would drive up to Torrence and visit the graveyard. The next page showed Pop aboard ship: lying on his bunk with a bottle of beer. Standing in the galley with his mates. Posing on deck with an American flag blowing behind him.

The black coffee was beginning to eat her stomach, so she rummaged around for breakfast. His refrigerator was a dump. Two half-eaten macaroni and cheese casseroles. Four wobbly orange-brown carrots. A crumpled plastic bag containing three pieces of yellow squash stewing in their own effluence. She and Fran should have done more than pick up a few things at the market. A carton of eggs. She reached in hopefully. Expiration date: August. Oh, she shook herself. A few weeks ago, her first reaction would have been fury at the incompetence of this man to do his own housework—for surely his fridge had been a mess for years. Now she was simply filled with sadness at the irredeemable state of things—his body, his refrigerator, their entire family. Perhaps she was getting carried away by the metaphor. Toast, there must be at least some bread.

She didn't inspect the loaf of sliced rye carefully. It felt stale, of course, but that would be remedied in the oven. She washed the counter while the bread was toasting, then ate the slice dry, reluctant to search for jam or butter. She would excavate the fridge later, she promised herself, before he got up, after her stomach was settled.

Sun washed through the kitchen window causing Cora to marvel at the degree of comfort, even happiness, such physical pleasure brought. She poured a glass of orange juice and, more alert now, returned to the living room to make the most of this time alone.

He had always kept financial records in the top left drawer. Her hand shook as she picked up the green plastic checkbook and the neat stack of bills beneath that. She must know how much money he had, she told herself, she needed the details in order to be helpful.

Clearly Aunt Min had been right. With several hundred dollars in the savings account and a few hundred in his checking account, he must have transferred his money as well as his house to the boys. The checks were predictable enough—utilities, church, groceries. But one frequent notation was puzzling: AFN. The signature on the back of these checks—Oswaldo Steward, Chairman, AFN—offered no clarification.

Ring. Ring. The damn phone. She looked around before remembering it was in the kitchen, then ran to answer it. Follie raced down the hallway, barking.

"Hello," she answered brusquely, remembering too late that it might be George. She wasn't prepared to talk with him. She would pretend he had reached the wrong number.

"Cora?" A woman's voice.

"Yes," she answered tentatively. It could be Connie or Ally. Or Tommie.

"Oh, I'm glad. You sounded different."

"Who *is* this?" she stemmed the anxiety in her voice. Her eye was caught by a brochure in a pile of newspapers on the kitchen stool: Americans for Freedom in Nicaragua.

"It's Sara, Sara Riley. Don't you remember—we met on the beach." Her voice lifted. "Don't you remember—we grew up together."

"Sara!" Cora leaned against the fridge, trying to settle her nerves. She didn't want Pop to stumble in and find his checkbook open. But she was, as ever, reflexively polite. "How are you?"

"I'm fine. Oh, sorry, did I intrude? How is your father?"

"He's napping at the moment. It's hard to tell how he is. And what about you? Did you decide about the job?"

"The job! Now that's a good, modest way to think about it. 'The Job.' I tend to think about it as 'The Future' or 'The End.' However, you're right, it's just a job. No, Richard and I are still weighing pros and cons. Actually, that's why I'm calling. I sort of thought you might be able to help. I don't know, give me some perspective from the other side of the world."

"Yes?" Cora was preoccupied again by the filth of this kitchen.

"Oh, and I'd just like to catch up with you, learn about your life over the last two decades."

Cora fell silent. How often she had longed to call Sara. But she didn't know if she would be endangering Sara or herself. And as painful as the separation had been, she sometimes suspected the reunion would feel worse.

Sara tried again. "Can you believe it's been *decades* since we've seen each other?"

"Yes, I mean, sure, let's get together." Cora told herself it was silly to feel trapped.

"Well, how about tomorrow for lunch? I can drive into Grandview after my morning class. I've got an idea—let's meet at the Milk Barn and see if we can find any high school ghosts."

"Sure," said Cora. She tried to sound more friendly. "I'll look forward to it."

⁂ ⁂ ⁂

She had a hard time sleeping this first night back in the old house. Natural after all these years. She wasn't used to the noises—Pop's snoring from across the hall, the sap running through the new oak beams in the hallway, the distant, yet distinct roar of the ocean. Was Fran OK? Cora knew she would feel better when Fran moved here from Aunt Min's. Still, they all thought it would be best for her to have a few days alone with Pop first.

Her mind roamed. Damn Sara. Pop had been furious when he heard she was going out to lunch. Only here two days and already abandoning me, he had complained. Besides, did she know that Sara had married Richard Winton, a Commie lawyer from Chicago? Cora had simply heard him out as she scrubbed the kitchen, and she never did find a moment to ask him about the AFN. Once he had calmed down, she didn't want to get him riled again. She counted sheep. Waves. Evergreen trees. It *was* wonderful to be back. Her body relaxed in a way she had forgotten as she smelled the old wet needles and the ocean and the pungent brewery across the penninsula. Still, she couldn't sleep.

It was *stupid* to fret about lunch with Sara. It simply didn't matter what Sara thought of her. Cora wondered if Sara ever understood what a lifeline she had been in college. Cora would never have even got to college if Sara hadn't insisted and Dr. Riley hadn't persuaded Pop. She and Sara were going to grow up and become anthropologists together. Instead, she had dropped out of school and skipped the country. But Sara couldn't be mad at her—or even disappointed—after all these years.

SEVENTEEN ✳

Summer, 1968
Oregon, Washington, British Columbia

Cora set the bookbag on the seat beside her, glancing around the half-empty bus. "Express to Portland," the clerk had said. "You're lucky, lady, there're only two a week." She closed her eyes. Lucky.

Lucky to get an express, air-conditioned ticket to ride. North. Lucky there was only a two-hour wait in Seattle before the bus for Vancouver. This was how much he knew of lucky. What he didn't know was: lucky to have a bead on the border games because of two years' draft counselling. Lucky to have Amex contacts in Vancouver. Lucky the police were looking for a red-haired woman. Lucky that, although the felony murder rule could keep the case open forever and although Ralph's family was protesting the authenticity of the suicide note, the cops were slowing down. Lucky that they couldn't extradite someone for political crimes from Canada. She would be safe in Canada. North. Lucky.

The driver settled into his seat with the air of a man who enjoyed his job. He took off his jacket, set his blue thermos within arm's reach, adjusted the rearview mirror. As he turned the ignition key, Cora's heart jumped.

Canada, she closed her eyes and practiced calm. Open, green spaces. Three-party political system. Sanctuary to American refugees since the Underground Railroad. Just thinking of Canada was a respite. She breathed easier. Her body *would* relax. But this year she had become well aware of that line between dreaming and doing. Going to Canada had enormous consequences and filled her with terror. For the first time all day, she thought about Pop.

It wasn't as voluntary as that: Pop butted in.

He had been standing there at the front door the last time she went home. Anyone else would have seen him as a fat, aging, almost comically self-

163

important man watching his daughter cart away boxes of well-dressed dolls and scratched records.

"I'm telling you one more time, you drop this crazy radical business and this is your home again. This is a loyal American family with two boys risking their lives in the service; you should be ashamed of yourself . . . "

She remembered his belt buckle striking George. Unlike her brother, she would not be hospitalized. She would be banished.

"I never should have let you go to that Commie college where you got sucked into that pinko style."

Style! That's how he saw her commitments, an affectation of middle-class intellectual values. But in truth, she was just expressing her values—his values—in light of new information. He was right in one way: college was where the world became unbridgable, where the world had cracked open for her. But he was in no mood to talk principles.

Cora's hearing clicked off, and her eyes moved from his thin, mauve lips to his belligerent chin to the pocked door frame to the box-cluttered front porch. It wasn't a pretty house, but it was her home as much as his. What gave him the right to kick her out? The mortgage, for one thing, Sara would reasonably remind her. What gave parents the right to drag their children from place to place and proscribe their beliefs? Sara whispered she was too principled, too much of an idealist. Cora answered that she loved her father, she just disagreed with him. Didn't she have a right to her own ideas? Sara rolled her eyes.

Sometimes she did know enough not to argue with her father. And on this last day, she did not engage him. She thought of Mom leaving Pop for the hospital and Aunt Min leaving him three years ago to marry John Earle. This afternoon, Cora simply packed and observed, as if gathering evidence. She was surprised by the tenderness she felt for the ancient furniture and even the ornaments.

She took one last look at the ivory Ganesh, the sandalwood Buddha, the porcelain mosque, pondering her father's proclivity for collecting pagan souvenirs. As a child, she had played in reverent secrecy with the elephant and the fat man and the fancy house. As a teenager, she was pleased by their exoticism, as if their foreignness contributed to an explanation of the Casey idiosyncracies. In the last few years, she had grown profoundly embarrassed by these knickknacks, as she began to call them in front of her father. Tawdry neocolonial plunder. Right now the critique rang hollow, and when she was sure he wasn't looking, she approached Ganesh for one last touch. Then she peeked in his bedroom—at the Star-of-Bethelehem quilt Mom had made before she retired forever to doll clothes. She glanced at the crucifix over his bed. The palm leaves (which Mom had knotted at the base before she entered the hospital for the last time) remained faintly green.

"Come on, come on," he called from the front of the house, unwilling (afraid?) to come back and face her directly. "How long can it take you to pack a few boxes?"

Sara assisted silently, diplomatically, competently. Pop had always liked Sara, who came from the right kind of home. For her part, Sara used to describe Cora's father to their college friends as "gruff, but cute."

He refused to help Cora carry her life to Sara's car (he probably would have prohibited Aunt Min and Mr. Earle from storing her things if he had known about it), but he also wouldn't grant Cora the dignity of privacy. At the door, he watched as every last box was lugged from the house to the porch to the stationwagon. He stood by the broken swing, arms across his broad chest, as imposing as the pitted granite wolverine in front of the town hall.

Now Cora looked out the bus window and realized they were just beyond Diamond Point. It was a cruelly beautiful day with the brightest of blue Oregon skies. Weather so clean and warm it erased from memory a year of chilly rains. She was leaving today, leaving a place she had tried to make into home. As her mother had done. And just like Mom, she would never return.

Canada had been in her thoughts for some time now. She admitted to herself that while California had long been the dream, Canada had been the haven in the back of her mind. Canada was more exciting than California because it was a different country and offered a whole new life.

"Got a match?" A voice from behind.

She froze, engulfed by that last image of Ralph, staring into the burning draft files. Shaking herself, she turned to face the freak behind her. Freak, she liked this name hippies gave themselves. Sometimes she liked the self-deprecation. Sometimes she appreciated the accuracy.

"No," she lied, "I don't smoke."

"Not even good shit?" He winked.

She found herself ridiculously annoyed by this guy planning to smoke on the bus. She wanted to shout at him, didn't he have any consideration for other passengers? But the question was kind of ironic for an arsonist. Finally Cora responded and stared out the window at the anonymous highway, "Not even good shit." She considered the pleasures of riding in a bus so far above the road and remembered that sweet trip with Mom to meet Pop's ship in Coos Bay.

"We're going in the wrong direction." He was leaning forward, peering through the crack between the seats with the intensity of a burglar testing the safety of a dark corridor. His grey eyes were playful; his voice earnest.

The breath caught in her throat for a moment until she realized she had checked at the last two towns and they were, indeed, going North. She ignored him.

"All the shit's happening in Frisco."

Perhaps what she disliked about hippies was their limited vocabulary. Perhaps it was simply a squeamish objection to their recycled shit. Again she dismissed him.

"Be-in. Another summer of love. Flower children." His voice was sympathetically didactic. "Where are you from? Another planet?"

"Mars." She was taken aback by her own anger. "Shit's also happening in Detroit, Paris, Chicago and Prague this summer—if you read the newspapers." She thought about Sister Eleanor's Current Events class.

"Oh, a straight chick. Intellectual. A revolutionary?"

"Yeah." She forced lightheartedness into her voice. "Right up there with my sisters Emma Goldman and Rosa Luxemburg."

He paused, daunted by the European names or the dope or both. "Myself, I come from a normal American family."

Before he could answer another question, she said, "I'm kind of wiped out now. Think I'll grab a few z's." The language sounded satirical when she used it, but he didn't seem to notice.

"Right on," he sank back into his seat. She imagined his eyes as shiny ball bearings spinning down the bus aisle.

"Normal. American. Family." For years she had yearned after a normal American family where her mother wasn't crazy; where her mother wasn't dead. A family that took Sunday drives and regular summer vacations. The neighbors always said they loved Pop's Manhattan accent, but truthfully, they considered it a curiosity associated with his drinking and wandering. What would a normal American family be like—one with a father who sold insurance or worked in a bank and lived at home year round? Yet for all the anomalies the Casey story was perfectly normal—two boys in Vietnam; a father in a military-dependent job, a daughter exercising her New World prerogative of upward mobility through college. How normal was it to be an arsonist, a refugee taking the Greyhound to Canada? She sighed. Portland—60 miles, according to the green and white highway sign. She imagined it was more normal than most people would admit.

He got off at Portland "to check out a commune of weavers and potters." She declined the enthusiastic invitation to join him.

"Hey," he turned and shouted to her window, "hey, North is *not* the way to go."

She waved, strangely saddened to watch him disappear into the noisy city streets.

The bus moved faster between Portland and Seattle. She shifted to the aisle seat, stretched her legs toward the window, unbuttoned the top snap on her jeans and pulled down her inside-out sweatshirt. Too many late night chocolates, she shook her head. Well, that would change when she got to Canada. She had made a lot of resolutions for her new life.

Cora stared out the window, concentrating on arriving rather than on leaving, on the photographs she had seen of glorious Vancouver caressed by mountains. "Leaving home" was sentimental claptrap. Think about people whose homes were taken away from them—in villages destroyed by her brothers, her President, her taxes. At least in Canada she wouldn't bear the same complicity. She knew she would never return here, and was, as the freak intuited, an interplanetary visitor. She dreaded the idea of a cold bed in a foreign country, but maybe she had been sleeping around too much. In Canada, she would be more selective. Truth was, she felt a little tired of sex. She felt pretty tired altogether. Cora was saddened at leaving the coast (but the same water ran by Vancouver). She would ache for Sara (but she would make new friends in Canada). She felt exposed, forfeiting her citizenship (but wasn't nationality an imposed convenience of state bureaucracy?). The more she resisted each of these silly qualms, the more anxious she felt. Only her anger afforded any clarity, so she returned to that.

In Seattle, the Vancouver bus filled quickly. Just three more hours now. She thought about her grandparents crossing off the days as they sailed from Ireland to New York. Three more hours to freedom, she considered, although she had warned herself against excessive romanticism. A woman with tightly curled white hair was standing by her seat, asking something. Cora tried to ignore her, but found herself looking up, irritated by her courteous reflex. (She believed in the effective use of will—that if she concentrated in a certain way people would be at home when she telephoned, she would get the table she wanted in a cafe, she would not have to share her seat on the bus.) The woman was speaking more loudly now. In a Scottish accent. Ashamed of her selfishness, Cora smiled and slid over.

"Occh, thanks," the woman whistled spearmint air through her broken bottom teeth. "Quite a queue. I thought I'd have to stand the entire journey home."

Cora smiled weakly.

"Fiona's my name."

"I'm Cora." She found herself inquiring, "Where are you from?"

"The East Coast of Scotland." Fiona was catching her breath.

"That's a long way. How did you wind up in the Seattle Greyhound Station?"

"That's a long tale," she laughed.

Normally Cora remained aloof with strangers. However there was something gripping about the intense, yet modest, way Fiona recounted her story.

"Well, when I married Rob MacIvar, people said it was to escape my family: twelve there were then, in a farmhouse in Aberdeen. But truth was, I loved the man. And I suppose I was intrigued by his being a piano tuner. I wasn't really a farm lass by nature."

Cora was taken with the energy of Fiona's gregariousness and the pleasure of their sudden, easy intimacy.

Fiona lowered her voice. "Rob died, like so many others, in the
trenches. The Great War, we called it afterward, and I think it was the worst
I've seen. At any rate, I had a baby and postwar Scotland was no place to raise
her. So I accepted assisted passage to Canada as a domestic. Managed to put
Ramona through school and finally the music conservatory. She played beautiful violin. Ramona married, had a baby, then took up music again."

Here was someone with real problems, a real life, Cora told herself, absorbed by Fiona's equanimity and charmed by the sprinkling of Scottish and
Canadian words.

"A year after she joined the philharmonia, she discovered a malignant
tumor. Her husband left her. She died at a Christian Science hospital." Fiona
closed her eyes.

Cora patted the woman's hands, imagining her as an older Aunt Min.
No, she did not want to think of family. She concentrated on Fiona's brogue.

"Then there was Bobby to raise and that revived me. He's safely outside the music business! An electrician. Married to a lovely American girl. So
it's from their home on the Olympic Penninsula that I'm returning now."

Cora glanced out the window. Her heart leapt to her throat at the sign:
"Canadian Border—5 miles."

Border. Until now she had conceived of the border as something between her and the States, between her and the war, the police. But borders
were, by nature, two-sided. What if they wouldn't let her cross? Ridiculous.
She had worked it out. She had written half the draft resistance manual, for
Christsake. Of course her own crime was more serious than evading the draft.
There was no statute of limitations. As much as she wanted to, she couldn't
apply for landed immigrancy today. She would have to wait until she got another ID. She would just tell them she was on vacation and that would work
as long as they didn't demand to see her bulging suitcase. But they wouldn't
do that. Canadians encouraged tourism. Everything would be all right.

"Are you feeling OK, dear?" Fiona's reddish brows knitted a dramatic
fringe over her green eyes.

"Yes, why, oh, I guess borders just make me nervous. Silly, really."

Fiona nodded, her face drawn with unspoken concern. They filed off
the vehicle with their hand luggage. The bus driver snapped open the bag-
gage compartment, exposing an array of brown and grey suitcases. Her
patched green bag was hideously conspicuous.

He caught her staring. "In case they want to inspect something." His
voice was reassuring, "Usually they don't. Go in there with the white card."

"There" was a stuffy beige room with a faded blue linoleum counter.
The other passengers looked bored and hot. She pretended to be bored
and hot. Suddenly the office was all too familiar: smelling of cigarettes,

stale instant coffee, mildewing files, typewriter ribbons. Poor Ralph. Crazy Ralph. Her eyes spilled with tears as she staggered two or three steps.

"It's all right, dear." The voice woke her. "It's all right, I'm here."

The thought surfaced despite Cora's best efforts to suppress it—Fiona could easily be an agent. The cops were getting more clever. They had hired those black men to infiltrate the Panthers and the Muslims. And what would they have to pay an old grandmother to ride the scenic bus between Seattle and Vancouver? She would do well to keep her distance from Fiona.

The border guard was slim, alert, efficient. He waved most of the people back on the bus, but had told a ponytailed hippie to step aside. They were interrogating him in a glass-walled office. Stupid kid, she thought, if he were dodging the draft, he should have cut his hair. The guards weren't supposed to ask if you were resisting the war, but they could turn you away for looking unsavory. She glanced aside now lest she somehow be associated with him. She could hear George jeer, "Always looking out for number one." She *had* to cross this border.

Now she was two people away from the guard. She could see he was checking each name against a log. Traffic tickets? People finking out on their taxes? They couldn't all be *political* outlaws. She must settle herself. Calm down. Assume a slight indifference. Prepare to smile. They always liked girls to smile. Rehearse the lines.

"Here for the summer. For the long holiday." She heard herself speaking to the guard. He looked about five years older than she, and his eyes were skeptical.

"Holiday?" he inquired.

Was he French Canadian? What was the word in French? *Vacances.*

"I thought Americans didn't say holiday. We get thousands of people here, and no one is ever on holiday. All of them are on va-ca-shun."

Swell, she had metamorphosed from a dangerous terrorist into a target for his anti-American pot shots. Out of the corner of her eye, she watched the hippie, now released from the glass box, slouching toward the bus. She smiled at the guard. "I grew up with a mixed vocabulary—because my Pop's parents were Irish."

"Mine, too," he brightened. "Where from?"

"Clifden."

"We're from the Dingle Penninsula. You'll find a lot of us in B.C. Welcome to the far west of Eire."

She smiled broadly, naturally, amazed and pleased that it had been her father who escorted her across the threshold. Western Ireland, she shook her head. Who cared as long as it wasn't the U.S.?

Fiona smiled as she returned to her seat. "Borders are such a nuisance." The old woman raised those eyebrows. "People just create trouble for themselves."

"Pardon?" Cora asked. She was feeling a little woozy and wasn't sure she had caught the old woman's meaning. Fiona didn't seem tough enough to be an agent. Then, Cora didn't know much about agents or borders or even terrorists.

"We're all one race. We all own land. It's just human arrogance to build fences. And it's such a waste of a nice summer day."

"Yes," Cora nodded courteously, gripping each of Fiona's words to steady her from the waves lapping through her belly. God, she felt wretched. Well, what did she expect if she were going to eat french fries and drink three bottles of Dr. Pepper for breakfast? Oh, Christ. Oh, she opened the bus window just in time to vomit over the side. The right side, she noted, the side *away* from the immigration office. They weren't going to admit plague victims. She leaned back and closed her eyes, her face flashing hot, then cooler and cooler as the sweat seeped down her thighs and along her neck. Just nerves. Aunt Min was always warning her about being high-strung. But she wasn't *crazy* like Mom, just a little *stressed*. She had been throwing up every day for weeks. She could still smell the smoke in the draft office.

Fiona watched attentively as Cora recovered, then offered her a spearmint. Cora accepted the candy with gratitude and observed her breathing return to normal as soon as the driver started the bus.

When they finally reached Vancouver, the first thing Cora noticed was the cleanliness of the station in comparison to terminals in Seattle and Portland. The floor was swept; the garbage bins were only half-full; there was room on the benches. The next thing she noticed was a gorgeous blond man with a red beard. They made eye contact, and he waved a copy of *Soul on Ice*. So this was Gordon, the Amex representative. Vancouver was looking more and more attractive.

Fiona observed the exchange and smiled. "Good, you've found your friend. But just in case you need anything," she handed Cora a tightly folded slip of yellow lined paper, "here's my address and phone number. Burnaby isn't as exciting as Vancouver, but just in case."

"Thanks." Cora slipped the paper in her pocket, a little wearied by the woman's concern. She pecked Fiona's rouged cheek and was struck by the familiar scent of Aunt Min's Evening in Paris.

"Take care of yourself," Fiona's voice faltered momentarily as she patted Cora's shoulder. "Be gentle with yourself."

"Yes," Cora nodded distractedly, "you too."

She didn't want to keep Gordon waiting. It was time to start her new life in Canada.

EIGHTEEN ✴

Summer–Fall, 1968
British Columbia

Lying on the lumpy bed in the large roominghouse, Cora felt in her jeans pocket for the reassuring slip of yellow paper with Fiona's number. Gordon had said he wished he could take her to dinner, but he had an editorial meeting at *The Georgia Straight* tonight, and he suspected she wasn't into meetings yet. She had to admit she was into a bath and a nap.

Fiona said to call any time, but that would be too easy. Besides, Cora felt she and Gordon had a good momentum, hitting it off right away, bantering, laughing, talking politics. They made a date—well, maybe not a date—who knew if he had a wife and ten kids, but he *had* offered to show her Stanley Park tomorrow—after his union work and before the commune meeting. He had said there might be an extra place at the commune if so-and-so left for the Maritimes. Cora had simply nodded and hoped the Maritimes beckoned sooner rather than later.

An hour before sunset, her small room was dim. Drawing aside the beigish curtains, she examined the window critically, more amazed than appalled by the grime. Cora turned around, bumped her shin on the green suitcase and found tears streaming down her cheeks. Ludicrous to take this dump so seriously. After all, she was safe. The cops could look for that mystery woman, but they would never get her. She had made it across the border. She had enough money to pay this room for a week until she got a job. She had two friends. God, she wanted to talk with Sara, who would be expecting a postcard from California any day now. Would she ever be able to tell her friend what happened? Had they lost contact forever?

Mind on the present, she remonstrated. Gordon had told her the bathroom was down the hall. She had nodded, she hoped without surprise. What did she expect—the Biltmore? Now as she stepped from her room she puz-

171

zled—right or left? Wsssh. Wsssh. The loud, mechanical sneeze of the toilet drew her forward. A small man with three days' growth of beard exited, smoking a cigarette. Camels, she noticed, Ralph's brand. The bathroom window was open, making this much brighter than her own room. She tore off toilet paper and placed it on the seat, taken aback by the sanitary reflex. Ah, the bladder muscles relaxed. She had been drinking a lot today—to quench the nervous thirst of the journey. Three or four bottles of pop. Her tongue explored the sugar lining on a back tooth and she felt sick to her stomach. Hot, sticky, oh, yes, a *bath* would bring her back to life.

From this distance the tub was gray. Nearby lay a tattered rag and a jar of Ajax. Maybe later she would have the spirit to scrub it. Maybe once the sun went down, the tub wouldn't look so bad. A walk—that should revive her.

Cora felt better the minute she hit the street. Air, people, music, honking horns. She had never lived in a large city with crowded sidewalks, congested traffic and yammering construction drills. Of course she would get used to it all. Used to the pale, fair citizens with their pleasant accents. Used to the strange spelling in the newspapers and the different candy brands and multicolored money and five contiguous time zones. She was going to become Canadian. Exhausted, she considered going to her room, but the thought of the bathtub kept her walking these city streets.

◦ ◦ ◦

Vicky's Cafe was familiar enough and Cora felt lucky to land a job after just five days. She and Vicky liked each other immediately, perhaps because Vittoria Montali had also crossed the border. The small solid Sicilian in her early forties was willing to take a risk on Cora because she remembered her own first week in Vancouver years before.

"Is a good place, Canada. More opportunity than in your country now." She looked at Cora expectantly, and when her new waitress wasn't forthcoming, she didn't pressure her. They got along fine.

Serving meals in Vancouver wasn't a whole lot different from waiting tables in Oregon. Of course there were certain regional peculiaritites, such as fresh cream served with fruit. Customers seemed a little friendlier here. Maybe that's because she was.

Gordon had a lot to do with Cora's sense of well-being. At first, he was simply acting the good comrade: looking out for her, introducing her to a few people, taking her to films. By the second week, she hoped it would turn sweeter than friendship. She recalled her resolve to go slower with the guys here. On the other hand, there was something different about Gordon. Something special. She didn't want to lose him because of an abstract resolution.

One night they stopped for a pitcher of beer on the waterfront. The moon was three-quarters full; the stars were bright and riotous, and the Greyhound ride seemed years away. Cora loved to look at his large, competent, graceful hands; orange and yellow hairs licked up the long fingers.

They had fallen silent, watching fishing boats dip and sway, listening to a new Beatles song from the bar. She didn't notice who made the first move. She took his hand or he took hers, but suddenly her heart was thudding; her breath was short, fast.

They began to see each other every two nights, every night. She joined the Labor Solidarity Coalition. Late in the evenings, he taught her about the differences between the Canadian left and the American left. Here, above the parallel, Canadians knew that "international union" was a euphemism for "American union." Here in a three-party system, there was a halfway realistic dream of socialism. And a solid history of collective politics.

Gordon, himself, was different from the American men she had known. More talkative than her brothers. More sensitive than guys in the movement back home. He loved to hike, called himself a birder. He played beautiful classical guitar. Often at night, after making love, he would play several pieces for her. Odd, she thought, that his taste ran to liturgical Bach.

The sex was terrific. Cora let herself feel the loneliness she had experienced with other lovers lately. Perhaps that had been her fault; she had been guarded about everything this summer. In contrast, Gordon was tender, inventive, passionate. He was even conscientious about birth control, said he didn't think it should just be the woman's responsibility, but was glad she had an IUD. What Cora liked best—although she never said, not wanting to threaten him—was that he slept curled around her, anchoring her safely to this peaceful room in

Vancouver,

British Columbia,

Canada.

* * *

Sometimes she felt exhausted after serving lunch, but Vicky was understanding. Culture shock, the older woman would laugh good-heartedly, waving Cora to take a coffee break in the back booth. On days like this, she put in extra time cleaning up, even though Vicky insisted it wasn't necessary. Cora knew Canada was not perfect, but she allowed herself to think it was close.

Within three weeks of her immigration, Gordon invited her to move into the commune on Flinders Street.

The rambling brick house was such a relief after her tiny room in grime city. Gordon's renovated attic filled with light from high arched windows. His taste was minimalist—double mattress on the floor, clothes neatly piled in old milk crates, several bulky cushions covered with Indian paisley. Teasingly, he said he had asked her to live with him because she hadn't had time yet to collect much clutter. Fine. This stopped her from thinking about the clothes she had left behind. (If only it could help her forget about the people.) This spare life was politically responsible and aesthetically gratifying.

Certainly there was plenty of distraction from the other residents, and she made a mental catalogue for the letter she could not write to Sara or Ron or George or Pop: Elana, a smart, beautiful woman with coils of honey brown hair, who had taught English in Teheran for two years, decorated her room with Persian fabrics. Craig, a serious rocker, had converted his chamber into the Janis Joplin hall of fame. He drank endless bottles of 7-Up and was always losing his glasses. Walter, a thin, dark graduate student in marine biology, kept his ten-foot aquarium in the hallway between the kitchen and the bathroom. Even though Cora slept two floors above, she could hear the glug glug of the water pump when she awoke at odd points in the night. But this noise didn't bother her, nor did the music nor the midnight conversations nor the sexual moans nor the giggling in front of the television. She cherished the vitality of Flinders Street, the purposefulness of political debates, the fun of dancing, the sweetness of five scraggly people hungover together at breakfast.

But something was wrong with her stomach. Initially she blamed the queasiness on the fire, then on roominghouse water, however, after a month in the commune, she was, if anything, feeling more nauseated. She had postponed the doctor because of cost and because she didn't want to risk being caught by the provincial health scheme. Vicky was worried about her. Elana said to check out the free clinic.

Gordon had planned to accompany her, until an emergency editorial meeting surfaced. With a worried face, he dropped her at the door of the old warehouse, nodding to the clinic windows three flights up. She told him she'd be fine and didn't mind taking the bus home. Silly to be bothered about going to the doctor, she told herself. Probably it was just an allergy. These people wouldn't care about papers. They wouldn't ask a lot of silly questions.

"Age?" inquired the grey-bearded doctor.

"Twenty."

"Weight?"

"One hundred fifteen. I think."

He was efficient, slightly bored. Cora guessed she wasn't nearly as interesting as a LSD overdose or a case of tenement tuberculosis. She felt silly being here suffering from what—nervous tension?

"Gaining weight?"

"Maybe a little."

"Regular nausea?"

"Yes," she was relieved that he seemed to be on a track.

"Tenderness around the breasts?"

"Yes."

He raised his eyebrows.

She sank back. This was the *wrong* track.

"Last period?" His voice was almost sarcastic.

"Oh, no." She explained that she had had the IUD for a year.

"Last period?"

"Well, about three months ago. But I'm not regular. Sometimes I go for six months . . . "

He withdrew a green perscription pad from his drawer and began to write. "Let's be sure." He handed her the slip. "Take the test this afternoon, and you'll have the verdict in a few days."

"They're running tests," she told Gordon and Elana over dinner. "I'll know in a few days."

"What do they think it is?" Elana frowned.

"Oh, probably just nerves. Probably nothing," she reassured them, struck by the tinsel-flimsiness of her words.

⋄ ⋄ ⋄

"Sergeant Pepper's Lonely Hearts Club Band;" "Lucy in the Sky With Diamonds;" "I Am a Rock." Finally she was learning the words to these songs. She had been too busy in Oregon—waitressing, studying, agitating. Of course she was busy here, too, but the northern days lasted longer; her pores opened. She particularly liked the new Dylan album.

Yet even as she claimed the music, she grew wary of cultural imperialism. What a pleasure to learn that Ian and Sylvia were Canadian. "Wake up Jake;" "You Were On My Mind."

"Really?" she asked Gordon one night as she lay in bed, listening to Walter's stereo through the floorboards. "They don't make much of their Canadian identity in the States." She learned to say "the States" rather than "America."

"Part of the Canadian mediocrity complex." Gordon explained that many Canadian artists passed as American in order to sell their wares. He praised the progress of Cora's nationalization. Some U.S. radicals were as bad as High Republicans. They immigrated to Canada, assuming they would run the movement here, and they had to be reminded of the border.

Still, Cora observed, there were plenty of Americans who did not have to be reminded. Every week the commune sheltered a passing draft dodger or deserter. The deserters were especially grateful to be above the 49th parallel and especially anxious about being sent back. (Sometimes she fantasized opening the door late at night to Ron or George, giving them refuge. But she blocked those thoughts because they sent her on a path of endless obsession.) Although it was illegal to extradite people for political reasons, members of the RCMP had been rumored to take personal excursions, delivering recalcitrant soldiers to Washington State. This intensified Cora's belief that certain identities transcended nationality—police and politicos among them.

The day after the doctor's appointment, Cora revived. Maybe she wouldn't bother to check the test results. Well, she could hardly make the

Saturday appointment because it was the day of the big September peace
march. How had she forgotten that? Her allergy, or flu, had cleared up now
anyway. Again, she fell easily into the pattern of staying up late strategizing
and making love; working all day at the restaurant and joining Elana to prepare the big communal suppers.

Vegetarianism was a revelation to Cora, who had been raised to believe
in meat and potatoes as ancillaries to the Apostles' Creed. She had never
thought about the oppression of ranch animals and the general "humanist"
arrogance of her diet. For the first time she tasted curry, chili, coriander. You
could make a hundred recipes with beans. A good thing, too, since she and
Elana and Craig brought in the only steady wages.

Gordon was simply too committed to hold down a routine job, and Walter was deep into his dissertation. She loved the smell of their kitchen at 7
P.M., still sweet from the bread Walter baked during the day, now swelling
with savory spices.

The September peace march was thrilling. Never before had Cora seen
so many people protesting—once again reminding her that she was in a big,
cosmopolitan city, a world apart from her life at college or in Grandview. Surprised to see the group of Vietnam vets against the war who had come up
from Seattle, Cora longed to ask if any of them knew George or Ron. Instead
she counted the contingents: Quakers, Maoists, feminists, American expatri-
ates, dropouts, rebels . . . "Amnesty for Deserters and Resisters" read the
lavender sign carried by a tall black man. What would Ralph have thought
about all this?

The commune didn't have much time for TV, but they usually checked
out the late CBC news, which, although it was bourgeois and simplistic, was
so much more tolerable than American reporting. Still, she couldn't escape
American *news*. The war had a nightly spot. And the campaign loomed everywhere: Tricky Dicky versus Hubert the Hump. What a choice. Then there
were endless legal battles of protestors in Newark and Atlanta and Chicago.
No news from Oregon. She could feel safe that the FBI had closed the case,
or she could remember that one small town draft board was hardly news-
worthy in comparison to these big city actions. Just because they weren't reporting it, didn't mean that the FBI wasn't investigating it. Poor Ralph. Even
his death didn't warrant coverage. She observed a strange and pleasant
change in herself: she steered clear of the Americans who came through the
house, instead concentrating on Canadian issues and fresh bread and the music of the Perth County Conspiracy and her passionate new world guide, Gordon Winters. She had been deliriously happy when Elana told her Gordon
wasn't usually monogamous like this. For Cora's part, if she ever committed
to one man, she would want someone as smart, socially active, sexy and gentle as Gordon. Maybe it *wasn't* too soon to think about a commitment.

◊ ◊ ◊

The small room looked more like an insurance agency or a minor government bureau than a medical lab. As Cora sat forward in the semicomfortable metal and leather chair, she realized that she had never been in an insurance office or a government bureau. She had lots of abstract ideas, but little worldly experience. She was too young, and she had never met a notary public. Clearly, she was too young to have a child. Clearly, God knew that. She noticed God had appeared at odd moments since she arrived in Canada.

The walls were covered with pale blue rice paper and decorated with Cubist prints: Picasso, Braque, Léger, and . . . she couldn't quite identify the large one in the chrome frame. Her concentration was disrupted by the faces of other women awaiting sentence. The heavy Italian holding a little girl on her knees looked tired but relatively calm. Across from her a woman with silver blond hair smoked nervously and flipped through *Vogue*. Late thirties, Cora surmised, good time to have a kid. You'd be prepared mentally and financially. You'd know something about the world, at least about insurance offices and government agencies. The third woman was young and thin, like herself, like she used to be. Ever since her visit to the clinic, Cora had had to admit she was gaining weight. At first she thought her jeans had shrunk. Now she cringed at her own denial. Realistically, this girl was ten pounds lighter than herself and in for a happier verdict. Suddenly, she ached for Sara, who had steered her through so many hoops. Her eyes filled as she thought of never seeing Sara again.

"Mrs. Casey," the secretary called her to the desk. Cora walked to the small glass window with a timidity she remembered from the third grade when Sister Marion held her after school. Mrs. Casey. Mother was Mrs. Casey. Mrs. Casey was a mother . . .

"Here are your results," the woman sounded cool, though not unkind. "Sorry it took so long, but we expected you several weeks ago, and your lab record got filed away."

Cora could not believe how long this explanation was taking.

"We advise people to get the news from their physician. Of course, you're welcome to stay here."

Inadvertently, Cora looked at the other three women: one-by-one, each lowered her eyes. "No, thank you," she forced a confident smile, "I'm already late for an appointment."

The woman behind the desk considered her momentarily. "Very well." Her voice was more manicured. She handed Cora the green envelope as if she were doing her a favor.

Cora finished half the tuna sandwich and Coke float before fishing in her bag for the envelope. This would be her last Coke float, she vowed. She would go on a diet right away. Using the knife as a letter opener, she slit the envelope with obsessive precision. In the past she had been a careless ripper-opener of letters, but she had planned many new disciplines in this revised northern life. The slip inside was the same green color as the envelope, her verdict immediately visible.

Pregnant. With child. Expecting. Knocked up. Bun in the oven. *Enceinte.* Carrying. Fertilized. Cora sensed—imagined?—a movement in her belly, a strange feeling she couldn't control. Her body was no longer hers. She didn't notice anything had happened until she heard the "Oh, no" of the man in the next booth. Glancing down, she saw that the cracked linoleum table was covered with vomit.

Fall, 1968

Cora looked around her pale yellow room at the back of Fiona's cottage, telling herself to cheer up. She was lucky to be in this cozy house in Burnaby. She was lucky to keep her job. She was lucky to be in good health. She was lucky she hadn't lost that slip of lined paper with Fiona's number. Still, she had never felt so alone in her whole life. Who could have imagined the nightmare of the last year: Ron going to Vietnam, Pop disowning her, Ralph killing himself. Herself an arsonist, an exile.

Her mind wandered back to the Flinders Street commune. At first, Gordon had been ecstatic about the baby news.

She had to tell him the truth. "They say I'm three months along, which means . . " It could have been James or Peter or . . .

"Hey, hey," he cradled her on their mattress. "Who cares whose sperm it is. Children belong to everyone. That is, if you're into sharing."

She laughed and laughed, burying her head in his golden furry chest.

They drank a bottle of champagne and made passionate love. Afterward in the room dimly lit by jasmine candles, he talked about dusting off his carpentry skills to build a crib.

For weeks they played with names—Samora, Fidel, Huey, Bernadette, Clara. She recovered from the "morning" sickness and found herself getting wider. Suddenly she was full of energy, easily able to keep up with her shift at Vicky's Cafe and the commune housekeeping and her political work.

Then in October a cold wind blew through the house. Despite going over and over the story with Fiona, she could never figure it out. Sometimes, she thought the negative atmosphere had to do with that deserter from New Jersey who flipped out on meths. Everything happened so quickly: Gordon explaining to her the gossip about the agent, saying that as the only American in the house now—of course it was ludicrous—she was a likely suspect. And it would be better for everyone if she cooled it a while in another place. No one else in the house was saying much. Elana simply nodded in agreement with Gordon that it wouldn't be a bad idea for her to crash somewhere else.

Cora hadn't expected Fiona to remember, but the old woman took her in immediately, as if she had been waiting. What would she have done without Fiona these last two months? Every day she waited for Gordon's call. Every night until she fell asleep sitting up. Elana had visited her after a couple of weeks and took a letter to Gordon (maybe her other notes had been intercepted in the post?). He responded with a phone message at Fiona's while Cora was working at the cafe. He would be in touch soon. Never fear. But he didn't call again. Elana started to drop by the cafe. They went to movies together. Afterward, they talked about everything except Gordon. Elana began to act annoyed when Cora asked after him. Desperate not to also lose Elana, she stopped inquiring.

Cora tried to shake her depression. It was a beautiful Sunday; maybe Fiona would like to take a walk. She heaved herself up and headed slowly toward the living room.

Fiona sat by the radio with her eyes closed, listening to "Highland Reel," her favorite program. Every Sunday afternoon when the house was filled with this Scottish dance music, Fiona spent two hours in her mind with Mr. MacIvar, practicing strathspeys and flings. Normally Cora found this ritual touching, and she was careful not to intrude.

Now she sat in the rocking chair, opposite Fiona, trying to get in the mood.

"Oh," Fiona said, "you gave me a start. How are you, Cora?"

"Fine. Don't let me interrupt."

"Not at all. Would you like a sweet?" She extended a cut glass plate piled with hard spearmint candies.

"No thanks," Cora raised her hand to halt the dish before it came within smelling distance. After two months with Fiona, the scent of spearmint made her sick. Now, fearing that she had been too abrupt, she said, "Fiona, you know I am so grateful. I don't know what I would have done without you."

"Enough of that." Fiona reluctantly drew away from the music, pouring herself a fresh cup of tea. "I've cherished the company. This house is too big for an old woman."

Cora noticed that Fiona kept a mint in her mouth as she drank the tea.

"Besides, you insist on paying your share. I still think you should be saving your wages to take care of the wee one."

Cora shook her head. "You only accept a token. We'll be OK." She patted her stomach, curious about the security the word *we* provided.

"If you don't mind my asking," Fiona began hesitantly.

Cora walked to the window. Yes, I do mind your asking, she wanted to say, for when Fiona had this nervous voice she was usually about to inquire after her family.

The phone jarred them both. "I'll get it," Cora said, with relief.

"Hello, Cora?"

"Elana, how are you?"

"Fine. Just called to check in. You sound a little down."

Cora stared at the blue and white cornflower wallpaper in the kitchen. She closed the door. "Oh, well."

"Well, what?"

"Well, I guess I was thinking about when I might come back to the commune."

"What's the matter, is Saint Fiona getting on your nerves?"

"No, I just want to come back." She rushed ahead recklessly. "Gordon and I talked about having the baby at home . . . "

"Listen, Corey, there's something you need to know."

Cora wanted to put her hands over her ears.

"I won't wait any longer for Gordon to be straight with you. You can't come back to the house because . . . "

"Because the new woman is in his room." Cora finished the sentence herself.

She didn't get hysterical, as Gordon might have feared. For a day or two she argued with herself that monogamy was bourgeois. Then rage cleared her head and her eyes grew dry with bitterness. But she would not explode. She had followed her fiery temper once too often. This time she closed down.

Winter, 1969

Other people would have called it a breakdown, she knew, even as she was going through it, for one part of her was always detached, watching. Cora thought about her spell as a lapse, like lapsing from church. Everything was, just, well, a little exaggerated. Such as her dreams. She was walking across tundra, from Yellowknife to Baffin Island to St. John's. It was a long walk, but she wasn't tired. Or cold. There were so many fires. Campfires. Bonfires. Napalmfires. Strange to see steaming rainforest in the arctic. Everything smelled of smoke. She had been trying to get her father to quit smoking for years. She thought of Los Alamos. Dresden. The San Francisco earthquake fire. Jack London. You needed fire in the wilderness, to maintain body temperature. Of course there was hell. Flaming hell.

Did she want a drink, Fiona was asking.

Wasn't she sleeping?

A baby wailed.

Baby?

Her baby.

No, it was so cold. She was delirious. Cora tried to go back to sleep, then realized that if she wasn't asleep, she was awake. She lay in bed shivering, seeing Sara's face. Sara; she missed Sara so much.

But this wasn't Sara. She had a man's body. A big, hairy man's body and a black and gold Omega watch. Impossibility/possibility: two sides of the same word, growing out of one another. Was Canada now impossible? God, it felt hot in here.

No, Fiona said, you must keep on the covers. She pleaded with Fiona not to call a doctor who would lock her up like Mom. Fiona agreed to keep her out of jail as long as she minded the covers. Was she awake again? The baby was gone now. Where would an old woman get a baby? Cora brushed the hair from her forehead, fingers caught in an oily mass of knots. How long had she been in bed?

"It's good to hear you talking." Fiona said.

"Yes," Cora tested her own voice.

"How are you feeling?" She bent over to tuck the covers around Cora's shoulders.

"Fine, fine, did anyone say I wasn't fine?" Cora barked, puzzled by the panic in her voice.

Fingers cracked in the background. The room smelled terribly smokey.

From the back porch, a baby wailed.

Fiona's eyes were small with worry. "I'll be right back, let me check on the wee one."

It was always like this: they were always leaving her. Mom. Mom didn't even say good-bye. Pop—going and coming and going. George and Ron. She told them not to go, warned them about the fires. It had been the same fire that had taken Ralph and now Gordon. Go to hell, Gordon. It had been her fault. She wished him damned, wished them all damned.

"He'll be just fine." Fiona entered with a pot of tea. She was wearing a blue dress now. Rain pinged on the window. Was this the same day the baby cried? Babies cry every day, she told herself. She must be going crazy. No, she was not in a looney bin. She did not know how to sew. George was wrong about her being nuts. And about so many other things. Wrong.

Fiona poured sun into her cup. The old woman wore a red flannel bathrobe and smelled of lavender.

"How are you feeling today?" Her friend inquired.

In the background, Cora heard a baby gurgling. Pain ripped across the back of her head. Her baby. She would not leave her baby.

Cora stared at the stranger she felt she had known all her life. "I have looked deeply and found sanity."

"Very well, dear."

Cora sat up and accepted a cup of tea. "Yes, I'm very well. How is my baby?"

Fiona's mouth softened. "I'll be just back." Her voice caught with excitement. "I'll be just back with the bairn."

Cora kept dropping below the surface that week but continued to fight her way to the top where she heard giggling and crying and wailing. Her family had been waiting for her to fall, had pegged her as the one to follow Mom, but she was choosing to be sane. It was a choice—for deep down she had also found madness—that she would have to keep making for the rest of her life.

○ ○ ○

The baby would be named Fiona. When it came. Of course she realized the noises this week had been imaginary. Here she lay still expanded like a balloon. But she knew it would be a girl and she would name her Fiona.

○ ○ ○

Cora regained her grip two weeks before the water broke. It had just been a lapse, she told Fiona, who, as a solid Presbyterian, did not understand the concept of lapsing. She did understand labor, however, and proved the best of companions as the taxi veered and reeled to the hospital. She sat in the fathers' room as Cora panted and screamed and pushed. When Cora floated up to present tense, she imagined Fiona, sucking on her spearmints, smiling as the men passed out cigars.

"Fiona," she said, presenting her baby to her friend.

The old woman shook her head. She was honored, she said, but her name was unfashionable for a 1960s baby. How about her secret name, what she had always dreamt of being called.

So the child was named Françoise.

Spring, 1969

It rained the April day Fiona took them to the train station. The West Indian conductor nodded enthusiastically when Fiona asked if she might help Cora on the train with the big, patched suitcase. Cora felt so exhausted from Fran's crying that she let Fiona persuade her to get a berth rather than a coach seat for the three-day journey to Toronto.

Passengers pushing. Conductors shouting. Porters flashing in and out. The baby crying. Fiona crying. Cora crying. She hung on to Fiona as they hugged good-bye. Of course it was the right thing to go to Toronto, to take the job at Fiona's cousin's restaurant. This would make a good, fresh start for herself and Fran in a new city in their new country. Of course, she argued back to herself, it also made sense to stay here, where she had friends like Fiona and Vicky and Elana. The memories of Gordon—which rocked between tenderness and fury—haunted her whenever she walked downtown. What if she ran into him? What if she didn't? She couldn't bear the possibility of another lapse. Thus instinct—and perhaps a little cowardice and perhaps a little adventure—drove her further east, further away from Grandview. Back and forth she went with these thoughts as the train was grinding to a start. The whistle sounded. Cora looked outside to see Fiona waving and dabbing her eyes with a white lace handkerchief.

٭ ٭ ٭

Fran finally settled down when they reached the Fraser Canyon and Cora stared incredulously as the train balanced along the rim of this earthen rift. She felt a terrible sadness at leaving Fiona.

Cora looked out at the green trees insisting spring into the winter hillside. A hawk flew beside the train for a few yards. The far mountains were still peaked with snow. British Columbia, Alberta, Saskatchewan, Manitoba, Ontario: a whole new world to learn. Her daughter would study this geography in school. Fran's face revealed tiny movements: pursed lips, wrinkled nose, eyes rolling beneath the transluscent lids. So calm. So trusting. Such red hair.

Elana had crocheted the pale green baby dress. "You have to do something with your hands at meetings," she had shrugged when presenting the delicate outfit to Cora in the hospital. "And I've given up smoking."

Now Cora ran through her list of reassurances. Fiona planned to come to her cousin's for Christmas. Elana, who had a brother in Toronto, promised to visit. Meanwhile, they would all keep in touch. Sunday phone calls were cheap. And there was always the post. Cora fought back tears.

The thin Ukranian woman across the aisle was going to visit her family. Cora understood there was a huge Ukranian population in Alberta, and she wanted to know more about it. But the woman was fascinated by Cora. "You're brave to go to to Toronto alone."

Cora didn't think she was brave. There was a difference between necessity and courage. Besides, she wasn't alone.

VI

NINETEEN

Fall, 1988
Oregon

"Maybe you could pick up a six pack and some of those cheese Doritos on your way back from the high school reunion." He watched TV as he instructed her.

"Sure, Pop. I might also experiment by buying something nourishing." She bent down to check the hem of her flowered cotton skirt. Was she too dressed up? Maybe she should have worn pants. She pulled a silver barrette from her pocket to hold the long black hair off her face.

"Don't be gone all day."

"I'm just having lunch with Sara," she bristled in spite of herself. She hated buying him alcohol. Still, he wasn't going to turn sober in order to make a saintly exit.

"Who knows how long women can talk?"

"Sure, Pop." Cora kissed his bald spot. "See you around 3:00, OK?"

He did not answer.

Follie began to bark and continued yapping frantically as Cora rolled down the driveway.

She was grateful for her father's cantankerousness. Pop had always been fueled by anger. Sometimes when she heard the old crank yell, she could forget about the increasing frailty. Sometimes.

Waiting at a traffic light, she found her attention drawn to a stout man with a blanket around his shoulders hobbling across the street. He looked uncannily like Ralph. No, she could see that his nose was much longer and his jawline softer. Would Sara bring up the subject of Ralph? Probably not, he had never really been her friend. She had likely forgotten most of the details of that ancient incident.

A car honked from behind. She shifted into first, proceeding to the Milk Barn, reminding herself that she had no idea of Sara's college memories.

The Milk Barn looked much the worse for wear with its fading sign and weathered grey siding. She was surprised that it was still functioning, given that the town not only had a McDonald's but also a Burger King and a Jack-in-the-Box. Who wanted to hang out in this antediluvian cafe when you could have all the neon, rock music and MSG you wanted at the sleek chain restaurants? Well, the old place had an ambience. She remembered afternoons she and Sara and Margaret and Kate used to spend here talking about boys. Then that last spring in high school when they all came here *with* their boyfriends. Michael Kelsey wasn't exactly a date, but he had had as much aversion as she to being labeled a social retard, so they made an unspoken agreement to escort each other to required places. She was still astonished when she thought about him trying to kiss her after the senior prom, but she suspected that had something to do with the jug wine they drank behind the gym while everyone else was twisting and shouting.

Cora had trouble adjusting her eyes to the light as she walked in. The same old Milk Barn. She smelled the chocolate syrup and ketchup and hamburger grease. Boys returning from Vietnam had said they dreamt about Milk Barn hamburgers in the swamps. Yet another reason not to go to Vietnam, she had joked to Ron, who hadn't laughed. Cora's heart stopped as the waitress turned around. Gretel—still here after all these lifetimes. The tough, wiry woman must be in her eighties now. How many high school romances had she chaperoned? Of course it was unlikely that Gretel would remember her, and Cora, not wanting to risk disappointment, looked away. But Gretel waved, nodded and pointed to the corner booth where Sara was sitting, flipping through yellow juke box cards extending from the wall.

"Thanks Gretel."

The juke box ground to a start. "A hank of hair and a piece of bone and a walkin', talkin' honeycomb."

Cora made her way across the room of diners, all her generation or older, she noticed. Grinning, she waved to Sara, who waved back. She was flooded with fondness for this friend, whom, she now remembered, always managed to arrive everywhere even earlier than herself.

Sara was handsomely turned out in a green wool knit dress and paisley silk scarf. Her hair was drawn back from her face. She looked like a professor, Cora thought. She found herself inspecting Sara for signs of aging—gratified, then sympathetic, as she noticed the wrinkles and slight fatigue in this very familiar face.

Cora slid into the booth. They held hands, beaming.

"Never thought I'd see the day," Sara was shaking her head.

Cora studied her nervously. She noticed that Sara frosted her hair and that her tiny gold earrings bobbed up and down as she talked. She had never before thought about the ears and the jaw being so closely connected.

"Come in, Cora. Same old Cora." Sara was laughing. "You always used to get distracted like this."

"I did?" The familiarity eased her suspicions. "My daughter complains about that too."

"To think we're all grown up with children. God, I need a drink, why did I suggest a soda fountain?"

Laughing, they both looked more relaxed. Suddenly Gretel was standing there, notebook and pencil in her spotted, competent hand.

"Cheeseburger and a Coke, no fries, please Gretel," Cora said automatically.

"I'll have the same," Sara grinned.

"Let's not be too grown up yet," Cora said, remembering her resolution to keep the conversation superficial. "Gossip first. Whatever happened to Becky Murdoch?"

As they proceeded through the names, Cora was surprised to learn how many of her high school girlfriends had stayed in Grandview. Only one or two had gone as far as Portland. Cora tried to hide her disappointment. Who was to say her life was any better spent? Still, she didn't stop comparing.

Sara was grinning. "I always thought you'd recover from your modesty, Corey. It seems you really had no idea who you were in those days, what you might accomplish."

"Did you?"

"Oh, yes, but then I've taken a much more predictable track—from doctor's daughter to lawyer's wife; from school valedictorian to college professor. You were always more idiosyncratic, more original . . . I don't know."

Cora tried not to hear, "crazy," "dissociated." "Original," Jacques also called her original.

"So tell me about *your* 'track,' " she switched the focus back to Sara. "About Richard and your girls. What are their names? Did you bring pictures?"

Once Sara got going, she talked nonstop. It had always been like this. Cora enjoyed the photos and the description of her family and the discussion of her career trials. But it was hard to keep concentrating because Sara's parameters were so alien: problems with the two houses and the prep school tuition.

Sara checked her watch and changed the topic determinedly. "So you've been working as a journalist? Corey, you were always great at writing. I used to think you'd wind up doing Broadway plays."

"You did?"

"Sure, you were so good at understanding people's relationships. You figured out the motivations of kids in our group long before I did. I was still caught up arguing ideologically. And you had, I don't know, a more practical, common sense attitude."

Were they going to talk about Ralph? She could feel her face flushing. "What I want to know," Sara paused and took a breath.

Here it comes, thought Cora, summoning the answers she had practiced about why she had left so abruptly and had never been back in touch.

"What I want to know is how did you find the courage to do it?"

"Do it?" Cora swallowed the last of her Coke, then sipped the iced water.

"Go to a new country. Start a life by yourself. Take a risk at becoming something as . . . well, as unpredictable as a journalist."

"Oh," Cora pursed her lips and opened her eyes wide to keep from laughing. "*That*. You think I'm a fool?"

"No," Sara searched her face. "Maybe it's just that compared to you, I feel like such a cop-out. Maybe I'm glad you exist and at the same time I wish you didn't."

"But, as you said," Cora frowned, "we began from different places."

"Hmmm," Sara let her eyes wander over the cafe. "You know, I've hardly asked you about Jacques . . . or Fran. How old is she? And your Pop? How is he doing? There was such a rift before you left. Remember when I helped you move out of the house? How are you two getting along?"

❋ ❋ ❋

Follie's barking welcomed Cora as she hauled the two brown grocery bags from the car. The television was going full blast. As she set down the bags and fumbled for her key, she heard voices. Pop and . . . she couldn't make out the other one. She wasn't prepared for this; the boys weren't due from Medford for a couple of days. Oh, it had been stupid to go off to lunch with Sara. She felt completely unsettled by the afternoon: revealing too much to Sara, making Pop mad and leaving an opening for George and Ron. What did she expect, that they would ambush her as she walked in the house? Taking a long breath, she opened the door.

Fran was sitting, lotus position, on the ottoman shaking her fist at Pop, who was pretending to be angry. Cora felt that peculiar jealousy again as she saw how easily her daughter could talk with the old bear.

"About time," he growled. "Did you get the beer?"

"Would my life be worth anything if I came home without it?" Cora winked at Fran.

She shifted the bags into the kitchen and called out, "Beer, Pop? And what will you have, Fran?"

"Nothing, Mom." Fran followed and lowered her voice, "I thought that after you caught your breath we could take a little walk. Maybe check out that state park Aunt Min was talking about?"

"Leaving me again," he barked. "What do you think this place is, a heliport?"

Fran shrugged, regarding her mother seriously.

Cora whispered, "Can it wait until tomorrow?"

No, Fran shook her head firmly.

Too many worlds converging—Pop, Fran, Sara, soon George and Ron. Cora wished she could simply step offstage for an hour and crawl into bed with Jacques.

"OK, let me get Pop a snack and change into my jeans. I'll be right with you."

He accepted the tray. "You're going again, aren't you?"

"Just for a quick jog, Pop. You know young people, they need exercise." The flimsy explanation seemed to pacify him. She poured herself the last of the coffee and handed her keys to Fran. "You drive."

Once they got to the bottom of the hill, Cora asked, "Everything OK at Aunt Min's?" She had hoped for another night alone with Pop, but if Fran was unhappy, there was no reason they couldn't pick up her things and take them back to Pop's.

"Yes." Fran's voice was taut. "Let's wait until we're in the woods to talk."

Puzzled, but too tired to press further, Cora listened to the tires scrunch along the gravel road.

Fog hung low and the wind was still strong. Mist washed their faces as they trudged north through a stand of Douglas fir. Fran walked fast, as if setting after a particular goal. Absently, Cora wondered how she would maintain her spikey coiffure here in damp Oregon. Maybe Tommie would recommend her barber. She hoped not, because she did, in fact, agree with Pop that Tommie looked like a concentration camp refugee.

"You OK?" Cora asked again.

"Sure," Fran nodded, glancing over her shoulder. "But I've got some news about family politics."

Annoyed by the cryptic response, Cora waited.

"Apparently Edie is starting a local youth chapter of AFN."

Cora regarded Fran closely. "AFN?"

"Americans for Freedom in Nicaragua. It's a far-right organization. Don't you remember we saw a special on them in the motel—in Utah or Colorado—they interviewed Vietnam vets, businessmen, some conservative politicians?"

"Yes." Cora remembered vaguely a night last week when Fran had been plugged into the television while she, herself, lay in bed, exhausted from a day of driving, longing for darkness and silence. Of course she should have been familiar with them from her work on the Central American piece. She had spent so many years trying to become a Canadian journalist, putting blinders on the American perspective, and she guessed she had achieved some dubious success.

"What's more," Fran lowered her voice. "Uncle George—George—has been involved with the group. It's really quasi-illegal stuff. Run by some rich reactionary named Rhinehart."

Cora reflected on her initial unfavorable impression of Edie. She also felt a strange, unwelcome loyalty to George. What was Edie—or Fran, for that matter—doing gossiping about his illegal activities?

"You OK, Mom?"

"Sure," Cora tried to sound ironic, "it's heartwarming to discover patriotism in the bosom of one's family." She remembered the broadcast now—about a private group that had been pressuring Congress to send troops to Central America, which had supplied arms to anti-Communist mercenaries long before Lieutenant Colonel North entered the picture.

The mist had thickened to light rain. A thin shard of light sliced beneath grey clouds along the horizon. Simultaneously, they turned toward the car.

"How did Edie come to tell you all this?"

"I don't know. I think she was trying to win me over."

"Win you over?"

"Away from Tommie. Sibling rivalry, I guess. Anyway, Edie really believes in this stuff and thought I'd be impressed by the *seriousness* of the cause, and she's strange about her pride in George's involvement and all."

Cora considered the astonishment on Fran's face, wondering if her daughter was, for the first time, beginning to understand their sticky, tangled family.

As they reached the car, Cora asked again, "Are you sure you're all right at Aunt Min's? I mean, do you want to move in with Pop and me tonight?"

"No," she shook her head, ducking into the front seat. "Besides, tonight I have a coffee date with Tommie. Who knows what I'll learn there."

Cora engaged the windshield wipers and concentrated on the road.

"She wants to take me to some local antique curiosity called the Milk Barn."

o   o   o

Cora found herself whistling as she made the salad. Well, perhaps she was just relieved Fran was OK.

She hated this AFN business. Hated that her family was involved in it. But what could she do? She thought about Georgie Boy on the pitcher's mound. Hey, Georgie Boy, Georgie Boy. What could she do? Georgie Boy was going to win one game or another, one way or another.

She looked forward to the evening with Pop. Who knew what would happen when the boys came? Given George's talent for tortuous delay that could be weeks. Was there something particular she wanted to discuss with Pop? No, there was everything. Everything in their small window of time. Really, they should be talking more about the cancer. But he detoured whenever she got near the topic.

He was watching the news when she brought in the steaming plate of chicken, broccoli and boiled potatoes. She thought to herself, this is probably the healthiest food either of us has eaten in weeks.

"Hmmm," he said, not taking his eyes off the screen.

She collected her plate and sat on the couch watching Robert MacNeil interview Harrison Salisbury.

"Best news on TV," he announced between bites. "The most objective."

She disagreed. "None of them are objective. But these public TV types are more intelligent."

He didn't speak for a long time, intent on his dinner. Her heart swelled with domestic pride.

"He's Canadian, you know?"

"Robert MacNeil? Oh, yes." She smiled, appreciating the friendly gesture. "How about a little more chicken? Or the potatoes—they're your favorite."

"Yeah, OK," he was absorbed in a report about the federal budget deficit.

Over coffee, she finally dared to say, "Do you mind if we turn off that thing for a while?"

He contained his surprise. "Well, I guess if I've seen the local news and an hour of MacNeil-Lehrer, I don't also need Dan Rather. But you'd be surprised, sometimes CBS has something completely different on."

"I'm sure."

All of a sudden he was rambling. "I was thinking about the family just this morning, about how after Louise died and Min came to help with the children. Ron broke his arm—his right arm—soon after that, and it was a tough year because we were in a new house." He continued for ten minutes, describing their move step-by-step. "People said it was crazy to move at a time like that, but I thought we'd all go nuts if we didn't leave. Min was awful good. The children all loved her."

"Yes, Pop," she spoke calmly despite her distress at being described in the third person. "I was *there.*"

"Of course you were." He picked up a bottle from beside his chair. She noticed for the first time that he had put a six pack on the floor between the recliner and the end table. He was halfway through it. Slllop, he twisted off the cap. "You know you're part of me."

"No. You're part of me."

"Flesh and blood," he countered.

"But it goes the other way. I inherited characteristics from *you.*"

"You're so smart, you're the one with the college education. You explain inheritance to me."

She dredged up dominant and recessive genes from a sophomore biology class.

He listened intently. When she finished, he repeated, "You're part of me. I knew that. Even during the last twenty years, I always knew it. You had to come back."

Astonished, she wondered whether he was saying that her return had been genetic destiny.

"I always had faith in you," he continued, answering everything at once.

TWENTY ✸

Summer, 1983
Toronto

July 1. Not the wisest of times to move in Toronto. Cora hadn't checked the thermostat, but it was sweltering, even at 7 P.M. However, she hadn't exactly *chosen* this time. She had never been adept at choice. The wind seemed to move her. Or circumstance. Sweat trickled down her cheeks. She could hear Pop now. "Just not used to a real day's labor." With this, she heaved another box from the car to the sidewalk in front of the house she and Jacques and Fran had found to rent in this downtown Italian neighborhood.

On top of the box was the old, framed photo of Fiona holding "wee Fran," as she called her fourteen years ago. Fiona would approve of this move—out of an impersonal apartment and into a real community. In fact, Fiona would have a chance to see for herself, for when she phoned last week, she had promised to come for Christmas.

These modest, multicolored rowhouses were occupied by large families and dogs and cats. The old man across the street, Mr. Caputo, seemed as friendly as he was curious. Delicious dinner smells seeped from neighbors' houses—garlic, oregano, tomato—big meals even on a hot night. The yards were cluttered with tricycles and baby carriages and birdbaths. People *lived* on this block. It felt so much more vital than the high rise she and Fran had been occupying on the edge of Cabbagetown, although she would miss the character of Parliament Street. Not surprisingly, Jacques—with his network of political friends—had been the one to find this place.

"More books?" Jacques called from the top floor window of what was to be Cora's study. Study, the idea of an entire room for her work was extravagant to Cora. It seemed absolutely necessary to Jacques.

"Only a couple of more boxes," Cora called up, moderating her volume so as not to disturb the neighbors.

"Be right down," Jacques yelled back in his ringing Quebecois accent.

And he was right down before Cora unloaded the last box. Cora was almost as impressed with his boundless energy as she was with his fine brown eyes.

"How's it going, *chérie?*"

"How *can* you be so buoyant in this heat?" Cora asked.

"Hot? This is nothing compared to Montreal."

"You say the same in winter," Cora laughed. " 'This is nothing compared to Montreal.' " She smiled with the pleasure of having known Jacques an entire winter and spring.

"*C'est vrai.* Toronto is nothing compared to Montreal in any way, except, perhaps, the case of its rapturous American immigrants."

"Oh, please." Cora closed her eyes.

"Hey, Jacques," Fran leaned out a second-story window, "I thought you were going to help me with the stereo."

"I'll be right up," Jacques shouted back.

"The stereo?!" exclaimed Cora. "This is her idea of priorities: plugging in the stereo?"

"Pretty, these Americans, yet a little stodgy." Jacques shook his head and shifted the box on his hips. "Music is good for unpacking the soul."

"OK," Cora heard Aunt Min in her voice, "but not too loud."

Jacques laughed his way into the house.

Cora continued unloading, thinking about her first meeting with Jacques on the high school track near her old apartment. Well, it was hard to pinpoint the *first* encounter because she had been noticing Jacques out of the corner of her eye that autumn for several weeks before they spoke, watching the big-boned dark man lope by as she had plodded along in her modest jog.

They had been jogging at the same time for perhaps a month before Jacques slowed down to talk with her. Cora knew she was in trouble, because she could barely maintain this speed in silence. How could she carry on a conversation and run at the same time?

"You'll get more mobility if you position your hands this way," Jacques was explaining.

Cora liked his accent almost as much as his body.

"And if you hold your back a little straighter, it will be easier to breathe."

But she didn't care for his instructive tone. A current of irritation crossed Cora's face. Perhaps Jacques noticed.

"Otherwise you have good form. You been running long?"

Cora couldn't shake her annoyance at this man whom she just met—finally met—starting out with a criticism. "Running from a lot of people for a long time." Maybe if she were brusque enough, the guy would piss off.

Jacques hadn't come the next day or the next. Later that week, he was finishing his run as Cora arrived. He waved to her in a wide, friendly arch before beginning warm-down exercises.

Cora waved back, disappointed the contact would be so brief.

The following week, Cora made a point of arriving earlier and on the second day, caught Jacques before he began running.

"Thanks for the tip," she sounded cordial, but not eager. "The running's going better now."

"*Bien sûr,*" Jacques smiled.

It took two months for them to find the time and courage to have an orange juice *après* track.

The body of Cora's car rose higher and higher as she removed boxes, the axles groaning with pleasure. "Sorry, Irma," Cora whispered because not even Fran knew she talked to her car. "I won't let this happen for a very long time again." Oh, god, she hoped this was true. She hoped she wasn't making a mistake moving in with Jacques. After Gordon, she had never again lived with a lover. How did you keep from getting in each other's hair all the time? Would sunny Jacques find her too shy? Too intrusive? Maybe she would hate Jacques's housekeeping. She already knew he shed newspapers everywhere he went. Maybe the romance would wear away more quickly when their toothbrushes slouched in the same glass each night.

While she would like to pin all her doubts on Fran and how the move would affect her fourteen-year-old daughter, the truth was that Fran liked Jacques and was always complaining about their cramped apartment. No, these worries about living with Jacques were all her own.

"We'll save money this way," Jacques replied when Cora said perhaps they should wait until Fran graduated from high school.

"I'll be at the printshop all day," Jacques answered when Cora said she needed time and space to write.

"I'll buy you earplugs," he said when asked if he planned to play Nana Mouskouri day and night. Nana Mouskouri was a great favorite of Fran's as well.

So it was that Jacques, Fran and Cora began to house hunt and much too soon for Cora's equilibrium, found the *perfect* place—two bedrooms, a living room, a study, a garden—on the west side of town.

"That's it," Cora sighed to Irma. "The last load. Now, let's see if they're making progress inside; if there is life beyond the stereo." She picked up a lamp and a wastebasket.

Entering the living room where, indeed, Fran and Jacques were still fiddling with the Victrola, Cora demanded, "What is that weird smell?"

"Dinner from next door," Fran raised her eyebrows. "Smells good, eh?"

"No, I mean that kind of incensey smell, like something burning."

"Oh, that's the sage. To clear away old spirits and make the house tran-
quil." Fran said matter-of-factly.

Cora set down the lamp, then the wastebasket. Shaking her head, she
went back to the car.

Fran and Jacques dashed in front of her.

"Beat you down," Fran laughed.

"Not on your life," Jacques roared.

Cora closed her eyes, imagining two broken necks at the bottom of the
stairwell. Within seconds, it seemed, they were bounding up the steps toward
her, each effortlessly transporting two boxes. Cora moved aside.

"*Voilà!*" Jacques slapped his hands together. "I think this calls for a
gelato. Yes, Fran?"

"Sure. How about you, Mom, wanta go down to College for some ice
cream?"

"No, I think someone should stay here in case the plumber calls."

"Aw, Mom, he's not going to come in the evening."

"You never know! And you'll be the first one to start complaining about
the shower."

"No way," Fran huffed.

"You know I'm right," said Cora.

"Yes, Ma'm. But we'll bring you something, eh? What would you like?"

"Well, I wouldn't say no to an amaretto and chocolate combo."

" 'Sadeal. Back in a flash."

Cora held her breath as they raced down the stairs again. She reminded
herself that she had never seen anything with a broken neck, not even the
ducks George had thrown off the roof. She felt so lucky right now, listening
to the two of them chatter on their way out of the house. What had she done
to deserve Jacques? She reminded herself that he wasn't perfect. He talked
too much, was a fitness freak and could be overly cheerful, but given the scale
of personal defects, she could cope.

She lugged a last box down the hall. Kitchen utensils—from the Salvation Army, Woolworths, a sale at Eatons—and mismatched glasses. Grinning,
she thought about the elegant china and crystal she had imagined herself acquiring by the time she was grown up. Was she grown up now? Now that she
had a teenage daughter and a partner and a running automobile? Opening
the back door, she felt a breeze and sat down on the garden steps.

Tomatoes ripened on the back vine—a legacy from Joe and Dacia An-
drotti, who had moved their family to a new tract in Etobikoke. The sharp,
pungent aroma calmed her. Next year she would plant basil and tomatoes together. Perhaps a few ranunculuses over by the fence. And a double-dug bed
for herbs if she got really ambitious. She closed her eyes.

She had come this far and it was OK. All her doubts had been pointless. She remembered when she and Fran arrived in Toronto that spring of

1969; remembered how disappointed she had been to learn that Fiona's cousin worked way up in North Toronto. Yet, if she hadn't lived there, she might not have got the job at York University and started to take courses and then got her degree and met Mr. Rose who gave her the first assignments and . . . And if she hadn't written that article about draft resisters, she never would have met Oscar, who, aside from being one of her dearest friends, had found an apartment for herself and Fran. And if she hadn't been living in that apartment block, she never would have met Jacques and . . .

"Ice cream. Ice cream."

She listened to the two of them calling and giggling. She was lucky, she knew that. She should let them know where she was. But she needed one more minute of solitude. One more minute.

"Well, if it isn't Sloth herself," scoffed Jacques. "To think that we practically inhaled our gelato so you wouldn't be slaving here alone. Do you think we should let her have it?" He raised a magnificent eyebrow.

"Might as well," Fran shrugged, "both of us hate amaretto."

"Right then." Jacques handed over the half-melted cup of brown and beige ice cream. "What profound thoughts have you been spawning to deserve this?"

"I've been thinking how we met. About how I hung around the track waiting for you to show interest."

"Now that's what your Aunt Min would call an Irish lie!" Jacques set his hands on his hips.

"What do you mean? I did. I got there earlier and earlier until I found you." She sipped the melted ice cream from her cup.

"No wonder we met. I kept going later and later."

"I've heard this routine before." Fran turned. "Mind if I go fiddle with the stereo?"

"OK," Cora steadied her voice. She *did* want an independent daughter. "But don't . . . electrocute yourself."

"Yes, Ma'm, I'll do my best."

Jacques winked at Fran, then sat down on the stoop, hitting his hip against Cora's for space.

Contented and aroused, Cora took another long breath of tomato perfume.

"You OK?"

"Hmmm." Cora rested her head on Jacques's shoulder. She smelled the mixture of Badedas and Jacques's own scent.

"You're not too tired?"

"No, just a midthirties, midevening slump. Why?"

"You didn't mind that I mentioned your Aunt Min?"

"No, why?"

"Sometimes you get sensitive about her."

"I guess I feel guilty."

"But you write to her a lot."

"Every few months is a lot?"

"You told me you were out of contact for something like ten years."

"There was nothing I could do about that." Cora tensed. It had taken her months to tell Jacques the stories of her family, of the draft office. She had explained most of it. But there were still parts that revealed themselves at odd moments—as if her life had not taken place over time but rather had taken over time. She trusted him, as much as she trusted herself.

"Say now," Jacques ran his index finger gently down Cora's spine. "Who's criticizing? I think it was brave of you to write her the first time, every time for that matter."

"Aunt Min wouldn't tell Pop or the boys where I am. And the way I send letters, through Oscar's mother in Albany, they'd never trace me."

"All right, you're a coward. That's exactly why I fell in love with you. I adore cowards."

Cora shook her head.

"One thing I don't understand," he said.

"Only one?"

"Well," he began cautiously, "what does your Aunt Min say about the need for secrecy? Does she understand about the fire, about Ralph's death?"

Cora shrugged, "No, I doubt that she thinks about the subterfuge much. She just wants to be in touch. There's so much I want to tell Aunt Min. Partial contact like this is even more painful than no connection. If that makes sense."

"For a perfectionist, it makes complete sense."

"Jacques. Jacques, can you help me up here? I'm trying to reassemble the socket."

Their eyes widened.

"Reassemble the socket?" Jacques barely concealed his alarm. "Maybe I'll go up and check on Thomas Edison."

"I'd appreciate that." Cora used all her will power to stay put.

Teaspoons in the far right compartment. Then knives. Then forks. Soup spoons in the top. Tablespoons. Grapefruit spoons. Demitasse spoons. She had never seen so many spoons. Did the French eat more liquid foods? Or were they more fastidious? The things you never knew you didn't know until you shacked up with someone.

When the family was packing to leave Torrence, Cora recalled, she couldn't believe the amount of scraps Mom had collected. There were old dresses from Aunt Helen, for doll clothes, of course. But also small swatches for quilts and hook rugs. The basement closet was filled with scraps.

Pop had made George throw away his comic book collection. Cora thought her brother might explode, but he had learned by then how to humor Pop, had developed an almost military art of obedience. Cora imagined that this had stood him well in Vietnam. Yes, sir, and into the fire went Batman, Archie, and some of the more adult books that she was sure Pop had never seen. Everyone had to leave something behind.

Nana Mouskouri was belting it out from the living room. Not so loud, though, that Cora wouldn't hear a bloodcurdling scream if Jacques and Fran were being electrocuted. Everything was probably all right, she told herself, and closed the door. She switched on the radio and swiveled the dial for the CBC news.

Time passed swiftly as Cora unpacked dish towels, tablecloths, napkins, pots, pans, mixers and dishes. She enjoyed being alone with the news of the world, but she was also happy when Jacques stuck his head in the kitchen.

"Are you planning to sleep tonight?"

"Is that an invitation?"

"The only one I'm making today." Jacques surveyed Cora's accomplishments. "Pretty good. Have you considered moving as a profession? Must pay better than journalism."

Cora's eyes welled with tears.

"Say, are you OK?"

"A little tired," she said.

"Then I insist that you accept my invitation."

Cora smiled and followed Jacques up to bed.

Cora listened to Jacques's slow, even breathing. Above that, she could hear Fran tapping her feet to the music that was coming through her earphones. She thought of Ron playing the clarinet. Outside, two blocks away, the College Street tram rattled by. The occasional truck screeched to a halt and then sputtered to life again. Nothing from next door, except the random noise of pipes. She was relieved to have quiet neighbors.

Her eyes adjusted to the darkness, or rather to the dimness, and she thought how pretty the room would look when they painted it blue and bought a couple of lamps.

Jacques stirred.

She kissed his ear gently.

He ran a tongue over her shoulder.

Cora held still, needing to contain herself a moment longer in this new bed, in this new house, in this new life. The humidity was thick and already she felt damp beneath the cool flowered sheet. Was the fan still packed?

He pulled back his tongue and bit her shoulder.

She turned and kissed his lips, then found herself kissing Jacques the length of his muscular body. His biceps. His hips. Calves. Toes.

Slowly, he entered her. They rocked. She squeezed him. Tight. Tighter. As he moved to her rhythms, she could feel their sweat wash together. He pushed deeper. She moaned softly, softly until she came with a burst of contractions, followed by quiet lapping, sighing. Then she could feel his own climax flooding her. Yes, Cora lay beside Jacques. Yes.

Blue paint. Running around the track. Soup spoons. Grapefruit spoons. Jacques's body inside her own. Amaretto plants in the back yard. Cora was very tired. Demitasse spoons. Yes.

VII

TWENTY-ONE

Fall, 1988
Oregon

She had never shaved a man before, but Pop seemed trusting as he closed his eyes and leaned back. She lathered his face with Colgate foam. Should she start under the ear—or beneath the nose or on the chin? She didn't want to shake his confidence or her own by asking, and suddenly it came to her—a scene over thirty years ago when he stood shaving in front of the bathroom mirror, surrounded by toothpaste, soap, shaving cream. She recalled the precise moment—the morning of her mother's funeral, for she had understood from there on out she would be looking to him for direction. She remembered, now, that he had started under the left ear; thus she began, noticing his shoulders soften as she set the razor against his cheek.

He had grown visibly sicker over the last two weeks, as if he were allowing himself to let go. Did it feel safer now that she was here, to relax, to die? She was grateful to think this might be so. Death, that was what they were all waiting for. The coldness of this thought steadied her. It was now safe to die. For him.

He had always used Colgate foam, and this scent was lush with memory. Although she had never considered it before, she had also remained loyal to Colgate-Palmolive products. Finishing the left side of his face, she applied the razor below his right ear. She itched to turn off the videotape, but *Wheel of Fortune* was one of his favorite programs, a good distraction from her fumbling ministrations.

His skin was barely pink beneath the foam. Today he was walking more slowly, speaking less. She imagined him as an enormous baby, wondering how she would be able to carry him when the time came. Cora was glad this was her father dying rather than her mother. Despite all their years together, despite the raging, the tears and now the frail, passionate hope of reconciliation,

205

she could detach from him in a way that would have been impossible with her mother. She, herself, would never look *quite* like this. Her exit would be different from his, and this knowledge secured their present intimacy.

"Ow! Oh, hell, watch it!" he exclaimed.

She stared at the tiny dot of blood easing carmine into white foam and stepped back. His blood was more a candy apple red than the deep wine color she was used to from Fran's cuts and scrapes.

"Oh, Pop, I'm sorry. Are you OK? Let me get you a cold cloth."

His eyes still closed, he grabbed her arm impatiently, "No, don't bother, it's just a scratch. Only be more careful, will you?"

She had never been as careful as she had in the last couple of weeks, tiptoeing around the past as she struggled to understand each day. She smiled inwardly at the absurdity of herself with a razor this close to Pop's neck. The next stroke was tentative.

He exhaled loudly.

She lifted the razor from his face.

"No, go on, it's not your shaving."

"You're in pain? Can I get you something?"

"Just a wooden box, and that not for a while yet."

"Oh, Pop." She took his hand, which was trembling, then looked up to see tears trickling down the freshly mown cheeks. Did the salt sting?

He made a fist and pounded his knee.

She waited.

"You better finish up or the foam's going to evaporate."

"Yes, Pop." She had done half his moustache when the doorbell rang. Her instinct was to ignore it, but he pushed her away. "Damn Jehovah's Witnesses. Shoo them off."

Follie ran barking to the window.

Still wiping her hands, she opened the door.

Cora found herself facing her older brother. She had been expecting him every day for two weeks now; still, she was startled.

Ron lingered behind, testing each car door to make sure it was locked. He wore earphones and carried a Walkman.

"Welcome home!" George grinned down at her, as if he had answered the door and were ushering her into a surprise party. He hugged her briefly. "Welcome to the prodigal daughter!" There was genuine affection in his eyes.

She smiled back, part calculation and part reflex, abashed by how good it was to see him. Those brown, almost black irises, were exactly the same. And unlike Ron, who had gained thirty pounds over the years, George was his old tall, slim self. The only difference was that he was balding like Pop. He tried to hide it by growing his hair long on one side and combing it over the top. This compensatory male style had always embarrassed her, and it made George seem unexpectedly vulnerable.

The two brothers walked past her into the house. George bent down to calm Follie. "You're no Tenk, but you're still pretty cute." He scratched the spaniel's neck vigorously.

Pop had wiped all the cream off his face and had adjusted his lounger to an upright position. If he had a seatbelt, Cora thought, he would have buckled it.

"Pop!" George patted his father's shoulder with the palm of his right hand.

She always thought her brother had such beautiful hands. Cora recalled his salad days on the pitcher's mound.

"How are you doing today?" George asked heartily.

"Fine, no thanks to you." His angry gaze was steady. "Or to that weak-kneed brother of yours."

Cora turned to see Ron, whose entrance she hadn't noticed, closing the door.

"Old man hasn't changed a whit, eh?" George addressed Cora. "I bet you feel right at home?"

"Yes." She watched him carefully.

"Hmmm, think I smell some of that cowboy coffee. Mind if I go rustle up some for Ron and me?"

Pop stared at the television.

Cora answered automatically. "Help yourself. I made it an hour ago."

When he turned into the kitchen, she noticed a bright red rash on his neck. Aunt Min said he had skin troubles from chemicals used in Vietnam, that the defoliants might have contributed to the slight muscular problems of his oldest son. Saddened, she wondered if they would ever get close enough to talk about these things.

"Hey," George called to Ron. "Fresh coffee. A woman's touch. Life on the ranch is looking up."

Ron sat down and focused on the television, still wearing the Walkman earphones.

"So, Corey, it really is nice to see you." George talked to her through the pantry opening between rooms. His voice had that familiar smokey slowness.

Annoyed by the tears in her eyes, she smiled, nodded.

"Ron tells me you have a beautiful daughter."

She stiffened.

"And that you're a journalist. I knew you would be a writer—you were always good at English."

Cora recalled long ago Saturdays in this house when she read novels and George and his friends shot baskets outside.

"You like life up there, in Canada?"

"Yes." She smiled, interested by her impulse to charm him. "I do."

"Beautiful country. Connie and I went up for the Winter Olympics. Lots of Americans in Calgary."

"Yes," Cora said, biting her tongue. "Not so many in Toronto. More Italians."

She changed the topic. "Do you like Medford?"

"Oh, yes. An all-American town. Good family values. Big enough to be interesting but small enough to be safe. You can't say that about too much of America nowadays."

He carried the mugs back into the living room. "Pop, are you sure I can't get you anything?"

He didn't lift his eyes from the television.

George patted his father's shoulder, then sat down next to Ron on the couch.

Leaning forward in the arm chair, Cora wished she had a mug to keep her hands busy, but she was too wired for coffee. She could feel George's fondness for her and reminded herself not to be seduced by sentimentality.

She glanced over at Pop, tapping her hand to her mouth as she observed the bristles on his chin and on one side of his upper lip. If the boys noticed, they weren't saying anything.

"I understand he missed yesterday's appointment at the hospital." George's voice was cool, formal.

Pop glared at him.

"You didn't mention an appointment?" she asked, despite knowing George would perceive her incompetence as ammunition to hospitalize him.

For a moment it seemed as if Pop wouldn't answer. He was concentrating on the TV, waiting for the wheel to spin down. Then he shifted toward her. "The doctor switched it to tomorrow."

He looked at George, then past him, "Some people think they know everything."

George shrugged and lit a cigarette. He winked at Ron. "Our sister's weathered pretty well, wouldn't you say? Hard to believe we're all middle-aged." He blew three perfect smoke rings to the ceiling.

"Yeah, Cora, you look terrific." Ron removed the earphones. "A lot younger than Sara Riley."

"Sara," she shot back. "What do you know about Sara?"

"Oh, Ally and I saw her on TV a couple of times. She's a big professor, you know, and gets interviewed about things like 'society and the American family.' 'American,' that's a laugh. She married some kind of Communist."

They fell silent.

George was staring absently out the window, the cigarette burning between his fingers. "Remember the day we moved in here?" he asked.

"Yeah," Ron said. "I remember unloading boxes for nine hours non-stop."

"Yeah, yeah." George maintained his maritime watch. "But what did you think about?"

"I missed the first house," Cora answered, "the 'old-fashioned' house."

"I wondered how I was going to cover the mortgage," added Pop, without taking his eyes from Vanna White.

"What about you?" Cora asked. "What did you think about, George?"

"I thought about that ocean out there, about how I was going to get me a sailboat and cross the Pacific." He looked back to her, his face becoming set again. "Stupid the things kids think about."

"Not really," said Ron, ambling back from the kitchen with another cup of coffee. "After all, you *did* cross the ocean—when you went to 'Nam. All of us crossed that ocean."

Cora cleared her throat. She caught Pop's quick, ironic glance.

"Well, almost all of us," Ron continued. "Anyway, that's why people have picture window views—to help them dream."

George cracked his knuckles, then looked at the time. "We better go pick up the girls or they'll be wondering what happened."

Ron gulped his coffee.

"Connie and Ally wanted to check out this antique fair in Florence." George filled in. "I thought it was just as well—nice for us to have a smaller family reunion first, before they joined us. We promised to take them out to lunch on that floating restaurant."

"We'll be back tomorrow," said Ron.

"Or the next day," George put in. "Can't tell yet. But we have time. I've got some business in the area. Ron's taking a small vacation. We'll see you when we see you."

"We're not going anywhere," Pop said.

Cora swallowed hard. You couldn't count on anything from George—that he would arrive at a certain time or on a particular day. After all, Ron said they had planned to come two weeks ago. He controlled people by surprising them. You never knew how long he might stay. She felt those familiar tugs of pity and fear she always experienced with George.

"What are you coming back for?" Pop kept his eyes on the television.

"Oh, I understand they show reruns of *The Donna Reed Show* on Wednesday afternoon and I wanted to bone up for 'Trivial Pursuit.' " George rolled his bloodshot eyes.

"God knows where you got your sense of humor." Pop shook his head. "I suppose I don't have no say in who comes through my door any more."

"Oh, Pop," coaxed Cora, "they're just paying a visit. You're always complaining no one comes to see you." She tensed, noticing her mother's tone and pacing.

"You too?" he asked.

She wondered.

"We'll leave you to argue the finer points of hospitality." George grinned. "See you."

"Right," Ron patted her lightly on the back. "See you later, Sis."

After they left, she waited for him to explode, but he continued, numbly, to watch the TV. She, herself, was too taken aback by a mixture of fondness and fear to react. Finally she said "Shall I finish the shave, sir? I think there were just a few whiskers."

"Naw," he grunted and turned off the television. "Naw." Slowly, he elevated himself from the chair. "I gotta get some rest. Didn't sleep so well last night." He limped haltingly toward the back of the house.

She considered the empty living room, sensing their presence still—the affection, antagonism, shared humor, separate memories, their completely different lives rooted in the same home—feeling again the mixed possibilities. Glancing out at the ocean, she recalled her own plans of crossing it. As a teenager, she hoped to visit Yokahama and Tokyo and the other Japanese ports her father had described. Later, she fantasized about traveling by train across India, learning a sentence in each of the official languages.

"Aggh," he groaned. She listened carefully, as she had listened for Fran's noises when she was a baby.

"Ahhh," he sounded more comfortable.

Best to leave him alone, she thought. It was even worse to pester him when he didn't need help, than to fail to be there when he did.

She collected mugs from around the living room. Pop's red mug was still half-full of black coffee. Ditto Ron's. George had drained his cup except for a few grains of sugar at the bottom. In the kitchen the hot water felt good on her hands. The Palmolive rose to rich, satisfying suds. She turned the radio on low and found Studs Terkel interviewing a jazz musician.

He slept for an hour, then two, and Cora found her peaceful afternoon filled with a faint menace. She tried to shake the dread by cleaning house, fluffing out cushions, dusting Ganesh and Buddha, straightening out her father's pile of newspapers.

Collapsing in Pop's chair, Cora picked up *The Heart of the Country* and began to read. But she couldn't concentrate. Her eyes were drawn to the television, perhaps because she was sitting in the recliner. So strange, the glossy, dark electronic face. She noticed a line of dust across the bottom of the screen, just above the shelf littered with video tapes. And below the shelf, the VCR machine she had learned to navigate so Pop could see last year's World Series again.

She stared at the screen which had been such a central member of their family. Her eye was caught by a new tape—she was sure it had not been there this week as she was plotting Pop's course through the World Series. "AFN" read the spine. Her breath stopped. Automatically, she knelt before the VCR machine and inserted the tape, modulating the volume so as not to waken Pop. Back in her father's chair, she watched.

School girls with red, white and blue pompons marched to "The Star Spangled Banner." Behind them, an all-male band competently played the national anthem. Then the camera cut to a young man speaking:

"We Americans for Freedom in Nicaragua thank you for showing your support by airing this film at your church, school or community group. Democracy is an international responsibility, and grassroots democratic support in America is the key to Nicaraguan freedom."

The speaker was a pale young man in a forest green suit. He stood on the stage of a school auditorium. Behind him were three American flags and four men, seated uncomfortably on grey metal folding chairs. First, she recognized George, appearing nervous and confined in his dark suit. Next to him sat someone who was dimly familiar. Someone she had known a long time ago, or maybe just a conservative spokesman whom she had seen on the news too many times. Cora hated it when her mind went muddy like this. There was something about this chunky, blond, bearded guy that bothered her. The other two men were also white and middle-aged.

"We rely on your financial, political and *moral* support for democratic rebels in Nicaragua. Of course we ask you to lobby your senators and congressmen, but we cannot rely on our leaders alone. Thanks to the generous contributions of people on this stage," he nodded deferentially to the bearded man, "we know Americans still are a grassroots society."

Who was that guy? Cora wondered. She noticed George grinning anxiously. She imagined the rash on the back of his neck glowing a deeper red.

"As you might suspect, we have our largest support from those who have put their lives on the line for freedom—veterans of World War II, Korea and particularly Vietnam. And I would like to introduce one of the troops right now, "The highly decorated Vietnam vet, George Casey."

Head down, George shuffled toward the microphone. Nervously, he adjusted the mike to his greater height. The first couple of words were lost as he stood too close. "That's blob, blob . . . " The microphone rang loudly. Poor guy, Cora thought, why didn't someone fix it?

George stepped back and tried again. "That's right, Bob. Those of us who fought in faraway swamps aren't going to stand by and watch democracy in our own hemisphere go down the tubes."

The camera shot to the men on metal chairs. Bob was rifling through his notes. The bearded guy was nodding vigorously.

"So we're using our expertise—as pilots, seamen, soldiers, to provide humanitarian supplies to the rebels. We await the day that our congressmen see the light and allow us to be more useful. Meanwhile, we can use your support to . . . "

Pop's door opened. A noise from Pop's room. Cora's heart stopped. Of course she wasn't doing anything wrong. Pop must have dug out the tape while she was shopping yesterday. Maybe he was going to screen it for her. She had a perfect right . . . Still, as she switched off the machine and replaced the cassette, her hands were shaking uncontrollably.

VIII

TWENTY-TWO ✳

Fall, 1988
Oregon

The bell rang. Cora hurried to open the door, thinking once more how her protectiveness about Pop's sleep was similar to the way she used to shield Fran during nap time. And the reflex was equally selfish. She could do with some peace today.

Through the window, she saw Tommie nervously rubbing her hands. Cora was, as always, taken aback by the girl's disguise. Why did she want to say 'disguise'? After all, if anything, she was *revealing* herself with shaved head and clean-scrubbed face. She looked angelic with her coiffure of soft yellow fuzz and her wide blue eyes. The rebel angel. The nose ring put off Cora a bit, but really, Tommie was only a little more extreme than Fran. She was followed up the path by her sister and her mother. Aunt Min walked slowly, carrying her big black purse in one hand and a foil-wrapped package in the other, as if they provided a balance and kept her from tipping over.

"Welcome!" Cora called, nostalgic for her refuge in Toronto. When she had told Mr. Caputo that final morning that she was going to the States, to see her family, she hadn't imagined the impending chaos. Now after twenty years of privacy, everyone was literally landing on the front step. A calculated risk, because with family the door must always be open.

"I baked you this banana bread," Aunt Min set the foil package on the kitchen table. "I remember you used to love it so."

"Thanks. Thanks. It's one of Pop's favorites too. He'll be pleased. He's, uh, he's asleep right now."

"Good, good," said her aunt. "We'll keep our voices low. Won't stay long. We're just running some errands."

"Can I get you something to drink?" Cora offered hectically. "How about some banana bread—from the best baker in Grandview?"

215

"No, no thanks," each said in turn.

Aunt Min sat down in the chair of her sister-in-law. Cora was struck by how much that chair suited women of the generation when one learned to sit erect, without crossed legs. Tommie lay sideways on the couch, her legs dangling over the end.

"I understand George is coming to visit tomorrow," Edie said from her perch on the ottoman. She wore a violet tweed suit and a faint pink blouse. Judging by the time of day, she had probably just been released from her job at Pine Top Savings and Loan.

"Yeah," Cora smiled, making a special effort to be warm to Edie, "he said he'd be back about three o'clock tomorrow. Or the next day."

"Back?" she sat forward.

"He and Ron stopped by the house yesterday," Cora said warily.

"Oh," Edie concealed her disappointment.

"Doesn't George tell his favorite cousin every little thing?" Tommie asked.

"You're jealous of my relationship with George," Edie pressed her cherry red lips together.

Cora's mouth widened.

"He's been like a father to me. A mentor. Since Dad died," she glanced carefully at her mother. "And he would have taken you under his wing, too, if you hadn't gone around flashing your radical ideas."

"It's a free country," Tommie stared at the ceiling, "Or so you say."

"You don't show the least respect for George. You should be honored to have a hero in the family." She turned to her mother. "Shouldn't she, Mom?"

"George is a good man," she pronounced, then nodded to Cora, "All my children are good. I've been blessed."

"Oh, give me a break." Tommie declared.

"See what I mean, no respect . . . " Edie began.

"Well, I think we've stayed about long enough." The old woman pushed herself up from the chair. "We don't want to wake up Uncle Roy."

Edie stood to help her mother. Tommie stayed put.

"You coming?" Edie inquired.

"Actually," Tommie sat up and glanced at Cora, "Actually, I think I need a little fresh air. Think I'll walk home if that's OK, Mom?"

"Sure, dear, whatever you like. But remember to be back by six o'clock. Fran said she'd have her surprise dinner ready for us by then."

Cora listened with interest. She hoped they liked macaroni and cheese.

"Yeah. Six. OK."

Cora and Tommie watched anxiously as Edie helped her mother to the car. When they had gone, Tommie turned to Cora. "I, I wonder if you have time for a talk. I mean if I'm in your way, I can disappear, but there's something . . . "

"Sure," Cora said. "Sit down." She retrieved her cup of cold coffee.

"Place looks good. You've done a lot of work fixing it up."

"No," Cora frowned, vaguely protective of her father, yet house-proud enough to be glad that someone noticed her contribution. All Pop noticed was the vacuum cleaner noise. "Just tidying."

Tommie arched her fair, almost invisible eyebrows, conveying zero tolerance for modesty.

They were silent.

"So how are you?" Cora asked.

"OK," Tommie nodded.

"What are . . . " Cora began.

"Still, he . . . " Tommie's words overlapped.

"Sorry, go ahead," said Cora.

"Still, he must be grateful to have you here." Tommie said.

"He, oh, Pop, yes, in his own way, I suppose he is."

"He's a trip, Uncle Roy."

"Yes," Cora laughed.

They fell silent again.

"Uncle Roy's asleep?"

"Yes, he went down, rather lay down several hours ago."

"I see."

Cora took in Tommie's pointed black leather boots, black slacks, dark purple sweatshirt, black and white scarf. Punk seemed to combine hippie and beat. Sometimes she found punks sullen, but there was a shy idealism about Tommie.

"Could we step out for a minute?"

This was beginning to sound like a Fred Astaire movie, Cora thought.

"Like on the back porch."

"Sure," agreed Cora. "Let me get a sweater."

Cora brushed pine needles off the picnic table benches and ushered Tommie to sit.

"Uncle Roy won't hear us?"

"No, we won't disturb him at all. His bedroom faces the front yard."

Cora breathed in the incense of fir and pine, allowing herself years of deferred Oregon nostalgia.

How strange to think she and Aunt Min were raising their daughters at the same time. Aunt Min here in coastal Oregon and Cora, herself, in clang-bang Toronto. How comforting it would have been to compare notes with Aunt Min about science projects, Girl Guides, swimming lessons, curfews. Still, Cora had to admit, she had been lucky to have Fiona and Elana calling from B.C. And what would she have done without those long nights sitting in smokey apartments hearing tales from other single mothers, levitating their collective consciousness? What would she have done without Juliet Mitchell, Germaine Greer, Florynce Kennedy and Margaret Laurence? Perhaps she had learned the most about endurance from Laurence's Manawaka women. How different would it have been to learn endurance from Aunt Min?

Tommie cleared her throat.

"Yes?" Cora said cautiously. "What did you want to talk about?"

"You understand family?" asked, demanded, the younger woman.

"Sorry?" Cora's voice was cautious.

"I mean you grow up with someone like a sister or brother, and you develop a kind of loyalty, right?"

"Usually," Cora offered.

"Yet sometimes, you also grow up hating them, you know?"

"I guess that's a basic psychological principle."

"But because of the first part—the growing up and the times together—you feel this allegiance."

Cora wished she hadn't opened the door today.

"Still, you can feel conflicting loyalty to someone else at the same time, right?"

"All sounds pretty feasible to me," Cora sighed.

"How do you know which part of your family—which part of yourself—to trust?"

"A universal quandry," said Cora. "But let's ground this a bit."

"Well," Tommie looked her over carefully.

Cora noticed how pink Tommie's scalp was beneath the blond fuzz. She wanted to advise her to pull up her scarf, but refrained.

"Well, I mean, I don't know why I should trust you any more than my own sister. But Fran suggested I talk with you. I don't know if I can trust Fran, for that matter. Frankly, I don't know who I *can* talk to."

Cora concentrated on breathing.

"It's like this. For the last three or four years, Edie has been caught up in this right-wing shit, like Young Americans for Freedom in the old days. Central American support shit. And, you know, I argue with her, although, really, after a while it's just an exercise. But this week, I learned something that sent me through the roof and I started looking closer."

Feeling trapped by the tall trees and the low grey sky, Cora wished that she had suggested they sit in the front yard where they could see the ocean.

"First things first. I found out Edie has been stealing money from Mom."

"What?"

"Maybe five hundred dollars over the last two months. You know, Mom's eyes are failing and Edie studied accounting in school and that's been her 'contribution' to the family lately—doing the books." She sighed.

"I see."

"But that's not all. She's been giving this money to AFN."

Cora recalled her conversation with Fran, her father's checkbook and the video. "George's group."

"Not exactly George's group—it's a huge national network. But yes, the one he's been working for."

"And in the process of finding out about Edie, I discovered a few details about George, that I, well . . . "

"Go on," said Cora.

"I think he's been transporting weapons illegally to Central America." Cora waited.

"It's a royal mess. Anonymous corporate donations. Veterans working as mercenaries. I mean it's a big deal, and George is right in the middle."

"Somehow."

"What?"

"Nothing." Cora wanted this to be a dream. Maybe she was really inside the house, napping in the room across from Pop's. Tommie's story was too grandiose. Too ridiculous. Too feasible.

"How do you know all this?" Cora pulled herself together. Maybe after all, Tommie was the crazy person.

"Putting different pieces together. Eavesdropping. Reading mail. Studying Edie's propaganda. Keeping up with the radical press. Talking to a few people."

Cora didn't want to know any more. She didn't want to know this much.

"Anyway, the reason I found out what I have is that recently there's been some kind of screwup. A guy George trusted ran off with some money, and he needs to cover it quick. He pressured Edie to take more money out of Mom's account this last month and it became obvious something was wrong. I mean, I'm no math whiz, but I could tell things were shorter than they should be. I confronted her, and she, well, told me more than she planned to."

Cora was thinking about how she had convinced herself over the years that she had exaggerated George's maliciousness. Just the sort of attitude a little girl would develop about her big brother.

"Sorry to lay this all on you at once." Tommie hunched forward.

"Oh, no, I'm glad you felt you could trust me. Only I'm not sure where we go from here."

"Me either. I mean I can't come out and tell Mom. It would kill her to hear Edie's been stealing!"

Cora nodded.

"But I *am* going to make Edie quit AFN. I guess I could threaten to turn in her favorite cousin."

"That seems like a lot to take on." Cora cocked her head. "Which, I guess, is one of the reasons you wanted to talk to me."

"Think about it," Tommie took her elbow. "You don't have to make a decision right away, but think about it, will you?"

IX

TWENTY-THREE

Fall, 1988
Oregon

In preparation for the fraternal afternoon, Cora turned back to housekeeping. She tried not to think about Tommie's story for she always did the wrong thing when she reacted rashly. She would let the information simmer and then . . . God, she wished she could talk to Jacques. But Jacques and Oscar were on a camping trip in Algonquin Park, a trip the three of them had planned for months and that Cora herself insisted they take without her. She shook her head, recalling the terror after Ralph's death, desperately confused, yet unable to talk with anyone.

Cora fluffed out the couch cushions, once again taken aback by her reflex to present a perfect house to her sisters-in-law. Curiosity about these women almost overshadowed her dread. While she had never met Ally, she had known Connie briefly and found the older woman sour and demanding. She collected ashtrays, then picked up the newspapers next to Pop's chair.

Of course she didn't know when they would come. It would be George's decision; everyone else dangled from his string. How had this happened? Well, for years he was the "natural" authority in a manless house, Pop's proxy while he was at sea. They all fell into the habit of following his lead. George had never developed the finer skills of consultation. He knew about orders—how to receive orders, how to give them. Perhaps it was as reflexive as that. Or perhaps deep down, he thought only he knew what was right. He didn't care if you disagreed or if you had other commitments. What if she had said, "We've agreed to go to Aunt Min's house then." or "I had planned to take Pop for a ride"? He might have shrugged. He might not have cared and said, "OK, so we won't see you this trip," as if she had simply dropped down for a vacation.

"Stop it. Stop *it*." She stood in the middle of the living room and scolded herself. "Stop it." He was simply her older brother. She had been an adult for twenty years. It was a silly psychological reflex to get caught in these nets of resentment.

The phone rang. Damn, Cora thought. Pop would be sure to waken now.

"Hello."

"Hello, is Mr. Casey there?"

"Yes," she faltered. If it were important, he would be furious at missing the call. "Just a moment, I'll check."

She tiptoed down the hallway to find him sound asleep under the quilt. For a moment she listened to the slow, soft snoring she had remembered from childhood and felt safe. One breath in; one breath out. Taking; giving. Hang on Pop. Reluctantly, she returned to the phone.

"I'm sorry, but Mr. Casey is unavailable. May I take a message?"

"Yeah, John Mumford here, from Coastal Real Estate."

"Yes?" She reached for a pen.

"No message, really. He told me he'd be stopping by there today and . . . "

"Are you calling Roy Casey?"

"No, I thought he was in the hospital. No, George. Tell him John has a buyer for the house."

"Would you like his number in Medford?"

"No, Ma'm, I have to make arrangements for showing the house in Grandview. I have to talk to him while he's up here. Anyhow, don't bother about the details, just tell him to call, OK?"

"OK."

"You know when he's going to be around?"

"No." Cora stared out the window. Her voice gained strength. "I don't know his plans."

Despite the panic roiling in her stomach, she resisted the meaning of the telephone call. Maybe John Mumford was confused. Or maybe George did real estate business in this part of the state too. He was probably more successful than she thought. Or maybe she had got the message wrong. Jacques was always chiding her for getting messages wrong. She would have made a terrible secretary.

                          o o o

Fran was the first to arrive.

"So I'm going to meet the whole circus?"

Cora grimaced. "The entire acrobatic team. I wish I knew where the safety net was."

"Ah, come on, what can go wrong?" Fran flung her hands in the air.

Clearly Tommie hadn't told her the latest details.

"Let's go make coffee," Fran said. "If there's one thing I know about this family, it's that they have a thirst for muddy water."

Cora was beginning to think that this was the only thing she herself knew for sure.

The bell rang.

Fran opened the door.

Cora approached the living room shivering. How cold the afternoon had grown. There they were on the steps: her thin older brother and his plump wife and her chunky younger brother with his birdlike wife, all of them wearing friendly, calm, weekend-outing sorts of faces. "Welcome," called Cora, the treacherous first mate admitting pirates to the ship.

She became irritated that people were holding open the door so long. It would be a disaster for Pop to catch a chill. She supposed Pop was going to get up and hold court eventually, in his own time.

"Cora," Ron reached for his sister's arm. "This is Ally Patterson. Ally, this is Cora."

Cora was taken aback by her own surprise that Ally had kept her name.

"What's doing?" Ally, small, bright-eyed, extended a cordial hand. "Nice to meet you."

"Good to meet you, too. My daughter, Fran."

"Hi there, Corey," called Connie. "Long time no see."

"Right, hi there," Cora waved across the room, relieved the distance between them precluded a hug. Her sister-in-law had grown bigger and blonder over the years.

Each person claimed a seat, as if settling in for the duration, thought Cora. In the middle of the room, Pop's chair was conspicuously vacant.

"His Highness going to honor us with an appearance this afternoon?" asked George.

"He's napping right now," said Cora.

Everyone fell mute.

The material differences between her two brothers came into focus. Lanky George, slouched sideways in an overstuffed chair, wore faded green gaberdine slacks and a bulky grey sweater. His shoes were scuffed. Ron wore new casual clothes from the pricier pages of L. L. Bean, almost too new. How ironic that he had become the most successful member of the family. Did this give Ron a better footing with George, or did it create more tension? Maybe if George hadn't done that extra time in the army, if he had come back to the U.S., he might have made it into the majors, at least he might have had a better start. Touched by his defeated pose, she wondered when had he given up and why. She was struck by how much she cared and by how little she could do.

"How about some coffee?" asked Fran.

"Attractive kid," said Ally as Fran stepped into the kitchen. "She looks like you."

"Good thing, too," George said, "because I bet they don't know who the father is."

Cora could tell her brother had been drinking. She tried not to feel frightened by his lucky guess. And there was no point in being embarrassed, for this part of her history would be much less shocking to her sisters-in-law than other chapters.

Connie lit a cigarette and handed it to George. "Here's something to keep your mouth busy." She lit one for herself.

Grateful for the defense-of-sorts, she asked Connie, "I guess your kids are a little younger?"

"Sophomore and Junior in high school," she admitted formally, as if Cora were an IRS auditor.

Cora retrieved a sense of self by thinking of her life in Canada: Jacques waiting for her in bed at night. Oscar telling terrible jokes over the gourmet dinners he cooked. Elana phoning about successes and failures and diets and gossip. All these people knew her, loved her. She had a life beyond this family.

Ally rushed in to compensate for Connie's coldness, "And Fran is, what, eighteen?"

"Nineteen," corrected Fran, carrying a tray of mugs.

"Listen." George nodded, sucking his cigarette. "As long as the old man is in the sack, we might as well have a heart-to-heart."

"Yeah," Ron cleared his throat. "Cora, we need to talk with you."

She sipped the coffee—"Yes?"—and tried for a Meryl Streep coolness.

"Pop simply can't stay at the house. He's got great insurance. The hospital is the only place for him at this stage."

"Why are you so certain?"

"We've been taking care of him for the last year," George flared. "You just got here. Why do you think *you* know what's going on?"

"Yeah, Ally and I have been spelling each other," Connie glanced around critically. "Coming here every other week to clean the place. And put up soups and casseroles for him in the freezer."

"We simply can't continue doing it." Ron pronounced.

"*You* can't continue doing it? Sounds as if it's been your wife." Cora sucked in her lower lip.

"Oh, I didn't mind," Ally began, then looked doubtfully at Ron. "I mean, Ron's right, of course, it would be better for your father in a real hospital. I only meant I don't mind supporting Ron, after all . . . " She took a sip of coffee instead of finishing the sentence.

"Listen, Cora, we're all busy people, so let's get to the point." George rocked the top half of his body back and forth through a cloud of smoke. "Pop is dying. He belongs in the hospital, not in a drafty old house."

Cora snapped before she thought better, "Particularly not in an old house that's being sold out from under him."

"What?" asked Ally.

Connie and Ron stared at flecks in the shag rug. George looked Cora directly in the eye.

"When a man gets this sick," George spoke slowly, "responsibility passes on to the children."

"Responsibility *and* money." Cora steadied her voice. "Sometimes children get impatient."

"Cora, hold on here," Ron spoke nervously. "That sounds like an accusation."

"Does it?"

George coughed a deep, rocky cough. "I think what's needed here is some fresh air. How about a walk around the block?"

Fran shot her a warning glance which Cora pretended not to see.

"Sure," agreed Cora, "let me get my sweater."

As they strolled down the gravel driveway, Cora noticed that a breeze had come up this afternoon and wished she had worn her coat, but she didn't want to betray any indecisiveness. For some reason, she thought about that Sunday thirty-five years ago when he threatened to kidnap her to China.

"Bit brisk," he spoke with that familiar, tentative charm of his.

"Put a color in your cheeks, as Aunt Min would say." She found herself also being cordial.

"Look, Sis, let's be reasonable about this." His voice was muted, conciliatory.

"Yes." She felt a faint hope.

"What difference does it make to you if he spends the next month in a hospital or a house?" George asked gently.

"He has a right to die the way he wants."

"You've always been big on rights."

"What?"

"Nothing." Then, "Dying is dying."

"The way you die is important," she said. "So is the way you live."

"Always the idealist." He smiled fondly.

"And it's *his* house."

George stared through her.

"Your friend John Mumford called while you were driving over."

He didn't miss a beat. "Everything falls to the oldest son. I'm just trying to take care of business."

"Domestic and international," she said impulsively.

"What's that supposed to mean?" He stopped and took her arm.

She twisted away. "This is AFN *business*."

"What do you know about that?"

"I know," the words spilled out abruptly, "that mercenary forces have as much to do with democratic patriotism as your 'caretaking' of Pop has to do with family loyalty. Greed, it's all about greed, George."

He clenched his jaw.

They walked the next half block in silence.

George smiled ironically, "My sister, she always believed in morality."

"Don't you?" she demanded.

"No, no, not since, oh, about the eighth grade."

She shook her head at her own stupidity and his belligerence.

In a thin voice, he asked, "You still have a taste for pyrotechnics?"

"What?" She was the one who stopped now. She could hear Oscar's reminder about FBI prerogatives. She heard him laying out all the possibilities and likelihoods, explaining that possibilities were different from likelihoods.

"Don't know how much you know about AFN, about the people who are involved in it."

"Not much." She struggled for breath. Pop's snoring had been gentle. In . . . out. Like the tides. Hang on. Hang on.

"Some of our members are more discreet than others." He cracked his knuckles. "But some don't mind revealing their dedication. The chairman is Henry Rhinehart."

"Henry Rhinehart?"

"I believe he's an alum of your college. That, in fact, you knew each other in some political group . . . "

Cora blinked, placing him as the familiar bearded man on the AFN videotape.

"Seems he had a crush on you."

"Henry, yes, of course, Henry." Cora was back on a verandah overlooking the McKenzie Rapids. She buttoned her sweater up to the neck.

"Henry seems to have known you and your friend—what was his name, the one who 'committed suicide'—Ralph, pretty well."

"Yes," she said quietly.

"Says you and Ralph spent a lot of time together right before that draft board burned down. Lovers?"

She was silent.

"No, he said he knew Ralph pretty well in high school. Didn't think you were having an affair, at least not a sexual affair."

She waited.

"Henry keeps in touch with Ralph's family. It seems they never went along with that suicide story."

Cora looked away.

"I don't think Henry would want to find himself on the other side of the fence from you again."

"Is this some kind of threat?" She forced herself forward.

George didn't respond until they had reached Pop's driveway.

A sudden wind rose. Gently, he brushed the black hair from Cora's eyes. "Threat? I'm your brother, Corey."

X

TWENTY-FOUR

Fall, 1988
Oregon

It took all his strength to raise himself against the pillows in bed and once he had accomplished this, he closed his eyes for several minutes, gulping air. Cora saw Ron's lost expression in her father's face. Her own eyes were rimmed with tears before his opened. She turned away to collect his medicines and a glass of water.

The television hummed on his dresser. He watched it with the sound off, his face strained by concentration. She sat next to the bed, administering the pills.

He had grown paler than she imagined possible, given the wild flushes of his past. His face had lost all its ruddiness. These broken vessels in his nose pulsed a grey-blue color. He was fading—into the white sheets and the white walls. He was turning into a ghost before her eyes. She watched carefully to make sure he took enough water with the pain capsules.

"Follie?"

He seemed to be asking if she were Follie.

She lowered her head in embarrassed confusion.

"Follie. Where's the damn dog?"

"Oh." She steadied herself. "I let her out. She'll be right back. Shall I go look?"

"No," he said, taking her hand. "Stay here."

She sat, observing the electronic tabernacle. As programs and commercials filed past, she noticed she wasn't bored, more relieved not to hear the constant drone, privileged to keep vigil with Pop.

But she did worry. How seriously should she take George's threat of a court order to enforce his own power-of-attorney to register Pop in a "proper hospital?" She tried not to think of his more veiled reference to Henry Rhinehart. It had been two weeks since her brothers' visit. Still she did not believe George had given up. Just like him to come for Pop in the middle of the night. She found herself on guard after dark. Despite Fran's disapproval, she only slept in odd naps here and there during the day. What had happened to Follie?

She noticed Pop's eyes were closed, and his breathing had grown more regular. Gently, she let go of his hand, eager to stretch her legs.

The dog wasn't at the back door or the front. Well, Cora thought, it was a beautiful day, Follie was probably having a good time. Maybe Fran had taken her when she and Tommie went for a walk. Cora gazed down at the ocean: to the left she could see the lighthouse, and beyond that, a cargo ship. It was a perfect morning. Could she persuade Pop to sit in the living room a while?

Probably not. Cora collapsed in his reclining chair. Forget the view. He hadn't looked at anything for a week besides the television and the back of his eyelids. She considered her sloppy self in stonewashed jeans and ragged sweatshirt. She would brighten up for him this afternoon by wearing her turquoise sweater and braiding her hair.

She had been here a month; it seemed much longer and not long enough. Cora feared she would make it back to Canada in plenty of time to avoid American Thanksgiving. Pop's pain was increasing horribly, although she was administering more than the prescribed dose. Was George right? Would he be more comfortable in a hospital? Should she give in? Well, this wasn't the point. It wasn't her decision.

If friends were really God's compensation for family, Cora thought how she had felt especially grateful for the call from Sara this week. After offering her shoulder, Sara asked in that direct, no-nonsense way of hers, "Is it worth it, Cora?"

"Worth it?"

"Worth your grief and time and worry to see the old man out in his bitterness."

"Bitterness?" Cora asked vaguely.

"Sounds like he's become a closed, bitter old man."

"Yes, well, I guess I see some changes. I mean he's not Pope John XXIII, but I think he's moving a little from bitterness to . . . "

"Acceptance?"

"Maybe not that far," Cora squinted into the middle distance. "Maybe resignation."

"That's progress?"

"Yes," she smiled thinly. "For him, for us, that's progress."

"Cora. Cor-a," he bellowed with impressive strength.

She checked her watch to see that she had been away ten minutes. He wasn't due for his next pill for another hour. But if he wanted one now, who was to stop him? She hurried toward the back of the house.

His eyes were shut, and he had slid down on the pillows. She would have to change the pillow cases again this afternoon because they were crusted with yellow drool.

"Oh, Pop, let me help you get more comfortable." She reached to straighten the pillows.

"No, I want to lay flat." He looked at her like an angry boy.

She had tried to think of him as a boy when she bathed him, tried to ignore the exhausted flesh, the rashes, and the smells. She concentrated on those baths with Ron years ago and her distraction made these ministrations easier for Pop and for herself.

"OK, whatever you like, Pop." She could feel the fear in her face. "How's your pain? Would you like another humdinger?"

"Humdinger," he said, almost inaudibly, a smile tracing his lips. He pointed impatiently to the faded green collar of his pajamas.

She unhooked the top button and he sighed.

"Are you OK, Pop?" Stupid question. "Is there anything I can do for you?"

"You can lie here." He patted the bed. "Hold me for a little while."

Her hands trembled. "Yes," a quavering voice. "Yes, of course." Resisting some deep, unnamable fear, she perched on the bed and fiddled with her troublesome shoelaces. Then she obediently lay down on the Star-of-Bethlehem quilt and stretched her arms around her father. Her black hair stuck to his drool on the sheet. She closed her eyes and held tightly.

"They want to take me away," he said loudly.

She was encouraged by the strength in his voice.

"You won't let them take me away, will you?"

"No," she whispered.

"There, look."

She raised her head, assuming Follie had found her way back into the house.

"Look, there."

Cora looked all around her father's bedroom, but saw nothing. When she turned back to him, he was absolutely still.

She lay with his body for a long time.

* * *

Cora kept telling herself to get up, but she was weighted to the bed, alone now in a new way. She stared into the mirror, studying the odd parts of the room that were reflected—the top of the window, a corner of the seascape she had painted him when she was sixteen. Also the crucifix with the pale green palm leaf—knotted in only the way Mom knew how.

Cora was heavy with sadness for both her parents. For their deaths. For their lives in an ill-conceived marriage. For their three children.

She remembered Mom sucking on the rubber glove amidst the litter of bus tickets and the roaring of Pop's impatience. "I'll always be with you," she had said once. When? Cora couldn't recall, but she did remember the vague sense of threat that had accompanied that promise and she closed her eyes now.

TWENTY-FIVE ✷

Spring, 1955
Oregon

Cynthia didn't look like a nurse. She wore a brown jumper over a beige blouse. Her hair was drawn in a brown page boy. The only thing white about her was her skin; it was the pale, milky kind that made Cora think more of a patient than a nurse. What sort of people were taking care of her mother?

Cynthia was excessively friendly as she led George, Ron, Aunt Min and Cora past the residents' mailboxes (Cora preferred the term "patient" because it sounded less permanent than "resident."), through the shiny cafeteria and into a blue office with blue couches and chairs.

"Make yourselves comfortable," she invited in a singsong voice.

Cora wondered how she could speak and smile at the same time.

The Cynthia person was talking to Aunt Min. "Mrs. Casey is making great strides. In the last month we've halved her medication. And she's sewing beautifully."

Cora heard a faint, high-pitched sound. She wasn't going crazy. It was Ron, whistling under his breath. George stared out the window, flexing his brows up and down as if lifting weights from his eyes.

Someone had to defend Mom.

"There's nothing wrong with our mother." declared Cora, pleased with the authority in her voice. "She needs a rest. We run her ragged, that's all. She only needs a rest."

George cracked his knuckles.

Cynthia regarded her closely. "That's right, Cora, your mother is a little tired now. She'll be better soon. But you—and I'm talking to all you children now . . ."

Ron stopped whistling and started to swing his leg back and forth.

237

"All you children should know she may be somewhat distracted today. That doesn't mean she doesn't love you. The medicine can make her a little confused."

Cora couldn't believe this Miss Cynthia was explaining that Mom loved them. Who was she, anyway?

"Do you have any questions?" She grew even more cheerful.

The room was silent.

"Perhaps we can see Louise now," Aunt Min spoke in her most polite tone. "We have to catch a bus back and that only gives us an hour."

"Yes, yes, of course. I had no idea you came all the way here by *bus*, with three children."

Cora tagged behind the others as they threaded their way through the hospital. Cynthia paused from time to time to explain that the room on the right was going to be a library, that the corridor on the left would eventually lead to a recreation room . . . that they really had no intention of accepting residents until the new wing had been completed, but there was such a demand. Cora didn't like the woman's high, witchy voice and wondered if she hypnotized her patients.

Mom was sitting at the window sewing a tiny green velvet coat. In the early afternoon sun, her red hair gleamed like a halo. Shoulders relaxed, her whole body was still, except for those capable hands, working swiftly through the rich fabric.

Cora took in the room through dry eyes. It was cramped but clean and neat—not like the rest of this construction site. She noticed that Mom had brought doilies from home and placed them on the arms of the institutional bedside chair. How suffocated she must be in this cell where there was barely enough space for a table, bed and a bureau. Cora saw she had taped last year's Christmas pictures on the wall by the door.

"Visitors, Louise," Cynthia said as if she were talking to a child.

Just as Cora was thinking about kicking Cynthia in the shins, Mom looked up—her face a carousel of fear, happiness and confusion.

Slowly, she focused on each of her children, "George. Ron. Cora." She nodded to her sister-in-law.

"What a nice surprise," she said slowly. Much too slowly, Cora knew.

Ron ran and sat on her lap. She held him with loose, tired arms. George waved coolly, studied the room, then perched on the window sill. Aunt Min fretted with the yellow roses she had picked that morning. Cora took a deep breath, walked over to her mother and began rubbing her shoulder.

Mom sniffed back tears, considering Cynthia carefully.

Why didn't the goddamned witch leave? Cora wondered in the language of her father. She wished he weren't at sea so much lately.

She saw Mom searching Cynthia's face for answers. What had this stranger done? Perhaps they could kidnap Mom when Cynthia left. When *was* Cynthia going to leave? Perhaps she could get George to trick Cynthia down the hallway. Aunt Min and Ron could whisk Mom out to the bus stop. She could lie in Mom's bed, pretending to be the patient until she knew they were safely riding home. Then she would sneak out in the dark . . .

"Don't you want to ask them how things are at school, Mrs. Casey?"

"Yes. Of course." Her voice was thick as well as slow. "How are things at school?"

Fall, 1955

Cora rushed ahead of Pop and Cynthia toward Mom's room. She couldn't stand Cynthia's whispery voice. Besides, she wanted to tell Mom how the gingham dress had fit Rosemary perfectly. When Mom came home, Cora would have the dolls all gussied up in their new outfits, sitting by the front door. Oh, she couldn't wait. Mom would be returning soon because she had been in this place long enough to get well.

The closed door alarmed Cora. It had always been open before. She thought there was some kind of rule about that, so the nurses could look in on you. Still, maybe Mom was changing clothes, getting ready. Cynthia told them in that sickeningly sweet tone that Mom "always looked forward" to their visits. Cora hoped she wouldn't be disappointed that the boys had stayed home again. Now frozen at the door, she wondered what to do. Silly, she told herself, just knock. She didn't want to alarm Mom, who seemed so fragile nowadays. Yet she needed to see her before Pop and Cynthia caught up. Cora continued to wonder about Cynthia's hypnotizing voice. What power did this ugly woman—who it turned out was not a nurse at all, but a social worker—have on her mother? She always regretted that she hadn't followed through with the kidnap scheme.

She could hear their footsteps.

Cora steadied herself, then knocked.

After an interminable wait, she knocked again. No answer. Cora reached down, tried the handle and found the door unlocked.

The small room was dark, except for splinters of light trespassing through drawn curtains. Was she asleep? Cora's eyes adjusted to the dimness. No, the bed was empty. Had she left? Maybe Cynthia had got her signals crossed. Maybe Mom was on an outing. Maybe she had escaped.

Cora could hear them rounding the corner. She detected a tiny sound from the far end of the room. Flick, flick. Flick, flick. Advancing toward the window, she saw her mother sitting on the floor in a blue summer nightie, doing macramé.

The grief in Cora's heart was almost immediately displaced by panic, for if Cynthia saw Mom like this, it would be much longer before they let her go.

"Come on, Mom, why don't you sit in the chair here." She reached down for her mother's arm. "This comfortable one with the doilies."

As she guided her docile mother to propriety, she had the peculiar sensation of not being recognized. Cora managed to switch on the lamp just in time.

"Isn't that nice, Louise is working on those beautiful macramé strands again." Cynthia turned to Pop and continued earnestly, as if she were recommending Mom for a job. "She's really the most productive of our residents. I'm hoping that next month she will be well enough to run a class for the rest of the community here."

Cora understood Cynthia had no intention of ever letting Mom return home.

XI

TWENTY-SIX

Fall, 1988
Oregon

Cora was asleep when the knocking started. Dreaming about being in Toronto with Jacques, she interpreted the sound as the clanking of water pipes. "Don't worry," Jacques told her, "It will quiet down. The Minellis must be taking a late bath." Knock, knock. Flick, flick. Knock, knock.

Cora opened her eyes and was back on Pop's bed. She wept quietly and aching with grief, she studied her father's still body. Tentatively, she touched his big, hairy arm to find cool indifference. Her breath came in short, tight beats.

Knock, knock, knock, knock, knock. More insistent now. Cora checked her watch: 1 P.M. Abruptly, she slid off the bed and fumbled for her shoes. No, they would take too much time. She bent over and kissed Pop on the forehead, reassured by the familiar smell of Aqua Velva, then covered his face with the sheet.

Knock, knock, knock, knock, knock, knock. Was this George, coming to take Pop to the hospital? She felt no spite, just gratitude that Pop had gone the way he wanted.

In the living room, she peeked through the venetian blinds, remembering her father's gesture when she arrived a month before. George wasn't anywhere in sight. Rather, two police officers—one female and one male—stood in stiff silence on the front door mat.

Knock, knock, knock.

"Oh, hello. Cora Casey?" The woman asked as Cora opened the door.

"Yes," she answered softly, as if Pop were asleep.

What did they want? Surely police wouldn't come to take Pop to a hospital. Had something happened to Fran?

They nodded to one another.

243

An accident? Was Fran all right?

"How can I help you?" she asked anxiously.

"I'm afraid you're under arrest, ma'm," the young man said.

Cora recalled teams of military officers who would visit women to explain their sons or husbands or brothers had been killed in Vietnam. But this was all wrong. She was the one who had to inform them. Of the death. Pop's death. His victory in staying home.

"You are under arrest for the homicide of Ralph Blake and for the willful destruction through arson of the Lock County Selective Service Office . . . " the female officer rattled on.

Cora felt she were watching a movie.

As the woman read her rights, Cora realized that she had known she would be arrested. At least since the AFN tape. Maybe since crossing the border. Long ago she learned the only protection was not being too surprised.

George had sent them. Fear hovered over her anger. George. He was such a bloody prick, her brother. George. She wasn't listening to the woman.

The officers were surprised when she directed them to the back room. For a moment, she wondered if they might also charge her with murdering Pop.

He lay there: cold, hard, large and still beneath the quilt, so many boulders under the sand. She hated sharing this intimate moment with the police. They viewed her father as a corpse, just as Cynthia so long ago had viewed Mom as a resident. Yet Cora found herself grinning—who cared what the cops thought—she had done a better job this time. She had protected Pop; together the two of them had won. Perhaps he hadn't had the life he wanted. But with her help, he had chosen his death. Tears streamed down her face again. She pulled a tissue from the bedside box.

The woman checked his eyes and his pulse, then turned to Cora with a mixture of embarrassment and barely masked irritation. "Your brother said your father was sick. He didn't explain how far along his illness was. I'm sorry."

The male officer mumbled that he would call her brothers to make arrangements and meanwhile would stay with the body. As the woman escorted her out the door, Cora turned to see the policeman writing his report, seated in Pop's chair.

* * *

Cora lay on her bunk, watching the portly guard walk back and forth the length of cells. The jail smelled of piss and disinfectant. Every sound echoed. The guard's shoes slop-slopped. Slop, slop on the grey concrete. Was this the beginning or the end? She faced prison as Pop had confronted death, resisting the inevitable.

No, Sara's husband had counseled her, never think like that. Never think you deserve to be here. Richard was a decent lawyer—bright, committed, energetic. She liked middle-aged people with that much idealism, and she hoped it was catching. Cora reminded herself she had friends here and Jacques would be down as soon as the airline strike allowed. She would have to be spirited, would have to summon the momentum of twenty years ago, if she were going to win her case.

The bed was too firm and too lumpy. The cell seemed cold, but Cora recognized the chill of fear. Guards here wore short-sleeved shirts. She distracted herself by picking up the book Sara had loaned her.

Tap, tap. Tap, tap. Tap, tap. The woman in the next cell had a maddening habit of knocking her bed frame against their common wall. Tap, tap. Tap, tap. Cora grew more or less conscious of the noise depending on her own mood. Was the woman deliberately annoying her? Perhaps she was a police officer trying to break her will. Or a deluded prisoner attempting to dig her way free? No, she was probably as bored and anxious as Cora. Tap, tap. Bored, anxious. Tap, tap.

Cora tried to read Sara's book, a book Sara had written, for Christsake—about women as managers in the family system. She felt proud of her friend, but found herself growing impatient with academic language. Well, Sara might find her journalistic voice too slick. No, this inability to concentrate had nothing to do with Sara's work. You couldn't focus on anything in this place.

Occasionally she would surface—as this morning to the noise in the next cell—and the terror froze her shoulders or wired her jaw. She wasn't afraid of physical torture or deprivation, but of the unreasonableness and the predictability of being here. She tried to conjure up images of the Pankhursts in Holloway Prison or of Ghandi in Delhi. But she knew she couldn't hold out like that. She lacked their moral courage, their support, their vision.

What did it mean to die? Did you check out? Give up? Fade away? This was hard to comprehend because she was so frightened of dying. Because comprehension implied some kind of continuing, an opening *into* something.

She turned over on the bunk, her eyes closed. Pop's death was—like everything else in his life—something he had accomplished. "Pop died at 10 A.M.," she said again and again to Aunt Min, to Fran, to herself. Not, "He passed away" or "passed on" unless you saw the passing in a sort of freeway sense—putting it into overdrive and *passing*. Cora had no doubt that he had chosen death, as he had chosen so much of life. It all came down to a kind of culpability.

This brought her back to blame, and she felt very tired. Tap, tap. The noise again. Tap, tap. Cora told herself she would not go crazy.

Now she had to accept his death—as she had had to accept the other manifestations of his will over the years. That Pop had died was one thing; "Pop is dead" was another story, one she could not believe. She could not believe he wasn't there, loud, offensive, unjust, passionate. She could not believe all his energy was *simply not there*. It defied the laws of the universe. It made her unbearably sad.

Perhaps the real dying happened when *you* let go of the dead person, when the sadness was less raw, when it was familiar enough to face, when you became protected by distance and cushioned by memory. She found herself fighting belief in his death—as if she were saving his life.

She had cried and cried yesterday and today. Cried without thinking. Down beyond the pain, the crying did more than bring relief; it provided breath. And because these were clean, comprehensible tears—with no trace of madness, neither her father's rage nor her mother's daze—she didn't mind other people seeing her cry. The tears were explainable. So much was explainable now that he was dead. Now that it was safe.

The noise had stopped. She sat up and began her yoga stretches. She would not let this place destroy her. She was a cobra now, breathing deeply, trying not to smell.

In some ways it seemed right to be locked away like Pop's body. As if she were making the trip with him, Pop was dead and she was numb. They were in limbo. Together.

XII

TWENTY-SEVEN

Fall, 1988
Oregon

The tapping from the next cell had ceased two days ago. Had they moved the woman? Executed her? Released her? Now Cora listened to the random clanks and groans of pipes, the whirring of fans, the squeals of carts and an occasional voice: epithet from a guard, expletive from another invisible prisoner.

The atmosphere was engineered to numb your curiosity and distance you from others—past and present. Jail reminded Cora of the emergency room in Toronto, where she had taken Fran a few years before for a broken wrist. The clinic was crowded with people enduring all manner of disaster— gunshot wound, dog bite, pneumonia—and the relatives of patients whose suffering had already admitted them through the double glass doors. For the first five minutes, Cora tried to imagine the personal lives behind the catastrophes. None of the patients met her glance. Gradually she became absorbed in watching *Dallas* on the hospital's overhead TV; the volume seemed to grow louder and louder until she felt as if she were alone in the room with Fran and J.R.

Cora worried about Jacques worrying about her. What could he do about a plane strike? Of course he would be here soon. To shake her ennui, she walked to the cell door and stared at the skinny guard pacing back and forth. She reminded her of Muldoon from *Car Fifty-Four, Where Are You?* Silly TV show. She had always identified more with Muldoon's squat partner, Tooty. Cora wondered what tedium did to a mind over time. Did it corrode your intellect as well as defeat your spirit? Fifteen more minutes until Aunt Min's visit. Fifteen more years.

Cora returned to her bunk and pretended to rest. She thought about her father again, then began to weep.

249

"Yeah, yeah, keep practicing."

She looked up to see the tall, thin guard unlocking her door. "Pretty soon you'll have a lot more to cry about."

Cora rose from the bed with forced dignity, steeling herself to conversation with this woman all the way to the visitor's room. Not conversation, abuse. "Traitor bitch," the guard had said yesterday, "I hate your kind for turning against our soldiers in Vietnam."

All the guard said today was, "Hurry up. You're just eating into your visiting time."

Cora glanced around at the winding staircases and on each floor, rows of cells, wondering at all the different stories here. The guard continued to mumble angrily. Cora ignored her, recalling her mother's pretense at ignoring so much of what went on around her.

The small, old woman stared down at her hands. Bent beneath the death of her brother, the imprisonment of her niece, Aunt Min had faded to a fainter grey. Cora could not believe she was bringing grief to the one person in her family who had always stood by her.

"How are you?" Aunt Min managed a smile.

"OK," Cora began talking before she sat down, conscious that the guard could curtail their visit at any point. "How are you?"

"Oh, a little tired, busy with the funeral arrangements. It's hard to believe everything goes so fast. Mass is tomorrow and I'm not nearly ready. People are coming over to the house afterward, you know."

"Yes," Cora nodded. While part of her was gratified that her brothers were not hosting the wake, she felt furious at them for dumping all this work on Aunt Min.

"Oh, Corey, I wish you could be there."

"I wish I could help you out. It must be exhausting, cooking and so forth."

"Oh, it's not that. People will bring food. Besides, I have Edie and Tommie—and this helping is the first thing they've agreed on in ages. But I wish you could be there at the funeral—for him. *He* would have wanted you there."

Cora thought how she had also missed her mother's funeral. How she had never had the chance to visit the grave since returning to Oregon last month.

"Jacques should be here in a couple of days." Aunt Min brightened her voice. "The strike is over."

"He called again!"

"Yes, the flight's all arranged. He'll be in Friday afternoon—just before visiting hours," she stumbled. "Of course by then Richard will have won his appeal on the bail. By then, you'll be with us at home."

"Home," Cora mused. "Yes, maybe."

They fell silent.

"You know I imagined the funeral before we crossed the border."

"Oh, yes?" Cora asked.

"And I guess I sort of thought of it as the end—with Grandpa dead, the air would be cleared, but . . . "

Cora waited. "But?"

"But then I got to like the old bear. Some things about him, anyway."

Cora nodded ruefully.

Silence again.

"Something happened after the funeral." Fran grimaced. "Something I have to tell you."

"Aunt Min, is she OK?" Cora demanded.

"Aunt Min, oh, yes, oh, it's nothing to do with her, not directly."

Hurry up, Fran, what is it? Cora could hear the guard calculating their disappearing time. "Yes?" she coaxed her daughter.

"It's about George." She took a breath.

"Yes?" Cora's eyes widened.

"Tommie turned him in." She regarded her mother carefully.

Cora felt red rise up the side of her neck. This was going too fast for her. The whole month had gone too fast. Her revenge was laced with fear. Fear for George or Tommie or herself, she didn't know.

"The cops came to Aunt Min's and booked him into jail. This jail, I guess." She looked around the green visitor's room and shrugged.

Cora thought how she never saw any of the male prisoners. How strange to think of George being here with her in the same jail. The idea frightened, pleased her.

Muldoon sighed in the corner.

"But he got out on bail last night."

"Naturally," Cora answered, bitterness rising in her throat. "Did they give him the Congressional Medal of Honor at the same time?"

How pathetic she had been, threatening George last week. Of course he would get out. She hadn't even been able to bring herself to report him, not even after it was clear how much he had betrayed Pop. Not even after she had been arrested.

"And he's back at Grandpa's house now." Fran said.

"Yes." Her mouth was dry. "I would expect that."

Fran's cheeks burned, "I want to tear his eyes out." She watched her mother cautiously, then lowered her voice. "Yet at the same time, he makes me sick and scared. I mean, he's part of our family."

"He probably feels the same way about me being his sister," Cora's voice was suddenly pensive. "In some ways I think the boys were injured more. In some ways I think I got away with . . . a lot."

"Time's up," Muldoon called from the corner. Far too loudly.

Cora turned to the guard. There was an honest directness in her gaze. Enough to give Cora courage to ask. "I think we have five more minutes, right?"

"All right," Muldoon nodded impassively.

"You know at the funeral," Fran said, "I thought how all of you had pieces of Grandpa, pieces of his spirit. George seemed to take his inheritance most literally, his political ideas and all. That and the drinking."

"Yes," Cora sighed. "That's right." She wanted to ask what *she* had inherited, but, she reminded herself, there wasn't much time.

Fran leaned forward, "It's going to be OK, Mom, I know it."

"You're going to be OK," Cora said, believing her fatherless daughter would be fine.

"No, I mean it. Richard said they have the suicide note from Ralph, explaining he did everything alone. It was reported that way in all the papers. His family is only pushing these charges out of guilt. They have no evidence about you. The drunk in the parking lot is dead now. No real evidence except that that silly Henry friend of George's says you and Ralph were tight . . . "

Cora frowned.

Fran shrugged impatiently, "I guess I shouldn't be talking about this stuff here, but it's all been in the papers, for heaven's sake."

It was Cora's turn to shrug.

"Oh, everything's been so confusing since we came here." Fran sighed. "So screwed up. I can't wait until we can go home."

"Home," Cora repeated numbly.

"When we get back home to Canada, everything's going to be fine."

Cora gazed gratefully at her hopeful daughter. She knew anything less than certainty would be betrayal.

Acknowledgments

A Walking Fire is dedicated to five old friends, Deborah Johnson, Eve Pell, Douglas Foster, Raul Ramirez and David Weir. I thank them for the example of their lives, for the stimulation of their arguments and for many good laughs over the years.

I want to acknowledge the artistic support of the Australia Council's Literature Board, the South Australia College for Advanced Education, Canada's Leighton Artist Colony, the Cummington Arts Community, the Virginia Center for the Creative Arts and Arizona State University.

Many thanks to Leslie Gardner and Carola Sautter for editorial encouragement, to Marcia Dillon and Gloria Litman for life encouragement and to Helen Longino for twelve years of provocative, patient and loving companionship. A number of people have generously commented on drafts of the manuscript. I am very grateful to Sandy Boucher, Julia Douthwaite, Jana Harris, Nancy Hellner, Elizabeth Horan, Deborah Johnson, Helen Longino, Mary Mackey, Joan McGregor, Eve Pell, Donna Perry, Kalima Rose, Susan Schweik, Madelon Sprengnether, Herb Trubo and Peggy Webb. Abundant thanks to Gretchen Scherer for proofreading assistance. While this book is informed by memory about and considerable research into period and place, many of the municipal and institutional settings (such as Cora's University) and all the characters are imaginary.

A Walking Fire is inspired by the memory of people of all nationalities who lost their lives fighting against or in the war in Southeast Asia. It is written with special gratitude to those Canadians who offered American women and men refuge and friendship during a period of turmoil, anger, fear and loss.